D1641747

Deleuze and Baudrillard

Plateaus – New Directions in Deleuze Studies

'It's not a matter of bringing all sorts of things together under a single concept but rather of relating each concept to variables that explain its mutations.'
Gilles Deleuze, *Negotiations*

Series Editors

Ian Buchanan, University of Wollongong
Claire Colebrook, Penn State University

Editorial Advisory Board

Titles Available in the Series

Forthcoming Volumes

Visit the Plateaus website at www.edinburghuniversitypress.com/series/plat

DELEUZE AND BAUDRILLARD
From Cyberpunk to Biopunk

∽

Sean McQueen

EDINBURGH
University Press

Edinburgh University Press is one of the leading university presses in the UK. We publish academic books and journals in our selected subject areas across the humanities and social sciences, combining cutting-edge scholarship with high editorial and production values to produce academic works of lasting importance. For more information visit our website: www.edinburghuniversitypress.com

Edinburgh University Press Ltd
The Tun – Holyrood Road
12(2f) Jackson's Entry
Edinburgh EH8 8PJ

Typeset in Sabon by
Servis Filmsetting Ltd, Stockport, Cheshire,
and printed and bound in Great Britain by
CPI Group (UK) Ltd, Croydon CR0 4YY

A CIP record for this book is available from the British Library

ISBN 978 1 4744 1437 1 (hardback)
ISBN 978 1 4744 1439 5 (webready PDF)
ISBN 978 1 4744 1438 8 (epub)

Contents

Figures

Acknowledgements

This book began its life as a doctoral dissertation. Books and dissertations are different animals, and acknowledgement is, above all, due to Andrew Milner, without whose generous supervision and mentoring both would have been impossible. I owe my sincerest thanks to Claire Perkins and Alison Ross. This book bears the impress of their wisdom and care. For their assistance and interest in this project, I warmly thank Ian Buchanan, Claire Colebrook, Steven Shaviro, Cathy Falconer and Carol MacDonald.

For their sufferance, personal support, professional stimulation and friendship I owe debts of gratitude to Sam Bateman, Lauren Bertacchini, Nick Karamanos, Rob Letizi, Janice Loreck, Deirdre McQueen, Lee McQueen, Michael McQueen and Luke van Ryn. I am indebted, too, to my father, Richard McQueen, from whom I inherited both my love of science fiction and the selected works of Marx and Engels.

Parts of this book have been published previously in different forms. A version of Chapter 1 appeared in *Science Fiction Film and Television* (5:2) as 'Adapting to Language: Anthony Burgess's and Stanley Kubrick's *A Clockwork Orange*'. An abbreviated version of Chapter 5 was published in *Science Fiction Studies* (41:1) as 'Biocapitalism and Schizophrenia: Rethinking the Frankenstein Barrier'. A version of Chapter 9 appeared in *Science Fiction Film and Television* (8:1) entitled '*Antiviral*: Capitalism of the Fourth Kind'. Chapters 3 and 4 share their titles with and began their lives in *International Journal of Baudrillard Studies*, although they now bear no resemblance to 'Seducing-Machines: Baudrillard, Deleuze, and *Crash*' (10:1) and 'Remote-Control Society: Baudrillard and Inversive Utopia' (11:1). I am grateful for the editorial labour of Mark Bould, Gerry Coulter and, especially, Sherryl Vint, all of whom steered these articles from peer review through to publication.

Preparation of this book was partially funded by a Monash University Postgraduate Publication Award.

Abbreviations

Works by Jean Baudrillard

A   America
CS   The Consumer Society: Myths and Structures
FF   Forget Foucault
FS   Fatal Strategies
MP   The Mirror of Production
PES For a Critique of the Political Economy of the Sign
S   Seduction
SED Symbolic Exchange and Death
SS   Simulacra and Simulation
TE   The Transparency of Evil: Essays on Extreme Phenomena

Works by Gilles Deleuze

DR   Difference and Repetition
FB   Francis Bacon: The Logic of Sensation
LS   The Logic of Sense
N   Negotiations: 1972–1990
PSC 'Postscript on the Societies of Control'
TI   Cinema 2: The Time-Image

Works by Gilles Deleuze and Félix Guattari

AO   Anti-Oedipus: Capitalism and Schizophrenia
K   Kafka: Toward a Minor Literature
TP   A Thousand Plateaus: Capitalism and Schizophrenia

Works by Gilles Deleuze and Claire Parnet

D   Dialogues

Introduction

This book will be an attempt at a cognitive mapping of the transition from late capitalism to biocapitalism.[1] It is a Marxian critique of science fiction, capitalism, psychoanalysis; an interdisciplinary work that aims to go to the heart of new currents in critical thought, science, technology, literature and cinema. It will do so by examining two science fiction subgenres, the established subgenre of cyberpunk and the emerging subgenre of biopunk.

Science fiction is a critical perspective from which to critique the mutations of capitalism. Mark Bould writes that science fiction distinguishes itself from other genres by offering a 'snapshot of the structures of capital' (2009: 4). Here, Bould follows Darko Suvin's extraordinarily influential *Metamorphoses of Science Fiction* (1979) and Carl Freedman's *Critical Theory and Science Fiction* (2000), both of which argue for the necessity of a dialectic between estrangement and cognition, without which the text qualifies neither as science fiction nor as Marxian. As Freedman summarises it, estrangement 'refers to the creation of an alternative fictional world that [. . .] performs an estranging critical interrogation [. . .] The *critical* character of the interrogation is guaranteed by the operation of cognition, which [. . .] account[s] rationally for [the] imagined world' (2000: 16–17). Against these prescriptive definitions, Bould writes that 'there is no necessary relationship between Marxism and [science fiction] – although there has always been a close one' (2009: 17). Dialectics are at the core of this book, but it is not its intention to verify the presence of this dialectic between estrangement and cognition. Rather, it will follow Fredric Jameson, who famously described cyberpunk as the 'supreme *literary* expression if not of postmodernism, then of late capitalism itself', 'fully as much an expression of transnational corporate realities as it is of global paranoia itself' (1996: 419 n. 1, 38). The consensus amongst science fiction scholars is that the cyberpunk movement has come to an end. Biocapitalism is the frontline of capitalism today, promising to enrich and prolong our lives whilst threatening to extend capitalism's capacity to

1

command our hearts and minds. This book will show that biopunk is emerging as the literary and cinematic expression of biocapitalism.

More narrowly, this book will be a critical intervention into the becoming-Deleuzian of science fiction (henceforth SF) of which there are two main components. The central novelty of Gilles Deleuze and Félix Guattari's two-volume *Capitalism and Schizophrenia* was the proposition that schizophrenia and capitalism animate one another. This clearly acquires a new relevance in biocapitalism. We are well into what was predicted to be both the biotech century (Rifkin 1998) and the Deleuzian century (Foucault 1977: 165). It is inauspicious that many of Deleuze's revolutionary concepts, such as the molecular, smooth space, the rhizome, the schizophrenic cell, the body without organs, becoming-animal and becoming-machine, have themselves become species of capital, in the forms of genetic engineering, xenotransplantation, mass communications networks, organ procurement and transplantation, and consumerist assemblages of human and machine. This, then, is the first component in becoming-Deleuzian.

Amongst critiques of Deleuze by such eminent Marxians as Alain Badiou (2000) and Slavoj Žižek (2012a) it was Jean Baudrillard who had in 1977 predicted that 'Deleuze's molecular typology of desire [. . .] flows and connections will soon converge – if they have not already done so – with genetic simulations' (*FF*: 35).[2] The background for these critical interventions is a more general phenomenon, where the popularity Baudrillard enjoyed in the 1980s and 1990s yielded to his now becoming 'distinctly unfashionable' (Browning and Kilmister 2006: 105) whilst the ascending popularity of Deleuze is signalled by the proliferation of 'Deleuze and X' titles, which this book both inserts itself into and distances itself from. In *Deleuze and New Technology* (Savat and Poster 2009) one encounters Deleuzian analyses of Baudrillard's preoccupations: simulation, terrorism, cyberculture, biotechnology, reality television, communications networks and mass media. Indeed, this book's cognitive mapping is conjoined to a missed encounter between Baudrillard and Deleuze themselves. Following his critique of Marx, *The Mirror of Production*, Baudrillard intended to write *The Mirror of Desire*, 'a true critique' of Deleuze that he ultimately decided 'wouldn't be worth the effort' (1993b: 58). Deleuze never wrote about Baudrillard, but Sylvère Lotringer – founder of Semiotext(e), and thus publisher of many things Baudrillardian and Deleuzian – has used the word 'despised' to describe his view (Lotringer 2001: 152).

When Lotringer moved to publish Baudrillard's *Forget Foucault*, Deleuze and Guattari threatened to sever all ties with Semiotext(e). To placate them, Lotringer modified the book with an interview with Baudrillard (Lotringer 2008: 9).[3]

Baudrillard is the second component in becoming-Deleuzian. Both Baudrillard and Deleuze have emerged as key references for examinations of SF in general, and of cyberpunk in particular, and SF was crucial to their theorisations of capitalism, psychoanalysis and Marxism. The becoming-Deleuzian of SF not only sees an increase in the number of Deleuzian analyses of novels and films, but is also characterised specifically by the substitution of Deleuze for Baudrillard in the analysis of particular SF texts, such as J. G. Ballard's *Crash* (1973) and the films of David Cronenberg, especially *Videodrome* (1983) and *Crash* (1996). These texts, formerly held to have a natural affinity with Baudrillard or, in the case of Ballard, a territory staked out by Baudrillard himself, have attracted scholars who dispute Baudrillard's negative emphasis on the technocapitalist invasion of the human body and mind, and replace it with Deleuze's affirmative and immanent concepts of desire, affect and schizoanalysis. In so doing, such analyses occlude the extent to which Baudrillard, Deleuze and the texts themselves provide a cognitive mapping of capitalism. The full extent to which Baudrillard has become a casualty of, and primary obstacle to, this becoming-Deleuzian is indicated by the way scholars find it mandatory to wrest particular texts away from him.

This book will be a prolonged engagement with SF, Deleuze, Baudrillard and others, including Jameson and Žižek, both of whom have contributed to SF studies, and will provide commentaries on Baudrillard, Deleuze, Karl Marx, Sigmund Freud and Jacques Lacan. To develop a Marxian, psychoanalytic and schizoanalytic programme, it draws on and expands the science-fictional thought of Deleuze and Baudrillard themselves. The grounds for the engagement will be what I have called becoming-Deleuzian, the transition from late capitalism to biocapitalism, and their cognate expressions, cyberpunk and biopunk.

Control

Deleuze's societies of control will provide the *mise en scène* of this book. In 'Postscript on the Societies of Control' Deleuze adds a successive phase to those described by Michel Foucault, identifying a 'higher-order of production' and newly dispersed systems of the management of people (PSC: 7). Foucault (1995) analysed pre-industrial societies of sovereignty and described their transformation into disciplinary societies, where the individual passed from one organised space to another (the school, the factory, the hospital, the prison). Where the *individual* once moved from one distinct *mould* to another, in societies of control, the *dividual* is now subject to perpetual *modulation* amidst communication technologies and speculative capital, liberated from the factory and the panopticon, only to suffer (and bizarrely and lovingly embrace) the carefully managed freedom of the corporation. New assemblages emerge: cybernetic and information technologies, pharmaceutical innovations, genetic manipulation and molecular engineering (PSC: 4; Deleuze 1988: 131).

Besides Foucault, it was William S. Burroughs who foresaw the emergence of control. In *Naked Lunch* (1959) Deleuze and Guattari find drugged and experimental schizophrenics with multipurpose orifices and reconfigured organs (*TP*: 166–7); in *Junky* (1953) they find both lines of flight and catatonic zombies (*N*: 23). In 'Control', Burroughs's society is harassed by media broadcasts and statistics, perpetually modulated by contradictory commands issued simultaneously, and 'conditioned to obey both commands automatically' (1974: 41). In 'The Limits of Control' he speaks of 'brainwashing, psychotropic drugs, lobotomy' and 'subtle forms of psychosurgery' (1998: 339). Unlike Baudrillard, who renders simulation society in more paranoid terms, for Deleuze, between discipline and control, there is 'no need to ask which is the toughest or most tolerable regime, for it's within each of them that liberating and enslaving forces confront each other [. . .] There is no need to fear or hope, but only to look for new weapons' (PSC: 4). This complements Burroughs's insight that control is 'partial and not complete'. While 'systems try to make control as tight as possible [. . .] if they succeed completely, there would be nothing left [. . .] When there is no more opposition, control becomes a meaningless proposition' (1998: 339). Control is a relative advantage, a process of constant, yet contestable, refinement and rearrangement of mechanisms. Finally, Deleuze writes that the 'conception of a control mechanism, giving the position of any element within an open environment at any given instant [. . .] is not necessarily one of science fiction' (PSC: 7).

Control societies are those of late capitalism and cyberpunk. *Cyber* is itself derived from the Greek word for control. Cyberpunk signifies a combination of real-life practices and a subgenre characterised

4

by the novels and short stories of Pat Cadigan, William Gibson and Bruce Sterling, and films such as *Blade Runner* (Ridley Scott, 1982), Larry and Andy Wachowski's *The Matrix* (1999) and those of David Cronenberg. Popular from the mid-1980s through to the late 1990s, cyberpunk dealt in mass-media technologies and the conjunction of gritty, urban experiences with virtual reality. Cyberpunks fashioned themselves as technonomadic, radical social outcasts and DIY computer hackers, solitary, yet united in virtual reality. Demanding total freedom of information and collective expression over cyberspace, cyberpunks sought to revolutionise society with cyberanarchy.[4] Gibson's *Neuromancer* (1984) remains the definitive work, where subjectivities and the economy are dispersed across the Matrix, a simulacral, virtual environment, and the Turing Police monitor artificial intelligences. Cyborgic, drug-addled corporate-criminal 'console cowboys' with compromised central nervous systems can no longer jack into the Matrix, contemptuously experiencing their own bodies as abject 'meat'.

Despite cyberpunk's confrontational veneer, its ideological weakness is its individualism, its often uncritical embrace of high technology, and its acceptance of, rather than resistance to, late capitalism. Cyberpunk's subversive strategies were quickly adopted by, and became indistinguishable from, the corporate structures they initially opposed. Describing the characters that populate 'cool capitalism', the 'marriage of counter-culture and corporate business', Jim McGuigan observes that punks 'constituted an extreme branch of the ironic tendency' whose 'subterranean lifestyle, hedonistic pleasure-seeking' and 'illicit drug-taking are all manifestations of cool' (2009: 7, 5). Cyberpunks transgressed the binaries of modernism and humanism: male/female, body/mind, nature/technology, human/ animal, white/non-white and self/other. Donna Haraway's cyborg is the ideal cyberpunk, wary of organic or political 'holism, but needy for connection' (1991: 151). Polymorphous, polysemous, often polyamorous, emerging from SF, the military-industrial complex and late capitalism, the cyborg wavers at every threshold: culture/nature, human/animal, organism/machine, man/woman. Blasphemous and ironic, the cyborg is also politically correct. When cyberpunk explored the triad of gender, race and class, it preferred the first two destinations, downplaying class and becoming complicit with the corporate arms of the culture industry (Slusser 1994; Suvin 1994); its duplicity was its fashionably alienated subculture embracing the 'high-tech tools of the establishment' it was 'supposedly alienated from' (Csicsery-Ronay Jr 1994: 183), and its marriage of New Age bohemianism and information technology presented cyberpunks as a 'streetwise technological avant-garde' rather than the 'privileged class' (Latham 2002: 228) they truly were.

Cyberpunk's appropriation of technology is a matter of consumerism and thus immediately enmeshed in political economy. Against their radical androgyny and promissory erasure of the technological-human barrier, cyborgs 'embody the libidinal-political dynamics of the consumerist ethos', incorporating the 'machineries of consumption' into their flesh (ibid. 1). Despite the multitude of interstitial, 'illegitimate' beings – clones, cyborgs, technotranssexuals, transhumanists and interspecials – cyberpunk's most radical claim was to be 'the literature of the simulacra', with the predominance of its 'disembodied techno-fantasies' (Vint 2010b: 230, 96). While it dramatises 'visceral encounters at the human/machine interface' (Hollinger 2010: 191) more often than not, embodied subjectivities are merely scaffolds for flights into virtual mindscapes, an 'electronic solipsism' that bears the impress of Marshall McLuhan, and 'marked by the same refusal to acknowledge the political reality of power and its operations' (Bukatman 1993: 191).

Cyberpunks themselves self-consciously adopted Baudrillard, Deleuze and others into their strategies. More broadly, they are part of SF's theoretical apparatuses, with Istvan Csicsery-Ronay Jr describing Baudrillard and Haraway as 'fusion[s] of SF and theory' (1991b: 389). In the recent *Fifty Key Figures in Science Fiction*, Baudrillard, Haraway and Suvin comprise the three entries devoted to theorists, and it notes Baudrillard's appeal for and affinity with cyberpunk, and that he 'reads like the peculiar blend of estrangement and cognition associated with' SF (Butler 2009: 22). The fullest treatment of cyberpunk remains Scott Bukatman's (1993) survey of 'terminal identity' texts and theorists, including McLuhan, Haraway, Baudrillard and Deleuze; and François Cusset cites Baudrillard, Deleuze and Foucault as the conceptual references for cyberpunk's 'blending of simulation, abstract machines, and the microphysics of power into a fantastic, futuristic world' (2008: 254).[5]

The Matrix famously includes a hollowed-out copy of *Simulacra and Simulation*, 'name-check[ing] for the cognoscenti *the* theorist of simulation' (Merrin 2005: 115). Although he inspired the film, Baudrillard dismissed it as 'the kind of film about the Matrix that the Matrix itself could have produced' and declined to be an adviser on the sequels (2005b: 201–2). Even *The Matrix*, expressly informed by

Baudrillard, has been the subject of becoming-Deleuzian (Diocaretz and Herbrechter 2006). Deleuze's machines and the virtual are put to work here, but we can easily dispense with this becoming-Deleuzian by referring to Deleuze himself: if 'behind every cave there is another, even deeper; and beyond that another still [. . .] a vaster, stranger, richer world beneath the surface, an abyss underlying every foundation' (*LS*: 146–7), then, as William Merrin points out, 'it is this possibility that the film rejects' (2005: 121).[6]

The Matrix was not the first time Baudrillard and Deleuze entered the popular imagination. With the publication of *Simulations* in 1983, 'simulation' and 'hyperreality' became 'passwords in the art world' of New York (Genosko 1999: 3) where a simulationist school was established. When Baudrillard publicly rejected and ridiculed them, humiliated artists organised anti-Baudrillard parties and rallied around Deleuze (Lotringer 2001: 152). While artists and activists have turned away from Baudrillard, contemporary cyberpunks claim Deleuze and Guattari as 'major philosophical and techno-scientific sources of progressive posthumanism' (Weinstone 2004: 10). Deleuze and Guattari 'hit the jackpot' with the rhizome, and *A Thousand Plateaus* is the 'philosophical bible of the cyber-evangelists' (Spiller 2002: 13, 96). John Marks explains that it is:

> not surprising that Deleuze and Guattari's work has been identified with aspects of cyberculture. For one thing, they seek to undermine the *molar* organisation of the organism, with its clearly defined and delineated body, in favour of a *molecular* plane of disorganisation. In an apparently analogous way, cybertheory often talks in terms of disrupting or even transcending the limits of the body. (2006: 194)

He adds that because 'many cyberspace enthusiasts also seem to embrace the free-market ethos of globalised neo-liberal capitalism', Deleuze and Guattari have found 'themselves co-opted into this alliance between cyberspace and cutting-edge capitalism' (ibid. 197–8).[7] The first part of this book, 'Control', will address these readings of Deleuze and Baudrillard within the control societies of late-capitalist cyberpunk. Distancing itself from disembodied techno-fantasies, it will analyse texts that attracted Deleuze and Baudrillard themselves, and bring renewed Marxian readings to those that are becoming-Deleuzian. Overturning the uses to which cyberpunks have mobilised their thought, these chapters develop the theme of control across language, perception, expression, production, consumerism, and pharmaceutical, televisual and cinematic assemblages.

Contagion

The twenty-first century was predicted to be both the biotech century and the Deleuzian century and, sure enough, Alexander Styhre and Mats Sundgren's *Venturing into the Bioeconomy* draws Deleuze's societies of control into active relation with biotechnology and biocapitalism (2011: 50; see Vandenberghe 2008; Sharon 2011). Biopunk signifies both the real-life practices and SF subgenre of biocapitalism. 'Contagion' is the conceptual axis of this part of this book. Contagion does not mean abandoning control, but crossing the threshold from late capitalism to biocapitalism, from cyberpunk to biopunk:

> The potent web of signifiers with which contagion is connected – resistance, immunity, colonisation, hygiene, blood, plague, hysteria – are concepts deployed poetically, theoretically, politically and scientifically [. . .] Spread[ing] by contact, contagion invites uneasy considerations of connections between things – people, animals, organic objects, inanimate objects – things which humans do not know, or always wish to know [. . .] Contagion requires contact, but it always implies more than this: it implies absorption, invasion, vulnerability, the breaking of a boundary imagined as secure, in which the other becomes part of the self. Contagion connotes both a *process* of contact and transmission, and a substantive, self-replicating *agent*, and is centrally concerned with the growth and multiplication of this agent. (Bashford and Hooker 2001: 4)

Contagion's polysemousness captures capitalism's distinctively biological qualities: its ability to render everything exchangeable, and the way globalisation spreads like a disease, encroaching on every aspect of our lives, at work and in our leisure time; spreading through communication networks, viral marketing and viral media; proliferating and replicating like cancer, whilst commodities like cigarettes and junk food conflate addiction and metabolic processes, psychic desires and physiological needs. In biocapitalism, viruses and pathogens are produced, patented and sold. Fascinating and repellent, contagion shifts across the borders and brings into contact aesthetics, media, poetics, theory, politics, economics, desire, science and technology. The second part of the book will be a critical intervention into these new challenges for Marxism.

Biopunk is animated by biopolitics and biopower, and the bioeconomy. In an issue of *Science Fiction Film and Television* dedicated to biopolitics, Sherryl Vint cites both Foucault and Deleuze to argue that ours is 'an era in which the speculative and the material are so entwined that neither can be understood in isolation', and that SF 'is in a privileged position to help us think through its anxieties and contradictions' (2011b: 161–2). Biopolitics is the aggregate of governmental, political, institutional and economic techniques that supervise and permeate the population, setting in motion its hygiene, birth rate and life expectancy. Biotechnology acquired cultural and economic relevance in the late 1970s and early 1980s, but capitalism itself would have been impossible without the biopolitical 'accumulation of men', the 'controlled insertion of bodies into the machinery of production and the adjustment of the phenomena of population to economic processes' (Foucault 1978: 140). Whilst the twenty-first century might well become the biotech century, biocapitalism does not signify a millenarian break in capitalism, but 'capitalism pursued by other (technoscientific) means' (Styhre and Sundgren 2011: 54–5). Similarly, for Nikolas Rose, the mutations of biocapitalism do not mark 'a fundamental break with the past', but 'a threshold has been crossed' nonetheless: 'Marxists and post-Marxists may disagree about whether "biocapital*ism*" is a novel "mode of production," but the existence and significance of biocapital, as a way of thinking and acting, cannot be disputed' (2007: 7, 34).

Unlike Deleuze – the theoretical foundation for Michael Hardt and Antonio Negri's biopolitics – Baudrillard is rarely invoked in this discourse. John Fekete claims that Baudrillard 'makes a huge contribution to the domain of biopolitics, though he never uses the term' (1994: 16) but without explaining why this might be so. However, in Timothy Campbell's introduction to Roberto Esposito's *Bíos*, he argues that biopolitics has come to denote two distinct approaches. On the one hand, Esposito's writings on immunisation and autoimmunity occupy the same conceptual space as Baudrillard, himself having much in common with Giorgio Agamben's sense of biopolitics as the thanatopolitics of Auschwitz (Campbell 2008: vii–viii). On the other, in Hardt and Negri's Deleuzian political ontology, the 'central role previously occupied by the labour power of mass factory workers in the production of surplus value is today increasingly filled by intellectual, immaterial, and communicative labour power' (2001: 29). Here, biopolitical production is not the production of commodities, but of 'ideas, information, images, knowledges, codes, languages, social relationships [and] affects' (Hardt 2010: 135). Private property here becomes tenuous, since biopolitical productions circulate without depreciating in use- and exchange-value.[8] Hardt and Negri have attracted numerous criticisms (Callinicos 2001; Fotopoulos and Gezerlis 2002) and their language clearly complements the New Age capitalist jargon of buying and selling 'experiences' rather than commodities, but their concept of affective labour underpins both the virtual labour of cyberpunk and that of biopunk.

For Rose, biopolitics is characterised by *molecularisation*, that is, thought which envisages and practices that manipulate life at a molecular level; technoscientific *optimisation* of the human body; new regimes of *subjectification* that produce biological citizens with new ethics and actions; the *somatic expertise* of biotechnological and biomedical professionals; and an *economics of vitality* of the bioeconomy (2007: 5–6). These five characteristics are symptoms of advances in the life sciences and technology: genetic screening, reproductive technologies, organ transplantation, genetic modifications, psychiatric drugs, genetic engineering, xenotransplantation and personalised medicine (ibid. 1). 'Contagion' will examine each of these features, for they compel us to move away from cyberpunk toward new forms of embodiment:

> The artificially enhanced body is no longer the cyborg [. . .] The new molecular enhancement technologies do not attempt to hybridise the body with mechanical equipment but to transform it at the organic level, to reshape vitality from the inside: in the process the human becomes, not less biological, but *all the more* biological. (Ibid. 20)

I will reinscribe these 'all the more biological', these *hyperbiological*, bodies into the control discourses of cyberpunk, distancing them from its delirious virtual prognostications. 'Contagion' will take them as models for biopunk subjectivity, locating them in the bioeconomy. By insisting on an intimacy between the 'artificial' body and capitalism, it rejects the dominant interpretative strategies of contemporary cultural studies. David McNally explains that 'lacking a critical theory of capitalism, much of cultural studies is hampered when it comes to explaining the intertwining of monsters with markets':

> In cultural studies, a giddy embrace of monstrosity is underway, as monsters are positioned as heroic outsiders, markers of nonconformity and perversity, representing all those marginalised by dominant discourses and social values. [. . .] [The] universal injunction to be on the side of the monster tends to trivialise real ethico-political choices, sometimes dangerously so. It is one thing, after all, to be on the side of the monstrous others like people of colour or sexual 'deviants' in the face of political persecution or repression. But it is quite another thing where multinational corporations [. . .] are the monsters in question. (2011: 10–12)

McNally provides a Marxian perspective from which to evaluate Jackie Stacey's *The Cinematic Life of the Gene* (2010). Stacey understands cinema and genetic engineering as technologies of biological and cultural imitation, and analyses films that dramatise cloning, such as *Species* (Roger Donaldson, 1995), *Alien: Resurrection* (Jean-Pierre Jeunet, 1997), *Gattaca* (Andrew Niccol, 1997), *Teknolust* (Lynn Hershman Leeson, 2002) and *Code 46* (Michael Winterbottom, 2003). These films are of the 'genetic imaginary', a 'fantasy landscape inhabited by artificial bodies that disturb the conventional teleologies of gender, reproduction, racialisation, and heterosexual kinship' (Stacey 2010: 8). These analyses unfold in Deleuze's societies of control, as do my own. But Stacey's opening move is to free herself from Baudrillard – for whom cloning is a symptom of technoscientific narcissism and capitalist simulation – in order to analyse new forms of identity through feminist and queer optics, so that *Gattaca* reveals less about the division of labour across a genetically determined class/caste system than about the politics of masquerade and impersonation.[9] Stacey shows how monsters and artificial bodies reimagine our biocultural assumptions, but this book insists that it is both urgent and necessary to stress that our biocultural horizons are shaped by the contradictions of biocapital. I will bring this renewed intimacy between the genetic imaginary and the economic and cultural matrices of biocapitalism to 'Contagion' to provide a theorisation of biopunk.

Kaushik Sunder Rajan's *Biocapital* details our moment where the life sciences represent a 'new face, and a new phase, of capitalism', and 'biotechnology is a form of enterprise inextricable from contemporary capitalism' (2007: 3). He unearths the dialectic between biotechnology and capitalism irretrievably '*overdetermined* by the capitalist economic structures within which they emerge' (ibid. 6). In a deregulated market driven by financial and technoscientific speculation and entrepreneurialism, biocapital is the exchange and circulation of new species of capital and commodities, and new forms of abstraction, labour and consumption. Biocapitalism remains a continuation of late capitalism, yet creates:

> a series of cultural transformations in the materiality and exchangeability of what we call 'life.' These transformations are created through shifting and variable use of market commodification versus public commons or public goods formation, both of which are disciplined by new forms of capitalist logic, conforming neither to those of industrial capitalism nor to those of so-called postmodern information capitalism. This is the

rationale for the term 'biocapital,' which asks the question of how 'life' gets redefined through the contradictory process of commodification. (Ibid. 47)[10]

These are the new contradictions of biocapitalism, recycling Marx's description of capitalism's ability to 'change continually without capital suffering the slightest alteration' (1950: 84) and the emergence of 'new classes, new conditions of oppression, new forms of struggle in the place of old ones' (Marx and Engels 1950: 33).

Biopunk is a new perspective from which to re-engage Marx's sense of a self-revolutionising yet perpetually exploitative capitalist mode of production. This book responds to the fact that there is no substantial scholarly material on biopunk or its relation to biocapitalism. But it is clear that biopunk's origins are embedded within SF, and most conspicuous in cyberpunk. Brian McHale's influential 'POSTcyberMODERNpunkISM' describes the difference between cyberpunk and biopunk as 'purely notional' (1992: 258). He writes that the '"bio-punk" sub-variety of cyberpunk SF makes available an entirely different, though complementary, range of motifs of the centrifugal self'. Where cyberpunk has its cyborgs, biopunk:

> 'grows' new human individuals in vats, or clones identical multiples of the 'same' individual [. . .] Where the machine-oriented variety augments and extends capacities through mechanical means [. . .] bio-punk accomplishes the same thing through bio-techniques, engineering new, reconfigured human types. (Ibid. 257)

Biopunk's emergence as a subgenre, rather than a tendency, is signalled by McHale's description of its generic figure, a 'living human being "possessed" by some alien, or under the irresistible control of some other human being' (ibid. 257), a description which bears little resemblance to the figures I will theorise.

An account of biopunk is necessary, not only because of the unsatisfactory character of McHale's reading, but also because the consensus is that cyberpunk is over. Embracing the simulacrum, cyberpunk was founded on an optimism about virtual reality. But, from the 1990s onwards, cyberpunks were forced to come to terms with a technology that 'remained frustratingly non-immersive', and 'the idea of the internet or cyberspace as a non-material, disembodied, and inherently liberating realm was found wanting' (Brians 2011: 124–5). Nonetheless, hyperreality's sensory overload 'wears matter out': it may 'live on as "[Cronenbergian] New Flesh," which may not be flesh at all, and may preserve of us what we admire least'

(Csicsery-Ronay Jr 1994: 192). For good reason, Graham J. Murphy and Vint called their recent collection *Beyond Cyberpunk* (2010), drawing attention to the urgent need for a form that responds to the distribution of power and subjectivity in our contemporary economy and technologised environment. In the wake of the false promises of the cyberpunk revolution, biopunk is a new fusion of real-life practices, science, technology, cultural theory and SF. To gain a sense of this subgenre, and its socio-economic and biopolitical valences, I will survey three elaborations of biopunk philosophy, alongside precursory and contemporary biopunk.

Affecting a radical break, Annalee Newitz declares cyberpunk 'passé. The Internet boom was a joke. Steve Jobs is a dink, Bill Gates is a fascist [. . .] What new techno-arts revolution will come next? [. . .] The answer has already arrived: it's the biopunk revolution' (2001: paras 1–2). Like garage-based cyberpunks, but unlike 'biotech corporate drones', kitchen-tinkering 'biopunks believe in the liberation of genetic data' (ibid. para 3), adopting as their theoretical references Evelyn Fox Keller and Haraway. Inspired by Octavia Butler's *Xenogenesis* trilogy (1987, 1988, 1989) – a mixture of aliens, biotechnology and queer and interspecies encounters – biopunk is 'pro-clone', and promotes the schizo-nomadic use of biotechnology that 'gets us out of the mommy-daddy-baby continuum' (Newitz 2001: paras 7–10). After Newitz, Meredith L. Patterson's 'Biopunk Manifesto' situates the movement as an evolution of cyberpunk, with biopunks 'building on the work of the Cypherpunks who came before us to ensure that a widely dispersed research community cannot be shut down' (2010: para 6). Biopunks are a community of autonomous researchers, biohackers and innovators, whose curiosity 'knows no ethnic, age, or socioeconomic boundaries' (ibid. para 7).

Critics have failed to warm to Paul Di Filippo's term 'ribofunk' (ribosome + funk), but his 'Ribofunk: The Manifesto' presages biopunk's discrediting of cyberpunk:

> Cybernetics was a dead science when cyberpunk was born [. . .] Punk was a dead music when cyberpunk SF was born [. . .] The next revolution – the only one that really matters – will be in the field of biology [. . .] Ribofunk must be as sensual as sex, as unsparing in sweat, cum, bile and lymph as the body is prolific in these substances. (1996: paras 1–3, 10)[11]

He traces the origins of biopunk to H. G. Wells's *The Island of Doctor Moreau* (1896) and thence to the biopunk tendencies in Greg Bear's *Blood Music* (1985) and Sterling's *Schismatrix* (1985)

(Di Filippo 1996: para 14).[12] Sterling's *Schismatrix* might profitably be understood as expressing biopunk's antipathy toward its antecedents, staging a conflict between Shapers, who use biotechnology, and Mechanists, who use software and cyberpunk technology to alter their bodies. Similar is the conclusion of *Neuromancer*, with Case, the protagonist, renovating his insides with new organs, whilst his simulacral, disembodied consciousness wanders the Matrix.

The impression one receives from these biopunk manifestos is of a movement still in its infancy which has the potential to intervene radically in our understanding of biocapitalism. Despite its hostility towards cyberpunk, biopunk risks repeating its mistakes: its anti-establishment, DIY punk posturing obscures biohacking knowledge contingent on access to specialised education; biopunks might operate from their kitchens but, as Marcus Wohlson's (2011) survey of DIY biohacking reveals, the vast majority of biohackers are already contracted or subcontracted employees of biotech companies. Biopunks are oddly convinced that their labour, even as deterritorialised biohacking, is unshaped by or unaccounted for in the political economy of biocapitalism, either as an addendum to commodity production or in the increasingly privatised and deregulated general intellect.[13] Above all, biopunks remain fascinated by the prospect of transforming themselves, but largely uninterested in revolutionising the fundamental structures of capitalism.

Biopunk tendencies can be found in the cyberpunk novels of Greg Egan (1992, 1994, 1995, 1999) but, like those of Walter John Williams, Butler and Bear, they are overdetermined by cyberpunk's preoccupation with virtual reality and their dependence on astrophysics and aliens. Against these are SF novels that engage the biopolitics of over and underpopulation, including Harry Harrison's *Make Room! Make Room!* (1966) and Richard Fleischer's film adaptation, *Soylent Green* (1973), William F. Nolan's *Logan's Run* (1967) and Michael Anderson's adaptation of the same name (1976), Paul R. Ehrlich's non-fiction *The Population Bomb* (1968), which inspired Michael Campus's *Z.P.G.* (1972), and P. D. James's *The Children of Men* (1992), the basis for Alfonso Cuarón's 2006 film. Like Aldous Huxley's *Brave New World* (1932) and Paolo Bacigalupi's Hugo and Nebula award-winning *The Windup Girl* (2009),[14] these biopolitical texts imagine futuristic dystopias rather than alternative cosmologies, whereas the works I theorise as biopunk unfold in the present, as alternative histories, or on appreciably shortened horizons. They thereby share aesthetic, thematic and narrative resemblances with novels like Robin Cook's *Coma* (1977), Max Brooks's *World War Z* (2006) and Ninni Holmqvist's *The Unit* (2006); films like *Parts: The Clonus Horror* (Robert S. Fiveson, 1979), *Gattaca*, *28 Days Later* (Danny Boyle, 2002), *The Island* (Michael Bay, 2005), *Daybreakers* (Michael and Peter Spierig, 2009) and *World War Z* (Marc Forster, 2013); or are contemporaneous with less science-fictional films such as *Contagion* (Steven Soderbergh, 2011). But biopunk is part of the SF canon, not just a cyberpunk tendency. I will develop this canonical line of argument, recasting as proto-biopunk Mary Shelley's *Frankenstein* (1818) and Wells's *Doctor Moreau*, and identify Karel Čapek's *R.U.R.* (1920) as the first biopunk text.

We can now make some meaningful distinctions between cyberpunk and biopunk. Both aspire to progressive or liberating DIY uses of science and technology otherwise available only to specialists in economically and socially powerful institutions and corporations. The protagonist of both is typically a physically, emotionally, culturally or economically 'disadvantaged' party, seeking retribution or vindication; one whose professional investment or intellectual curiosity affects a change in themselves or society, usually without the approval of governing institutions. In biopunk, the simulacra of cyberspace are replaced by genetic simulacra, such as clones; computer hacking becomes biohacking; the economy of virtual information is replaced by one of genetic material or digitised genetic information; and hyperbiological bodies replace cyborgs and disembodied consciousnesses. While I will follow the fortunes of biopunks who pursue social betterment, scientific curiosity and economic advantage, I want also to retain the more depreciatory connotations of the term 'punk' – working class, proletarian, exploited, conned – which, although valorised by punks themselves, are lost in the process of reappropriation. These punks are not necessarily invested in these changes, but are affected nonetheless, and their alienation is of a different order.

'Contagion' will be a critical intervention into biopunk and biocapitalism, mapping its antecedents, but mainly focusing on twenty-first-century texts. Each chapter will elaborate the fortunes of a contagious form: reanimated and sutured-together bodies, repressed desires, vivisected and xenotransplanted human-animal hybrids, interspecies and intersexual cybrid clones, the organ-factory working class, cancer-riddled consumers, the extracted organs of a cloned population, viral images, viral media, venereal bodies and minds, and biocapitalism itself.[15]

A Thousand Tiny Schizos

Essential to this book's analysis of Deleuze and Baudrillard, cyberpunk and biopunk, is schizophrenia. Rather than shorthand description for the postmodern experience, schizophrenia will apply meaningfully across a range of corporeal and psychological experiences, relating to both psychoanalysis and capitalism. Angela Woods notes that by the early 1980s, Deleuze and Guattari's *Anti-Oedipus* had:

> introduced new and politically charged models of schizophrenia into the academic establishment [. . .] Since then, virtually every aspect of late twentieth-century aesthetic and cultural production – including visual art, literature, television, cinema, architecture, and music – as well as the generalized subjective experience of postmodernity, has been understood through its lens. (2011: 183)

Deleuze and Guattari distinguish the clinically diagnosed schizophrenic from schizophrenia-as-process. The originality of this formulation is that, by placing desire into capitalist production, and production into desire, there is no distinction between libidinal and political economies. When Deleuze and Guattari call the unconscious a 'factory', they distinguish it from Freud's interpretation of the dreams and desires of his patients. His 'representational' thinking made two errors. First, in Freud's hands, desire plays itself out in a 'classical theatre' of myths and tragedies, chiefly the Oedipal narrative (*AO*: 24). Psychoanalysis becomes the task of determining which desires correspond to partial drives, always finding 'true' objects in mummy-daddy Oedipal characters. In so doing, psychoanalysis ceases to be 'an experimental science in order to get hold of an axiomatic system' (*D*: 86).[16] Freud's second error was to make desire a private, family affair and, to affect social relations, it must be desexualised and sublimated (*AO*: 293, 352).[17] Against this, desire *produces* (rather than represents) and is unattributable to Lacan's insatiable lack. If desire produces, then 'its product is real. If desire is productive, it can be productive only in the real world and can produce only reality' (*AO*: 26). If desire affects and is affected by the world beyond the Oedipal triangle, then society, politics, culture and economics are all products of libidinal investments.

What interests Deleuze and Guattari is the correspondence between ownership of private property and the confinement of desire to the family. Investing beyond the familial psychosexual drama, desire is a matter of capitalism. Capitalism sweeps away 'fixed, fast-frozen relationships', so that 'all that is solid melts into air, all that is holy is profaned' (Marx and Engels 1950: 36) – what Deleuze and Guattari call the decoding, deterritorialising novelty of capitalism. The schizophrenic is the product of capitalism, but both are subject to reterritorialisation, the reimposition of conformist social and corrective financial codes:

> Capitalism, through its process of production, produces an awesome schizophrenic accumulation of energy or charge, against which it brings all its vast powers of repression to bear, but which nonetheless continues to act as capitalism's limit. For capitalism constantly counteracts, constantly inhibits this inherent tendency while at the same time allowing it free rein; it continually seeks to avoid reaching its limit while simultaneously tending toward that limit. (*AO*: 34)

The schizophrenic process is capitalism's capacity to revolutionise itself, but the schizo goes one step further, evading reterritorialisation. The schizo is two things. S/he is a de-Oedipalised, asubjective process, bereft of an ego, neither man nor woman, an orphan, anarchist and atheist. S/he is also 'more capitalist than the capitalist and more proletariat than the proletariat [. . .] deliberately seek[ing] out the very limit of capitalism [. . .] its inherent tendency brought to fulfilment, its surplus product, its proletariat, and its exterminating angel' (*AO*: 34–5) – the immanent anti-capitalist tendencies of capitalism.

The task is to distinguish investments of desire that are either paranoid or schizophrenic, 'the ultimate products under the determinate conditions of capitalism' (*AO*: 281); between legitimate and illegitimate uses of the process, a schizophrenic breakthrough from a breakdown, deterritorialisation from reterritorialisation, molar from molecular:

> It would be a serious error to consider *the capitalist flows and the schizophrenic flows* as identical, under the general theme of the flows of desire. Their affinity is great, to be sure: everywhere capitalism sets in motion schizo-flows that animate 'our' arts and 'our' sciences, just as they congeal into the production of 'our own' sick, the schizophrenics [. . .] Our society produces schizos the same way it produces Prell shampoo and Ford cars, the only difference being that the schizos are not salable. (*AO*: 245)

The extent to which schizophrenics *are* for sale is one of the lines of argument pursued in this book. Indeed, both Jameson and Baudrillard have been highly critical of Deleuze and Guattari, drawing attention to the schizophrenic nature of consumerism since, for desiring-production, there is no meaningful distinction between the two, only the production and circulation of flows and affects:

> What the Frankfurt School theorised in revulsion [. . .] as the degradation of culture and the fetishisation of the mind has more recently been celebrated, in positive forms [. . .] What used to be denounced as commodification is now offered by Deleuze and Guattari as the consciousness of the ideal schizophrenic. (Jameson 2008: 375)

Deleuze and Guattari enjoin us to 'destroy Oedipus, the illusion of the ego, the puppet of the superego, guilt, the law, castration' (*AO*: 311). But making these the necessary conditions of an anti-capitalist revolution is, for Baudrillard, symptomatic of an 'intense sense of guilt which attaches to this new style of hedonistic behaviour and the urgent need, clearly outlined by the "strategists of desire", to take the guilt out of passivity' (*CS*: 35).[18]

The critical difference between Deleuzo-Guattarian schizophrenia and Baudrillard's is in the role of Lacan. Of Lacan's imaginary, symbolic and real, Deleuze and Guattari retain only the real as the domain of desire. Baudrillard's account emanates from a fidelity to and a departure from Lacan, namely the mirror stage. Lacan's mirror delivers the subject from a schizoid undifferentiation between self and other, organism and external reality (1977: 4–5). This process of identification with the ideal ego, eternally alienated by its simultaneous misidentification, forms a sense of anatomical coherency. Baudrillard's schizophrenia hinges on a technological retooling of Lacan: 'We lived once in a world where the realm of the imaginary was governed by the mirror [. . .] by theatre, by otherness and alienation. Today that realm is the realm of the screens, of interfaces and duplication, of contiguity and networks' (*TE*: 61). Screens, networks and communications technologies provide a richer, albeit simulacral, world of identifications unlike the mediation and opacity of the symbolic. With the mirror-become-screen, identification becomes interactive, unmediated, instantaneous and hypervisible.

For most, the preponderance of electronic communication and computer simulation means a subordination of the symbolic to the imaginary; for Baudrillard, they flatten the imaginary and the real into a single hyperreal, producing a 'digital Narcissus instead of a triangular Oedipus' (*S*: 173). Unlike the self-alienation of Lacan's mirror, the screens that absorb and harass Baudrillard's schizophrenic are communicative and communicable, so that we '*no longer partake of the drama of alienation, but [. . .] the ecstasy of communication*' (2012: 26). There is here a conjunction of Baudrillard's schizophrenia and Lacan's superego, a perverse, eternal injunction to obscene enjoyment. But, for now, Baudrillard's substitution of the mirror for the screen means that:

> We have entered into a new form of schizophrenia – with the emergence of an immanent promiscuity and the perpetual interconnection of all information and communication networks [. . .] A state of terror which is characteristic of the schizophrenic, an over-proximity of all things, a foul promiscuity of all things which beleaguer and penetrate him, meeting with no resistance, and [. . .] not even the aura of his own body protects him. In spite of himself the schizophrenic is open to everything and lives in the most extreme confusion. He is the obscene victim of the world [. . .] The schizophrenic cannot produce the limits of his very being, he can no longer produce himself as a mirror. (Ibid. 30)[19]

Many accuse Baudrillard's semiological and technologically deterministic theories of eclipsing the embodied subject, 'conjuring away the labouring bodies upon which the circuits of capital rest' (McNally 2011: 154–5). Baudrillard's delirious elaborations leave no room for human agency, but my own sense of his schizophrenic is as a subject who is frail, vulnerable, pitifully narcissistic, and lacking the ego boundaries and bodily integrity to ward off technological, ideological and, increasingly, biological intrusion. Chronically integrated rather than symbolically alienated, the schizophrenic lacks the psychic and physiological capacity to establish the necessary difference between self and other, between brain and body and screen; unable, perhaps unwilling, to extricate itself from the hyperreal.

Woods charges Baudrillard with striking off the embodied subject, that his '"pure screen" seems to exist independent of any fleshy reality', meaning that the schizophrenic's 'most basic material reference point is absent' (2011: 198). On the contrary, Baudrillard does not posit an absence as such, but rather a severe reduction to the body, attributable to the substitution of transcendence for immanence. The body is increasingly a vestigial addendum to the edifice of simulation, but this itself is a consequence of a 'degradation to a terroristic visibility of the body (and its "desire") [. . .] In a culture where appearances are desublimated, everything is materialised in its most objective form' (*PES*: 150–1).[20] In his earliest works, Baudrillard calls the body the finest object in the 'consumer package' (*CS*: 129). The confluence of desire, sexual liberation, advertising, fashion, hygiene, dieting and fitness guarantees that the energies, signs and gestures of the body become new sources of capital and novel fetishes, '"liberated, emancipated" to be able to be exploited rationally for productivist ends' (CS: 135). Later, in the crudest of Marxian reductions, Baudrillard is only interested in how the body is exploited by capital to produce use-, exchange- and sign-values (*SED*: 114). He thus conceives bodies in abstract and utilitarian fashion, as asexual and productive robots, and as pliable mannequins with interchangeable sex organs, producing surplus-value and sign-values that signify affluence, sexuality and fashion – and profitable 'differences'.

Wasps, Orchids and Simulacra

Having outlined the conceptual terrain of this book, I want to establish how Deleuze and Baudrillard will underpin a Marxian analysis of SF. This means identifying the parameters of their contributions to Marxism, and their relationship to SF. 'Schizoanalysis has one single aim – to get revolutionary, artistic, and analytic machines working as parts, cogs of one another' (*N*: 24). 'Is it our fault', ask Deleuze and Guattari, 'that Lawrence, Miller, Kerouac, Burroughs, Artaud, and Beckett know more about schizophrenia than psychiatrists and psychoanalysts?' (*N*: 23). Deleuze and Guattari find schizophrenics in modernist and high literature: Franz Kafka, Thomas Hardy, Malcolm Lowry, Allen Ginsberg, Arthur Rimbaud, Virginia Woolf, Henry James, Fyodor Dostoyevsky, F. Scott Fitzgerald and Herman Melville – writers that 'shatter the wall, the capitalist barrier. And of course they fail to complete the process, they never cease failing to do so' (*AO*: 133).[21] While he is fond of the absurdist literature of Lewis Carroll, Jorge Luis Borges and Alfred Jarry, Deleuze's interest in film is largely confined to European art cinema and the distinguished productions of Alfred Hitchcock and Orson Welles (*LS*; *TI*; 1998; 2012a). The exception to his otherwise refined taste is SF, especially with Guattari in *A Thousand Plateaus*, where they write that 'science fiction has gone through a whole evolution taking it from animal, vegetable, and mineral becomings to becomings of bacteria, viruses, molecules, and things imperceptible' (*TP*: 274). They cite *Frankenstein*, Daniel Mann's science-fictional horror film *Willard* (1971), *Doctor Moreau*, Ray Bradbury's *Fahrenheit 451* (1953), H. P. Lovecraft, Richard Matheson and Isaac Asimov (*TP*: 190, 257, 273, 308, 598 n. 23, 640 n. 57). With Fritz Lang's *Metropolis* (1927) and James Whale's *The Invisible Man* (1933) Deleuze theo-

Introduction

rises sound and image, and he speculates on the future of film itself
with Stanley Kubrick (*TI*: 224, 254). Moreover, in his preface to
Difference and Repetition, Deleuze writes that a 'book of philosophy
should be in part a very particular species of detective novel, in part
a kind of science fiction', for 'how else can one write but of those
things which one doesn't know, or knows badly? It is precisely there
that we imagine having something to say' (*DR*: xix–xx).

This gives us licence to read SF through Deleuze, but we should
also recall that for him the 'modern fact is that we no longer believe
in this world [. . .] It is the world which looks to us like a bad
film' (*TI*: 166) – a sentiment he shares with Baudrillard. Jameson
rightly points out that both Baudrillard and Deleuze have fostered
the culture of the simulacrum (2008: 500) but their conceptions
of it are entirely different. Baudrillard's simulacrum is one of mass
culture, mass reproduction, consumerism, the technological generation of images and scientific modelling; Deleuze's is grounded in anti-
Platonism, reserved 'for the contemplation of high-cultural texts and
speculative philosophy' (Durham 1998: 15). Their differences are
signalled by Brian Massumi with reference to Scott's *Blade Runner*
and Cronenberg's *The Fly* (1986). He rejects Baudrillard's 'nostalgia
for the old reality principle', which blinds him to the 'proliferating
play of differences and galactic distances. What Deleuze and Guattari
offer [. . .] is a logic capable of grasping Baudrillard's failing world
of representation as an effective illusion the demise of which opens
a glimmer of possibility' (1987: para 18). Nonetheless, Deleuze
abandoned the simulacrum, declaring it 'all but worthless' (2006:
362). By the time he wrote *What is Philosophy?* with Guattari, it was
given over to Baudrillard's use of the term, the 'shameful moment'
when the 'simulacrum, the simulation of packet noodles' became the
'true concept; and the one who packages the product, commodity, or
work of art has become the philosopher' (1994: 10).[22]

Deleuze maintained that he and Guattari 'remained Marxists':
'Any political philosophy must turn on the analysis of capitalism and
the ways it has developed' (*N*: 171). So, we need not go along with
Peter Hallward (2006) for whom Deleuze is an indifferent and apolitical philosopher.[23] Nonetheless, Deleuze and Guattari's subordination of class to minorities and micropolitics is a significant limitation
on their Marxian aspirations. 'A Marxist can be quickly recognised',
Deleuze writes, 'when he says that a society contradicts itself, is
defined by its contradictions, and in particular by its class contradictions' (*D*: 135). Rather than classes or contradictions, Deleuze and

Guattari privilege minorities and lines of flight. Following Jameson, the task is not to ask whether Deleuze is a Marxian, but 'to determine to what degree the thought of Deleuze moves within and endorses that problematic; or [. . .] to what degree the problematic of Deleuze includes the Marxian problematic and endorses Marxian problems' (2009: 190). Indeed, one of the most neglected lines in Deleuze and Guattari is that the 'power of minority, of particularity, finds its figure or its universal consciousness in the proletariat' (*TP*: 521) and it is this alliance between schizophrenia and class that I will critique and develop in this book.[24]

More than Deleuze, comparisons are consistently made between Baudrillard and SF (Hayles 1991; Rojek and Turner 1993: xi), especially George Orwell (Morris 1984; Norris 1990: 191; Flieger 2005: 21). His consonance with dystopia is particularly strong for Douglas Kellner:

> I prefer to read Baudrillard's work as science fiction, which anticipates the future by exaggerating present tendencies and thus provides early warnings about what might happen if present trends continue. It is not an accident that Baudrillard is an aviciendo of science fiction, who has himself influenced a large number of contemporary science fiction writers. (1994: 13)

The problem here is that it narrows the distance required to read SF critically through Baudrillard. In so doing, it oddly concedes too much to Baudrillard's own position that theory and SF have become indistinguishable. It also bolsters the consensus that Baudrillard has very little to offer contemporary social theory. Through overuse, imprecision and obsessive underreading, concepts like simulation have lost their psychoanalytical roots outlined above, and their economic foundations, to which I turn now.

The immediate obstacle for my Marxian use of Baudrillard is his hostility to Marxism, especially in *The Mirror of Production*. Stripped of semiological acrobatics, Baudrillard's basic insights – the foundation of a 'break' with Marx – are that there is nothing natural about needs or use-value, and that this last term ideologically reflects exchange-value, and that Marx underemphasises the role of consumption and wrongly analyses primitive societies. These are nothing that one cannot find in Louis Althusser and Étienne Balibar (1997) or are not accepted by contemporary Marxians, economists and sociologists (Boltanski and Chiapello 2007).[25] This leaves Baudrillard with two contradictory claims: first, that '*the critique of*

Introduction

political economy is basically completed' (*MP*: 51) and a new radical analysis is necessary; second, that today's capitalism is a '*later* mode', different 'in its structure, its contradictions and in its mode of revolution' (*MP*: 124). Baudrillard's revelation is, at bottom, the modest conclusion that vulgar Marxism provides an insufficient account of contemporary capitalism. Works that give a panoramic account of Baudrillard emphasise the nature of his break with Marxism, but nothing compels us to do so, especially if the break itself lacks substance.[26]

The 'Baudrillard Scene', largely indebted to *Simulations* and to Arthur Kroker and David Cook's *The Postmodern Scene* (1986), introduced a widely accepted, yet chronically partial, representation of Baudrillard as both prophet and advocate of the simulacrum, one reinforced by the popularity of *Simulacra and Simulation* and *The Matrix*. This caricature of Baudrillard is uninformed by the full translation of *Symbolic Exchange and Death* in 1993. Such is its importance, Gary Genosko writes that one 'can only imagine what the "Baudrillard Scene" would have looked like' had it 'appeared before the terms postmodernist and Baudrillard became synonymous' (1999: 88). The key work for Baudrillard is Marx's *Grundrisse* (1939). Extrapolating Marx, Baudrillard's 'end of production' is the absorption of living labour and production by dead labour, and the annexation of the general intellect by capital (*SED*: 15). As with 'flexible' capitalism and accumulation (Harvey 1989, 2006, 2010), Baudrillard points to '"job enrichment", flexitime, mobility, retraining, continuing education, autonomy, worker-management, decentralisation of the labour process' and 'domestic cybernetics' as defining a space where your 'quotidian roots are no longer savagely ripped up in order to hand you over to the machine'; rather, 'you, your childhood, your habits, your relationships, your unconscious drives, even your refusal to work are integrated' (*SED*: 14). '"Proletarian" wage-labour' increasingly becomes 'that bastard, archaic and unanalysed category of service-labour' that, rather than alienating, 'conjoins the body, time, space and grey matter' (*SED*: 17). Contrary to Hardt and Negri's optimism, this is the dawn of capitalism's '*real* domination, solicitation and total conscription of the "person"' (*SED*: 17).[27] From this perspective, Baudrillard theorises three orders of simulacra, which conjoin representational forms with economic determinations, spanning from the Renaissance to the Industrial Revolution, to industrial and consumer capitalism, to simulation (*SED*: 50–6), the post-Lacanian hyperreal: 'From now on

23

political economy is the *real* for us [. . .] It is the real *and therefore* the imaginary, since here again the two formerly distinct categories have fused and drifted together' (*SED*: 31).[28]

Like Deleuze, Baudrillard maintained a strenuous relationship with Marxism:

> Can you give up Marxism in the way you give up tobacco or alcohol? [. . .] The renunciation of the class struggle is grotesque: you can deny the class struggle or sacrifice it if you have to, but you can't give it up like an old skin or a childhood superstition [. . .] And what if, one day, the West were forced to revive Marxism, which is, after all, part of our heritage, damn it. (1994b: 53)

Marxism's inadequacy is, for Baudrillard, symptomatic of his conception of schizophrenia. For Baudrillard, the Marxian project hinged on alienated labour and the proletariat's desire for self-negation. But now that 'the sphere of labour has become hazy, [. . .] the concept itself has lost its definition', and 'lost in our "interactivist" sociality is precisely the negative element, and the possibility of a determinate negation' (2011b: 27–8). Marx remains 'irreproachable', but when Baudrillard writes that 'Marx simply did not foresee that it would be possible for capital [. . .] to make itself autonomous in a free-floating ecstatic and haphazard form, and thus to totalise the world in its own image' (*TE*: 11–12) he is simply wrong, for this corresponds exactly to the abstract and 'pure' forms of capital and capitalism Marx identified towards the end of the third volume of *Capital* (1894). These and other forms of capital, and how they mutate in biocapitalism, are pursued here.

Notes

1. I refer to Fredric Jameson's use of cognitive mapping as that which 'seeks to endow the individual subject with some new heightened sense of its place in the global system [. . .] in which we may again begin to grasp our positioning as individual and collective subjects and regain a capacity to act and struggle' (1996: 54).
2. Baudrillard pre-empts Žižek's wager that while 'Deleuze more and more serves as the theoretical foundation of today's anti-globalist Left and its resistance to capitalism', aspects of Deleuzianism, though 'masquerading as radical chic, effectively transform Deleuze into an ideologist of today's "digital capitalism"' (2012a: xxi–xxii). Žižek's critique owes itself in many ways to Badiou (2000), and the philosophical limitations and inaccuracies of both have been noted (Smith

2004; Buchanan 2008). Nonetheless, Žižek captures the tenor of many Deleuzian approaches to cultural studies and politics.

3. For competing accounts of Michel Foucault's reaction to Baudrillard, see Didier Eribon (1991: 275) and François Dosse (2010: 317).

4. See Eric Hughes's famous 'A Cypherpunk's Manifesto' (1993) and Christian Kirtchev's secondary elaboration (1997).

5. Nick Land's (1998) Deleuzian reading of Gibson's *Neuromancer* would be representative. Key to Land's mission was the accelerationist movement, 'formulated in the language of science-fiction and contemporary theory (particularly the work of Gilles Deleuze and Félix Guattari)' (Noys 2014: x).

6. Dialogue in the original script mentioned Baudrillard by name and quoted from *Simulacra and Simulation* (Merrin 2005: 119) which was required reading for the cast (Constable 2009: 1). *The Matrix* might seem a logical inclusion or starting point for this book, but I have no more to add to the contest, and enough ink has been spilt on the film's use and misuse of Baudrillard (Gingeras 2001).

7. Much like Baudrillard's simulation and hyperreality, 'Deleuzian concepts are now on display everywhere in prepackaged slogans: "smooth space" and "rhizome" freely circulate in the jargon of web designers, music producers, architects, and art critics' (During 2001: 166).

8. Here they put into overdrive Marx's claim that the socialisation of labour is incompatible with the mode of production (Marx 1982: 929). Deleuze seemed unpersuaded by Negri: 'The quest for "universals of communication" ought to make us shudder [. . .] You ask whether control or communication will lead to forms of resistance that might reopen the way for a communism understood as the "transversal organisation of free individuals." Maybe, I don't know. But it would be nothing to do with minorities speaking out. Maybe speech and communication have been corrupted. They're thoroughly permeated by money' (N: 175).

9. Glenn Rikowski summarises the claims of trans and posthumanists as the 'dissolution of hierarchies based on gender, "race" or any other ascriptive characteristics [. . .] The goal is individual *choice* of skin colour and texture, choice of the range of sexual organs and decision on overall body design. No single body is deemed superior; it is just a personal preference or fashion statement [. . .] In terms of its politics and economics, the transhumanist outlook tends generally to support neoliberal nostrums [. . .] There are real *social limits* to posthumanisation, limits set by *capital*' (2003: 130–1, 136).

10. Nancy Scheper-Hughes adds: 'At one level, then, the commodification of the body is a new discourse, linked to the incredible expansion of possibilities through recent advances in biomedicine transplant surgery, experimental genetic medicine, biotechnology and the science of genomics *in tandem with* the spread of global capitalism' (2004: 3).

11. Di Filippo is correct in his assessment of punk. All punks know that even the hardcore scene had broken down by the mid-1980s. Biopunks have not rallied around a particular form of music but, to me, the obvious musical correlate of, rather than inspiration for, biopunk is the extreme form of metal, grindcore, itself an outgrowth of hardcore punk. Grindcore is uncompromisingly aggressive and visceral in its style, song structure, instrumentation, imagery and mode of vocal delivery. Key bands include Napalm Death, Carcass, Pig Destroyer, Anaal Nathrakh and Cattle Decapitation, with their anti-capitalist, socialist and pro-vegetarian themes, and misanthropic preoccupations with genocide, drug addiction, pornography, nonconsensual biomedical procedures and technological domination. See Rosemary Overell's (2014) Deleuzian analysis.

12. Unlike other biopunks, Di Filippo emphasises nanotechnology, and while Bear's *Blood Music* is widely acknowledged as the first SF work to engage the becoming-conscious of nanotechnology, 'nanopunk' seems for now to be an unlikely prospect (Landon 2004).

13. We can therefore extend Matteo Pasquinelli's assessment of cyberpunk to biopunk: 'While the late public of digerati and activists are stuck to the glorification of "free" and "peer" production, good managers – and also good Marxists – are totally aware of the profits made on the shoulders of the collective intelligence' (2008: 91).

14. Andrew Hageman calls it 'cyberpunk, steampunk, agripunk, or some other genre (-punk or otherwise)' (2012: 285).

15. Where possible, I have analysed both novels and films in both parts of this book. First, because Deleuze and Baudrillard were interested in both. Second, the novels under consideration are overwhelmingly preoccupied with encounters with film and television. Cinematic treatments are therefore natural, if not essential, inclusions. Third, biopunk, like SF in general, is to be found across a range of media; I have suggested the type of music that I think corresponds to this subgenre, and I leave it to others to discuss comic books, television, video games and radio.

16. Deleuze and Guattari rightly note that Lacan dispenses with the Oedipal narrative, yet retains its structure (*AO*: 310).

17. Although this is not at all the case in Lacan (1998: 165–6).

18. Baudrillard 'knew' desiring production was 'basically a sophisticated (disembodied, deterritorialised) modern form of consumption' (Levin 1996: 100).

19. For a similar account, see Bernard Stiegler (2013). Critics have noted Baudrillard's debt to Lacan (Cubitt 2001: 46; Pawlett 2007: 58; Voela 2013). Baudrillard is not the only thinker to recast Lacan through technology; see especially Friedrich Kittler (1999: 15–16).

20. Referencing Herbert Marcuse's (2007) concept of repressive desublimation.

21. Paraphrasing Samuel Beckett (1989: 148).
22. While SF is something of an exception in Deleuze, his tastes tend towards the 'snobbish' (Buchanan 2000: 175). So, when Anna Powell writes that, 'surprisingly, Deleuze does not mention Cronenberg's work' (2005: 83), we should not be surprised at all given his comment that 'most cinematic production, with its arbitrary violence and feeble eroticism, reflects mental deficiency rather than any invention' (*N*: 60). Nonetheless, Lotringer surely overstates it by saying 'Deleuze probably regretted praising the simulacrum after Baudrillard used it to cancel every difference between the real and the referential' (2008: 20).
23. Guattari admitted that Deleuze did most of the 'sweating over capitalism' (2006: 137).
24. Thoburn rightly argues for a 'more appropriate tenor for the Deleuzian political than the popular image of unlicensed desire [. . .] After the deterritorialising joys of '68 [. . .] and the early English-language reception of Deleuze and Guattari's work, our more sombre times require a recognition of the increasing isomorphism of processes of complexity and difference to *capitalist* productivity' (2003: 3; see Jain 2009).
25. Baudrillard's metatheoretical accusation that because Marx's analysis is rooted in capitalism's assumptions it 'is led despite itself to reproduce the roots of the system of political economy' (*MP*: 67) is fragile deconstructionism.
26. Gary Browning and Andrew Kilmister add that 'hyperreality and the simulacrum, need to be seen not as a starting point for Baudrillard, but as the result of his engagement with critical political economy' (2006: 115–16).
27. The virtual mobility enjoyed by cyberpunks in Hardt and Negri's biopolitical production, Baudrillard's simulation and Deleuze's societies of control hinges on the so-called post-industrial society. For both Jameson and Baudrillard, cybernetic labour 'deprives people of their sense of making or producing [. . .] reality'. To 'insist on the mediation of the labour process', as I will in this book, is to 'dispel the banal and apolitical conception of a service economy' (Jameson 2008: 642).
28. I have omitted almost entirely from this book the concept of symbolic exchange, which is close to, yet formulated against, Deleuze. Rooted in Georges Bataille and Marcel Mauss, and animated by Freud's death drive, symbolic exchange is pitted against both 'materialist [and] desiring-production' to achieve (nothing less than) 'the extermination of value' (*SED*: 1). Because symbolic exchange 'puts an end to bound energies in stable oppositions' it is 'in substantial agreement with theories of flows and intensities, whether libidinal or schizo'. Yet, because 'capital is an energetic and intense system', there is an 'impossibility of distinguishing capitalist schizes from revolutionary schizes [. . .] Reversibility alone therefore, rather than unbinding or drifting,

is fatal to it' (*SED*: 5 n. 2). Baudrillard's symbolic is equivalent to Lacan's real, demonstrable in the confluence of Žižek and Baudrillard's responses to the terrorist attacks on the World Trade Centre. Both stressed that the attacks recalled Hollywood films. For Žižek, 'the unthinkable which happened was the object of fantasy, so that, in a way, America got what it fantasised about [. . .] It is not that reality entered our image: the image entered and shattered our reality' (2002: 15–16). For Baudrillard, 'fiction (from disaster movies, etc.) is part of our immune system; it protects us from reality by means of its double imaginary. It absorbs our fantasies. And the attack made our fantasies real' (2010b: 91). Disturbingly prescient, Baudrillard wrote in 1976 of its two towers that 'if there were only one, the WTC would not embody the monopoly' (*SED*: 69). Their destruction was 'not "real." In a sense, it is worse: it is symbolic' (2003b: 29). Agonistic spirals of humiliation and escalation are parts of Baudrillard's 'theoretical violence' (*SED*: 5) but largely remain theoretical.

Control

Cantlal

1

Viddy and Slooshy

If sight is perverse, so too is speech. (*LS*: 325)

In an interview with Deleuze, Negri observed that control 'relates to the most perfect form of domination, extending even to speech and imagination' (*N*: 174). The assemblages that characterise a society of control intervene at the level of speech and thought. Anthony Burgess's *A Clockwork Orange* (1962) is a meditation on control over language, expression and thought, but also technoscientific control, namely, the Ludovico technique, an assemblage of cinematic technology and pharmaceutical innovation the State uses to resubjectivise the criminal class. The novel is as famous for its ultra-violent aesthete, Alex, as for its fabrication of Nadsat, a fictional argot spoken by delinquent youths. Through Nadsat, sensations, affects and intensities are estranged, from sublime aesthetic pleasures to horrific violence, nauseous organs and images to new perceptions, new ways of looking and listening. Deleuze never cited Burgess, but he wrote at length about Stanley Kubrick, who adapted Burgess's novel in 1971. What interested Deleuze was how Kubrick initiated a 'cinema of the brain' (*TI*: 198) where the screen itself became a 'cerebral membrane' (*TI*: 121). Together, Burgess and Kubrick illuminate Deleuze's thoughts on literature and language, cinema and control, and allow us to trace their affinities with SF criticism and the genre's linguistic creations. This chapter will set aside Baudrillard,[1] who will return in Chapter 2, in order to place Deleuze into relation with SF, and explore what he means by control.

Minor Language and Abstract Machine

For Freedman, SF may be characterised by its generic narrative tropes, but also by the 'molecular operations of language itself' (2000: 36). SF distinguishes itself as a genre through its idiosyncratic use of language. Freedman selects the opening passage of Philip K. Dick's 1968 novel *Do Androids Dream of Electric Sheep?* to illustrate this:

A merry little surge of electricity piped by automatic alarm from the mood organ beside his bed awakened Rick Deckard. Surprised – it always surprised him to find himself awake without prior notice – he rose from the bed, stood up in his multi-coloured pajamas, and stretched. (Dick 1996: 1)

The 'stylistic register' of this passage 'marks it as unmistakably science fiction' (Freedman 2000: 31). The syntagm is peculiar because 'mood' and 'organ' are unlikely syntagmatic partners, but also for the fact that this 'mood organ' device has a quantifiable effect. These terms are not created *ex nihilo*, but acquire or inspire us to invest in them certain qualities, though we are unsure which for now. As Freedman observes of the passage, which he considers emblematic of SF's dialectical approach to language, the mood organ, a console-operated device that emits emotion-specific waves that affect the brain, is 'unknown in our own empirical environment' yet in the world of Dick's novel 'is an ordinary accoutrement of everyday life'. 'Casualness and estrangement' here work together: the 'unfamiliar and the familiar are held in suspension and [are] related to one another through the operations of a radically heterogeneous and polyvalent prose' (ibid. 31, 37). Dick's lexical manoeuvre disperses meaning, throwing into doubt history, humanity, sensations, affects and technology, thus making certain cognitive and imaginative demands on its reader. We read it, and SF more broadly, 'differently than we would read the language of mundane [non SF] fiction' (ibid. 31). Freedman's point is that this style forces unfamiliar reading relations, where otherwise routine grammar and words become ambiguous and estranged, what Deleuze and Guattari term deterritorialisation, or a line of flight. There is a particular effect at work in SF linguistics, whereby semiotic chains enact a double-coded movement. On the one hand, they highlight the stability of our own 'conventional' or, as Deleuze and Guattari conceive it, majoritarian language, concretising it by juxtaposing it with the foreign or minoritarian language. On the other, it simultaneously raises doubts about the majoritarian language that couches these peculiar words.

Against Ferdinand de Saussure, structuralism and the 'reduction of expression to the signifier' (*TP*: 74, 73) Deleuze and Guattari privilege moments when a major language breaks down, and a minor language creates new perceptions, affects and thoughts. They are not concerned with signification as an end in itself, deriving specific meaning from the sign, but with the conditions that make certain statements possible, and how statements interact in an assemblage:

'The minimum real unit is not the word, the idea, the concept or the signifier, but the *assemblage*. It is always an assemblage which produces utterances' (*D*: 51). The Platonic signifier aspires to an ideal representation of the thing itself and, for psychoanalysis, refers to the world of prohibitions. 'We've no use for signifiers [. . .] Flows of content and expression don't depend on signifiers: language is a system of flows of content and expression, intersected by machinic arrangements' (*N*: 21). SF is not a minor literature, but its linguistic creations, particularly those that develop comprehensive language systems, constitute a minor language. They are not unintelligible, but create isomorphisms and intersections with a major language. Major and minor 'do not qualify two different languages but rather two usages or functions of language' (*TP*: 115). Nadsat deterritorialises majoritarian English, creates when it corrupts comprehension, denaturalises perceptions, interrupts syntagmatic chains by making them break down, makes adjectives behave differently, and creates new sensations. A minor language does not comprise 'sublanguages, idiolects or dialects, but potential agents of the major language's entering into a becoming minoritarian' (*TP*: 117). Nadsat is a minor use of major language, just as English is a major usage of language. What interests Deleuze and Guattari is the becoming-minor of the major language, when a 'new syntax is a foreign language within a language' (*N*: 133). To enter into becoming-minoritarian is to be 'a foreigner, but in one's own tongue, not only when speaking in a language other than one's own. To be bilingual, multilingual, but in one and the same language' (*TP*: 109).

Minor languages are contestations over meaning and subjectivisation, ways that molecular, or schizophrenic, forms of organisation and expression contest molar, or paranoid, formations. Burgess makes a connection between the consumerist world of the molar bourgeoisie and how the nadsat are coded as a symptom of society:

There were more space-trips and bigger stereo TV screens and offers of free packets of soapflakes in exchange for the labels on soup-tins [. . .] And there was a bloshy article on Modern Youth [. . .] This learned veck said the usual veshches, about no parental discipline, as he called it, and the shortage of real horrorshow teachers who would lambast bloody beggary out of their innocent poops and make them go boohoohoo for mercy. All this was gloopy and made me smeck [. . .] Some starry pop in a doggy collar who said that in his considered opinion and he was govoreeting as a man of Bog IT WAS THE DEVIL THAT WAS ABROAD and was like ferreting his way into like young innocent flesh, and it was the adult world that could take responsibility for this with their wars and bombs [. . .] So we young malchicks could take no blame. (32)[2]

The counterpoint to Alex's violent and rapacious actions is his rejection of authority figures' accounts for his behaviour which absolve him of responsibility, for it is society's refined and civilising aesthetic productions that animate Alex's desire. Newspapers encourage 'A Lively Appreciation Of The Arts', for 'Great Music, it said, and Great Poetry would like quieten Modern Youth down and make Modern Youth more Civilised' (32). In Deleuzian fashion, Alex's schizes are immanent to the State itself. Ironically, Alex is the greatest aficionado of classical music, scorning pop consumers. By the same token, when incarcerated, Alex attends religious sermons and reads the Bible, outwardly to simulate signs of rehabilitation, but inwardly finding religious instruction sexually arousing, and it inspires fantasies of crucifixion, torture and humiliation. We can borrow Žižek's analysis of similar subjects: 'Since he speaks from the position of the *explanandum*, his remarks also effectively denounce the fakeness and falsity of the way the ruling ideology and its knowledge account for his acts [. . .] The excluded outsider is unmasked as the hidden model of the "normal" insider' (2012a: 169). Alex's schizophrenia is an expression of society's highest aspirations and deepest desires.

Numerous SF critics have argued for the specificity of SF's formal linguistic properties (Angenot 1979; Stockwell 2000). I suggest that the linguistic elements of SF are in concert with, and an augmentation of, Suvin's conception of SF as a 'literature of cognitive estrangement', in which estrangement is both the 'underlying attitude and dominant formal device' (1979: 4, 7). The supplementary point is what Suvin considers SF's *differentia specifica* (ibid. 63), the presence of a *novum* (plural: nova): 'A totalising phenomenon or relationship deviating from the author's and implied reader's norm of reality' (ibid. 64). Suvin continues:

> The postulated innovation can be of quite different degrees of magnitude, running from the minimum of one discrete new 'invention' (gadget, technique, phenomenon, relationship) to the maximum of a setting (spatiotemporal locus), agent (main character or characters), and/or relations basically new and unknown. (Ibid. 64)

The mood organ is a novum of the 'gadget' sort, since we presuppose its existence in the novel while it can also be cognified well enough in relation to our own empirical environment via the description of its workings. Beyond this minimal function is its shaping interpersonal and machine-human relationships. Broader still, the term 'mood organ' – the yoking of one sign to another is, in its linguistic properties, a novum – enacts the double movement whereby a minor language deterritorialises a major language. It is a new *thing*, and a new *expression*, 'effecting a shift in the perception of the world to which [it is] attached' (Stockwell 2000: 139).

Deleuze and Guattari write that 'crazy talk is not enough' (*TP*: 152) to justify a minor language, just as Suvin writes that SF can quickly amount to a 'semantic game without clear referent' (1979: 15). While the estrangement of the sign from its referent is a structuralist postulate, there is something more puzzling here at the internal level of the sign. The relationship between the two is arbitrary, but the internal components of the sign suggest one another (de Saussure 1960: 67). SF's use of minor language reveals that there is no strong relation between the sign's internal components, the signified and the signifier, but also that the former is questionable in itself. Through language, SF creates new concepts, things, perceptions and sensations. SF tends towards an 'aesthetic goal', whereby language may not be offered for decipherment, but serves to create 'a remote, estranged, and yet intelligible "world"' (Angenot 1979: 10). While this is persuasive, and I will be drawing on Angenot's analysis, Walter E. Meyers sees something more critical operating within the genre. He notes that a more developed SF text is likely to offer a new word without precise definition, bringing 'to the context in which it appears only the *associations* suggested by its *form*'. He adds that, if 'through the use of language the author adds an extra imaginative dimension and at the same time provides the reader with a new perspective from which to view his own society, something special indeed has been accomplished' (1980: 7, 8–9).

Burgess underscores SF's capacity to create minor language. The introduction of new units and syntagmatic chains are nova that imply a larger linguistic paradigm, a novum, what Deleuze and Guattari call an abstract machine. An abstract machine 'places variables of content and expression in continuity' (*TP*: 563) that operate within the assemblages of linguistic material. Abstract machines may open assemblages or close them. A minoritarian abstract machine can deterritorialise, whilst '*axiomatic or overcoding abstract machines*' perform 'totalisations, homogenisations, conjunctions of closure' (*TP*: 565–6). There are two elements at play here. First is the tension between the substantial and relational value of individual units, extending toward the new syntagmatic structures of a new language.

Second, units and syntagms are simultaneously enmeshed in a *'missing paradigm'* (Angenot 1979: 10) or, in this case, a 'missing' novum or abstract machine. On a unitary level, Nadsat words like 'oobivat' (from the Russian *ubivat*: to kill), 'smot' (*smotret*: to look) and 'shlaga' (from the German *Schlager*: a club or bat) are empirical symptoms of an abstract machine.[3]

Burgess's story is narrated in first-person Nadsat by Alex. Most of the words are modified from Russian, though there are also German, Latin, Dutch, regional Slavic, Gypsy, French and Arabic words, Cockney rhyming slang, and some invented words and expressions. To an anglophone they appear as borrowed neologisms, subsequently 'anglicised with free binding with other morphemes' (Stockwell 2000: 125). Importantly, they are 'couched' within the anglophone linguistic paradigm, the majoritarian abstract machine. One may 'viddy' films (from the Russian *vidyet*: to see) or 'slooshy' music (from the Russian *slushat*: to hear). These words are used throughout, spoken by other characters and related to us through Alex. Nadsat is not simply present at the level of the stray utterance, but is the abstract machine through which we interact with the world as Alex's language-as-consciousness moves through it, and we have no recourse to a world that is not mediated through Alex's schizophrenic utterances.

Nadsat is an absent paradigm, an abstract machine – a symptomatic component in the construction of, or an index to, the world. However, first-person narration complicates this. Alex is an unreliable narrator, said to have acquired Nadsat via 'subliminal penetration' (86), but his use of it is self-conscious. For an anglophone, Nadsat is a dizzying experience. Moreover, the implications of individual Nadsat signs are wide-reaching: through Alex, every sign, including those which the reader may identify as English, has the potential to become Nadsat given their mutual dependence in the comprehension of syntagmatic chains. Nadsat is what Csicsery-Ronay Jr calls 'a full-fledged mutant discourse in which the rules of syntax and word construction reflect radical social change at the level of language' (2008: 31). Nadsat and the world are commensurate, and it thus may be considered the minoritarian abstract machine.

For an anglophone, unaccompanied by a Nadsat dictionary, the (approximately) 200 Nadsat words seem, contra Jacques Derrida, to 'simply fall from the sky ready made' (Derrida 1973: 33) and the task is to internalise this language. The simultaneous presence of both English and Nadsat offers 'a partial recognition of our reality, but with sufficient alternativity to render the effect of defamiliarisation' (Stockwell 2000: 61). This relationship is isomorphic, where two domains of knowledge, one major-familiar, the other minor-unfamiliar, come into contact. The content of the Nadsat sign 'is really fixed only by the concurrence of everything that exists outside it' (de Saussure 1960: 115) – majoritarian English. Moreover, Stockwell suggests that 'all words are fundamentally implicated in other similar-looking words', thus 'readers often try to interpret them in terms of words they already know' (2000: 123–4). For example, the Nadsat 'viddy' suggests 'video' and, by extension, 'see' or 'watch'. The hopelessness of translating and deciphering signifiers in relation to other signifiers exemplifies Derrida's concept *différance* (1982: 11) but also Deleuze's concept of becoming, which does not privilege a point of origin, but movement itself. Here, meaning is in constant flux, and searching for it is an infinitely regressive and contagious process. For example, 'horrorshow' comes from the Russian *kharashó* for 'good' or 'well' yet is used adjectivally in relation to gruesome sex and violence. Thus Derrida: the 'meaning of meaning', in its 'indefinite referral of signifier to signifier', means that 'it will always signify again' (1978: 25). In this sense, recourse to a Nadsat dictionary thwarts translation, providing a host of new terms, both the foreign root and a few English equivalents.

Nadsat forces a new relationship that illuminates the overcoding of the majoritarian abstract machine and emblematises the shift from overcoding to becoming-minoritarian. For all his emphasis on arbitrariness, Saussure thought signs acquired relational stability by virtue of their difference from other signs, hence his aphorism that 'in language there are only differences' (1960: 120). Angenot observes that 'every "fictive word," no matter what its "etymology," will be read in a particular context. Surrounding elements irradiate virtual meanings on the opaque signs' (1979: 12). But this must be allowed to work in both directions: this reliance on difference between signs and the positioning of a major language in relation to a minor language contaminates the very majoritarian language we rely upon.

I am interested here in how a minor language works in film in relation to an abstract machine that overcodes expression, perception and sensation. Neil D. Isaacs notes that 'Burgess' dazzling use of language in *A Clockwork Orange* is the most obvious essential quality to be lost in a filmed treatment of the story' (1973: 124). By this he does not mean that Nadsat is absent from the film, since Alex's (Malcolm McDowell) voice-over narration is often transposed more or less word for word from the novel. However, the film is not construed entirely through his consciousness, as is the novel. Isaacs continues:

> More essential [. . .] is the use of that language by his persona. Alex's *voice* – not his vocabulary – dominates the book. The voice is mannered, achieving a kind of hyped musical quality through its many artifices. As such, it is the perfect vehicle for the appropriate and consistent tone with which it speaks. And in turn that tone of voice ideally conveys the ironic themes. (Ibid. 125)

With the obvious exception of the word 'book', this is something one could write about an actor's performance in a film. Vivian Sobchack finds the aesthetic experience of *hearing* Nadsat one of 'extraordinary imaginative resonance', a 'delicate balance between sense and nonsense, between logical communication and magical litany' (2004: 146). Indeed, Saussure said of the signifier in its phonic rather than graphic state that it 'is not the material sound, a purely physical thing, but the psychological imprint of the sound, the impression that it makes *on our senses*. The sound-image is *sensory*' (1960: 66). Burgess's own comments are worth considering: 'The light and shade and downright darkness of my language cannot, however brilliant the director, find a cinematic analogue' (1975: 15). Sobchack notes the irony in his self-assessment, which renders his work in '*visual* terms' (2004: 148) and insists on its acoustic plasticity. To give these words one's own inflection and then feed them back into the novel deictically is demanded of the reader. Extending this, without insisting on translation or suggesting that Nadsat signs work as substitutions, it is interesting to note that a great many of Burgess's words evoke the plastic, sensory qualities of cinema. To 'viddy' is to see, to 'slooshy' is to hear, to 'creech' is to scream, a 'goloss' is a voice, if something is 'gromky' it is loud, and a 'zvook' is a sound. Nadsat signs, especially verbs that evoke *sensations* rather than *things*, estrange their syntagmatic context, but also deterritorialise majoritarian sensation. How might viddying differ from seeing? What does a 'creech' sound like as opposed to a scream?

Below, we will see what Deleuze and Guattari intend when they describe what it is to become a subject of enunciation, that is, to be induced by language to conform and obey, to become an organism. More generally, though, we can make a medium-specific distinction along the lines of how enunciation functions as a narrative device. In literature, enunciation focuses on how narrative is communicated, largely via tenses and modes of address, be they first or third person. Transposed to film, 'enunciation has also come to signify the constitution of subjectivity in language, and secondarily, the production and control of subject relations through the imaginary link established between the narrator and the spectator' (Stam et al. 1992: 106). In literature, the narrator is a linguistic assemblage. This is not the case in film, where the narrator's mental activity is expressed verbally (cognition) and non-verbally (perception) (Chatman 1978: 181). Both literary and cinematic enunciation depend upon levels of mediation between the narrative and the narrator. In Burgess, direct access to Alex's language-as-consciousness comprises the entire narrative. Kubrick, however, shifts between objectively capturing the *mise en scène*, and combining verbalisation and perception into subjective states that bear the impress of Alex's enunciation. Seymour Chatman observes that 'by its nature, cinema resists traditional language-centred notions of the narrator', making a comparative form of enunciation challenging, since 'verbal activity furnishes no easy analogy with visual activity' (1990: 124). Yet, in Kubrick, language has a unique relationship with the image and they work together to produce subjectivity. With an emphasis on consciousness, we will see how Kubrick's cinematic treatment of language makes becoming-minoritarian possible.

The Ludovico technique is an apparatus of capture, a reterritorialisation. Nadsat is described by the doctors as the 'dialect of the tribe [. . .] Propaganda. Subliminal penetration' (86). This last comment is not entirely correct. Alex can moderate his speech, using minor and major language as it suits him. But the notion that Nadsat was acquired by subliminal penetration is revealed only when it begins to disappear, not from Alex's speech, but from his internal narration: even when Alex speaks English, this is secondary to his unspoken narration, which remains in Nadsat. The Ludovico technique manifests not when Alex is nauseated by ultra-violence, but when his unspoken narration becomes punctuated with English. He no longer slooshies, but *listens*, and the rozzes and millicents become police. The major language emerges as an assemblage that not only substitutes words but, at the level of thought and the body, modifies and normalises sensations and one's relation to authority. Although the nadsats distinguish themselves through language, the proper distinction is one of class antagonism. Kubrick's gangs are exclusively male, but in Burgess they are a mix of vecks (males) and cheenas (females), 'but not of the bourgeois, never them' (22). Bourgeois existence is characterised by police supervision during the working day and, at night, immersion in screens: 'The night belonged to me and my droogs and all the rest of the nadsats, and the starry bourgeois lurked indoors drinking in the gloopy worldcasts, but the day was for the starry ones, and there always seemed to be more rozzes or millicents about during the day too'; 'All this time, O thanks to the worldcasts on the gloopy TV and, more, lewdies' night-fear through lack of night-police, dead lay the street' (33, 45). It is important, then, that Alex's resubjectivisation will consist of similar State supervision and screen immersion.

Screening the Brain, Screaming the Body

Deleuze describes Kubrick's as a cinema of the brain where the psyche and its relation to the world becomes *mise en scène*: 'The identity of world and brain [. . .] does not form a whole, but rather a limit, a membrane which puts an outside and an inside in contact [. . .] confronts them or makes them clash [. . .] The insane violence of Alex in *Clockwork Orange* is the force of the outside before passing into the service of an insane internal order' (*TI*: 198). We see and hear Alex process the world, and we process it with him. For Deleuze, classical cinema was governed by the identificatory sensory-motor schema. When this schema breaks down, we access altered states of consciousness: 'The identification is actually inverted: the character has become a kind of viewer [. . .] He records rather than reacts. He is prey to a vision, pursued by it or pursuing it, rather than engaged in an action' (*TI*: 3). This cinema is one of 'liberated sense organs' (*TI*: 4) confronted with purely optical and aural situations (opsigns and sonsigns), becomings that bring oppositions into contact – subjective and objective, real and imaginary, mental and physical – and render them indeterminable. For Deleuze, the shot is consciousness itself, an 'objective illusion' (*TI*: 67) where the screen works as a brain, and vice versa. Moments when we share a character's point of view do not reveal the object perceived but the consciousness that perceives it: 'The eye's already there in things, it's part of the image [. . .] The eye isn't the camera, it's the screen. As for the camera, with all its propositional functions, it's a sort of third eye, the mind's eye' (*N*: 54). Adding to Deleuze's taxonomy of images, Patricia Pisters terms the neuro-image one where we 'no longer see through characters' eyes [. . .]; we are most often inside their mental worlds' (2012: 14). And we shall see that Kubrick's neuro-images are the cinematic equivalent of Burgess's narration.

The Ludovico technique marks a point of transition from discipline to control. After Burroughs, Deleuze suggests that control is emerging as the characteristic mode of authority, and this includes pharmaceutical productions and communications technologies. Alex makes this transition from discipline to control apparatuses. In the former, the objective is to mould the individual in accordance with the State. As the priest explains to Alex, 'you are to be made into a good boy [. . .] Never again will you have the desire to commit acts of violence or to offend in any way whatsoever against the State's Peace' (71). Yet the manipulation of Alex's desire has a greater affinity with apparatuses of control rather than discipline. In a control regime, individuals become 'masses, samples, data, markets, or "*banks*"' (PSC: 5), perpetually modulated, rather than moulded. The State's Reclamation Treatment takes place at a remove from the spatially circumscribed Staja (State Jail) in a medical treatment centre furnished with a cinema. Here, Alex is, on the one hand, depersonalised, rechristened as 6655321. On the other, the object of the treatment is less the macro-organisational effects of the power of spatialisation and the spatialisation of power, than the micro level of intensities at the intersection of simulacra, language and the organs. The Minister of the Interior – and we come to take this authority over interiority quite literally – elaborates the transition from discipline to control:

> The Government cannot be concerned any longer with outmoded penological theories. Cram criminals together and [. . .] you get concentrated criminality, crime in the midst of punishment. Soon we may be needing all our prison space for political prisoners [. . .] Common criminals [. . .] can best be dealt with on a purely curative basis. Kill the criminal reflex, that's all [. . .] Punishment means nothing to them [. . .] They enjoy their so-called punishment. They start murdering each other. (69)

The transition from moulding to the modulation of affects is underscored by the Governor of the Staja: 'If someone hits you you hit back, do you not? Why then should not the State, very severely hit by you brutal hooligans, not hit back also? But the new view is to say no. The new view is that we turn the bad into the good' (70).

Kubrick's film is intermittently narrated in first-person Nadsat by Alex. What interests me here is how the minor language enters into an assemblage with the neuro-image. Alex's language-as-consciousness is intrusive in the film (rather than constant in the

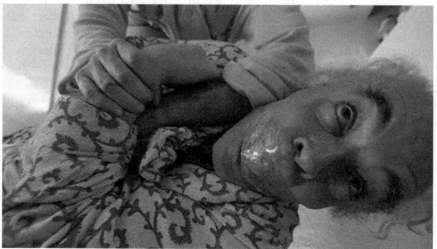

1.1 and 1.2   Stanley Kubrick, *A Clockwork Orange*, 1971. *'I'm singin', just singin' in the rain. Viddy well, little brother, viddy well.'*

novel) in its forcing of self-reflexive intersubjectivities. In both sequences there are forced relations of 'seeing', presented by shot-reverse-shot editing, and 'hearing', articulated in Nadsat. In Figures 1.1 and 1.2, Alex has just finished a gruesome rendition of the screen classic 'Singin' in the Rain', as a restrained figure, Alexander (Patrick Magee), is forced to bear witness to the rape of his wife (Adrienne Corri). In Figures 1.3 and 1.4, voice-over narration accompanies a

Viddy and Slooshy

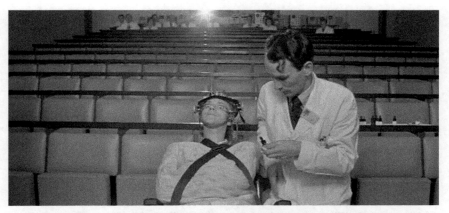

1.3 and 1.4 *'It was a very good like professional piece of sinny [...] It's funny how the colours of the world only seem really real when you viddy them on the screen [...] This was real, very real, though if you thought about it properly you couldn't image lewdies actually agreeing to having all this done to them in a film, and if these films were made by the Good or the State you couldn't imagine them being allowed to take these films without like interfering with what was going on. So it must have been very clever what they call cutting or editing or some such vesch. For it was very real [...] But I could not shut my glazzies, and even if I tried to move my glazz-balls about I still could not get like out of the line of fire of this picture. So I had to go on viddying what was being done and hearing the most ghastly creechings coming from this litso. I knew it could not really be real, but that made no difference. I was heaving away but could not sick, viddying first a brivta cut out an eye, then slice down a cheek, then go rip rip rip all over, while red krovvy shot on to the camera lens. Then all the teeth were like wrenched out with a pair of pliers, and the creeching and the blood were terrific. Then I shlooshied this very pleased goloss'* (77–8).

sequence in which the camera alternates between a restrained Alex and the screen, or, actually, the screen as seen by Alex. The film he watches shows a man being beaten by nadsats, later a woman being gang raped. This is followed by World War II stock footage and Nazi processions and iconography. The diegetic sound from the film Alex is watching – laughter, moans of dismay and reverie, and the sounds of blows falling – plays simultaneously with non-diegetic music – ominous acoustic rumblings that transform as the scene progresses. The two sequences, thematically and technically (their framing and composition) similar, are mirror images of one another: Figures 1.1 and 1.3 visually and sonically reflect one another, while Figure 1.1 is simultaneously the mirror of Figure 1.4, as Figure 1.2 is the mirror of Figure 1.3. The reversal of forced privileged points of perception enjoins the spectator to a perverse relationship as they experience and participate in both states. Both sequences feature phonological utterances inclusive and suggestive of Nadsat and, more broadly, the intersection of a major and minor language. This occurs diegetically in Figures 1.1 and 1.2, and non-diegetically in Figures 1.3 and 1.4. Kubrick thus brings to the screen and forces upon the viewer the deterritorialising properties of Nadsat. The intrusive imposition of Alex's didactic, direct address to the spectator in Figures 1.1 and 1.2 – 'viddy well' – and the voice-over narration and subjective inter- pretation of the intra-cinematic film in Figures 1.3 and 1.4 enjoin the viewer to a line of flight, deterritorialising the visual and phonologi- cal planes. It makes us both privy to a schizophrenic Nadsat linguis- tic consciousness, and abstracted observers of the corresponding abstract machine spoken by one of its subjects.

One of the foundations of Deleuze's approach to cinema is the rejection of linguistic models. Rather than applying structural- ist semiology, Deleuze claims that cinema has its own concepts. Linguistics reduces 'the image to an utterance [. . .] and then of course finds in it the linguistic components of utterances-syntagms, paradigms, the signifier' (N: 65). Yet, in Kubrick, there is a funda- mental relation between the image and what the word denotes or connotes. Deleuze argues that 'denotation functions through the association of the words themselves with images *which ought to* "represent" the state of affairs. From all the images associated with a word [. . .] we must choose or select those which correspond to the given whole. The denoting intuition is then expressed by the form: "it is that" or "it is not that"' (LS: 16). Against this process of selection and correspondence between word and image, the relation is better broached through the link between vision and sensation. Deleuze is interested in the interface between the brain and the screen, and more generally in sensation, the interval between instinct and cognition that 'acts immediately on the nervous system, which is of the flesh' (*FB*: 25). We viddy with Alex, but Nadsat also renders bodily sensations. In Burgess, Alex's aesthetic encounters and corporeal sensations are rendered in Nadsat. He neither elaborates on the objects he encounters, nor describes them in detail, but recounts their corporeal affects: 'I felt all the little malenky hairs on my plott standing endwise and the shivers crawling up like slow malenky lizards and then down again'; 'I lay all nagoy to the ceiling, my gulliver on my rookers on the pillow, glazzies closed, rot open to bliss, slooshying the sluice of lovely sounds' (22, 26).

In Kubrick, sensation is rendered more explicitly when we *see* and we *viddy*. In the first sequence we are explicitly told to viddy, sharing the perspective of Alexander, and the camera moves from Alexander's face to his wife's as she is molested. In the second sequence we share the gaze with Alex, who viddies instinctively. In both sequences, the camera is shaky, capturing the violence in an exploratory and declarative fashion, uncertain in its framing. The first sequence is brief, simultaneously suggesting immersion and repulsion. This is a forced relation of one who does not viddy instinctively – Alexander or the spectator who assumes an uncomfortable 'perceptual sympathy' (Chatman 1978: 159). The second sequence provides a formal contrast, and access to the neuro-image. Here a film is being projected within the film, but it is mediated through Alex's consciousness. Conflating Alex's perception and the camera, the gaze follows the trajectory of the thrusts and punches on screen, jerking left as the victim is struck on the right-hand side of the face, and vice versa. This is accompanied by Alex's Nadsat voice-over narration, giving us a privileged and unnerving perspective of a Nadsat construction of the world, less a perceptual sympathy than a schizophrenic neuro-image. The film thereby links minoritarian language with consciousness in its deterritorialisation of perception: like Alex we *viddy*, rather than *see*. There is a noticeable difference here between cinematic Nadsat and that in the novel. Stockwell suggests that SF neologisms often incite the reader to seek a 'linguistic correspondence', where 'words from similar lexical fields [function] as synonyms and [are] thus interchangeable' (2000: 142). In Burgess's novel, we can attempt to substitute 'viddy' with 'see'. But in Kubrick they are neither commensurate nor interchangeable. The film is essentially a meditation on control of perception, thought, language and, as we shall see, the body and its organisation. Alex's subjectivity is violent and alien, and by inhabiting both its language and how that language organises and experiences the world, the film facilitates the becoming-minoritarian of the spectator.

A major language is sustained by conventions rather than by convictions. It is 'not made to be believed, but to be obeyed, and to compel obedience' (TP: 84). Deleuze distinguishes the State from the majoritarian abstract machine. The State overcodes language, establishes boundaries and imposes significations. It is an assemblage that realises an abstract machine, 'organises the dominant utterances and the established order of a society, the dominant languages and knowledge, conformist actions and feelings' (D: 129). A major language comprises order-words, statements and corresponding social relations, 'the relation of every word or every statement to implicit presuppositions, [. . .] to speech acts that are, and can only be, accomplished in the statement' (TP: 87). The order-word function is a tool of subjectivisation: 'Forming grammatically correct sentences is for the normal individual the prerequisite for any submission to social laws' (TP: 112). But language is deployed in different ways according to different subjects. Deleuze and Guattari distinguish the bourgeois paranoiac from marginalised 'passionals', those 'who do not seem mad in any way, but are, as borne out by their sudden actions, such as quarrels, arsons, murders' (TP: 133), to which Alex belongs. The paranoiac is subject to the overcoding of the signifier, while the passional is subject to a 'postsignifying authoritarian regime' that normalises and controls language and behaviour:

> The various forms of education or 'normalisation' imposed upon an individual consist in making him or her change points of subjectification, always moving toward a higher, nobler one in closer conformity with the supposed ideal. Then from the point of subjectification issues a subject of enunciation, as a function of a mental reality determined by that point. Then from the subject of enunciation issues a subject of the statement [. . .] bound to statements in conformity with a dominant reality. (TP: 143–4)

The Ludovico technique is a postsignifying authoritarian regime that cultivates a certain type of subject, how they use language, their consciousness, and how language and consciousness organises the world. It does so because language and body form an assemblage. We can see how both majoritarian English and minoritarian Nadsat are themselves bodies. Deleuze expands the concept of a body to describe any collection of parts that interact to affect and be affected: 'biological, psychic, social, verbal: they are always bodies or corpora' (*D*: 52). When verbs-becomings move between major and minor poles, deterritorialising or reterritorialising, they create different affects in a body: 'When a word assumes a different meaning, or even enters into a different syntax, we can be sure that it has crossed another flux or that it has been introduced to a different regime of signs' (*D*: 117). Deleuze privileges verbs, because they embody his idea of becomings as transitory and mobile, expanding or contracting, expressing a state, or effecting change in body. When 'substantives and adjectives begin to dissolve', verbs-becomings form a 'language of events' (*LS*: 5). The viewer's primary access to this is the altered states of viddying and slooshying. The contrast between the camera's movement and framing, sometimes reluctant and skittish, sometimes austere and static, evokes Nadsat subjectivity via filmic enunciation. The haptic sensations of onomatopoeia in Burgess's Nadsat, such as 'glolp' and 'chumble', incite the reader to speculate as to how they are to be articulated: 'They entice the reader's participation in an alternative semiotics in which the sign refers, not to conventional and abstract meanings, but via its own palpability to corresponding qualities in the physical consistency, properties, and kinetics of things' (Goh 2000: 271). This is reflected in Kubrick, particularly in Figures 1.3 and 1.4, when Alex's consciousness constructs the image and he recounts his sensations. The camera-brain enthusiastically synchronises itself with the force and direction of violent blows, emphasising the corporeality of language-as-consciousness. The engagement of the spectator by means of eye-level matches invites a conflation of the viewer and Alex's consciousness rather than his vision and the spectator, making the viewer process the image through an estranged minor language. The Ludovico technique grasps Alex's linguistic unconscious, but also his body, organs, affects and intensities. The treatment is not intended to intervene at the level of psychic life, but at that of organic composition. The doctors explain:

> Your body is learning [. . .] The processes of life, the make-up of the human organism [. . .] What is happening to you now is what should happen to any normal healthy human organism contemplating the actions of the forces of evil, the workings of the principle of destruction [. . .] You're not cured yet. There's still a lot to be done. Only when your body reacts promptly and violently to violence [. . .] without further help from us, without medication. (81, 87)

Kubrick's film renders bodily control through performance, as Alex's physical movements become increasingly restricted as the narrative and the treatment progress. The stylised and choreographed violence, frenzied bedroom antics and perverse theatrical numbers are replaced by the pomp and ceremony of the Staja, its marches, inspections of bodily cavities, and striated architecture. The infamous scene of Alex confined in a straightjacket (which reverses his mastery over perception and space established by the film's inaugural tracking shot retreating from his unblinking eye) before the screen is part of the Ludovico technique and, thereafter, the interior shots are suffocating, caricaturesque domestic interiors, especially the family home. The gruesome films themselves are not a deterrence from committing violence. Rather, it is the relation between the biological – the serum injected, the nausea – and the image: the Ludovico assemblage makes for a microfascist relation between the organs and simulacra. Thus, Alex says: 'You're making me feel ill, I'm ill when I look at those filthy pervert films of yours. But it's not really the films that's doing it' (85). Deleuze and Guattari's concept of fascism will be treated in more detail in Chapter 4, but the key point is that fascism is not solely a mass or even ideological phenomenon, but molecular. This is literalised when Alex's desires and bodily organisation come to identify with their own oppression and repression. 'You're committed to socially acceptable acts,' Alexander explains, 'a little machine capable only of good':

> To turn a decent young man into a piece of clockwork should not, surely, be seen as any triumph for any government, save one that boasts of its repressiveness [. . .] Before we know where we are we shall have the full apparatus of totalitarianism [. . .] Will not the Government itself now decide what is and what is not a crime and pump the life and guts and will of whoever sees fit to displease the Government? (115–16, 118)

The film develops a complex assemblage, conjoining consciousness, the body, language and sound. By accessing Alex's consciousness, we note how sound and image, listening and seeing, affect each other. Deleuze argues that cinema has become increasingly 'legible', by which he means that films become increasingly self-referential, divorced from the distinction between real and imaginary, original and copy, objective and subjective. Opsigns and sonsigns are secondary manifestations of lectosigns, a concept Deleuze borrows from linguistics (Rodowick 1997: 80–1): 'The sound as well as visual elements of the image enter into internal relations which means that the whole image has to be "read," no less than seen, readable as well as visible' (*TI*: 21). Deleuze's proposition is that sound becomes visible; it is 'heard, but as *a new dimension of the visual image, a new component*. It is even for this reason that they are image [. . .] In so far as it is heard, it *makes visible*' (*TI*: 218). This line of thought is valuable for a comparative reading of Kubrick and Burgess, since the film literally makes images of sounds intimated in the novel, and hearing Nadsat is one of the film's unique sensations. While the filmic sounds themselves might confirm or reorient our assumptions about the novel's linguistic signs, the relation of the signifier to the signified, we should not disarticulate the filmic relation between sound and image: slooshying is as internal to viddying as viddying is to slooshying. So, rather 'than invoking the signifier and the signified, we might say that the sound components are separate only in the abstraction of their pure hearing. But, in so far as they are a specific dimension [. . .] then they all form together one single component, a continuum' (*TI*: 225). In the first sequence Alex brings the phonological aspects of Nadsat into relation with music. It is, as Sobchack puts it, 'unoriginal' music used 'originally', here emphasising the contrast of the sonic and the visual: 'Old movie memories are almost insupportably mocked. The violence and rape is done to the song and [. . .] we *are* victims of the violence done [to] our memories and associations' (2004: 212, 215). In the second sequence, we hear Alex processing the sounds of the film. His use of Nadsat makes us *slooshy* (rather than hear) the non-diegetic music, which turns from ominous to carnivalesque once Alex's attention is drawn to the blood.

The political force of becoming-minoritarian is revealed when we learn that minor language is the primary way its users distinguish themselves: their speech is unintelligible to the major language of the bourgeoisie and the State doctors. Minor use of language becomes politicised expression when it deterritorialises:

Freud himself stressed the acoustic origin of the superego [. . .] The first approach to language consists in grasping it as the model of that which preexists, as referring to the entire domain of what is already there, and as the familial voice which conveys tradition [. . .] and demands [the subject's] insertion. (*LS*: 221)

Nadsat short-circuits the normalising injunctions of the Oedipal family and the State. In Burgess, the reader's comprehension is always breaking down, stuttering and stammering. In Kubrick, the contrast between major and minor language is registered acoustically when sound and image become inseparable, but the relation sound and language have to the body is rather different. As we have seen, in Alex's experience, language and the body form an assemblage. Sound in Kubrick relates as much to Alex as to the viewer. For Deleuze, sound and language are, on the one hand, inseparable from the body; on the other, sound becomes independent of the body, insofar as it affects other bodies, so that it 'ceases to be a specific quality attached to bodies, a noise or a cry, and [. . .] begins to designate qualities, manifest bodies, and signify subjects or predicates' (LS: 214). Sound becomes a source of new affects that compose novel assemblages, and this is not confined to Alex, since we are made both his victim and his accomplice.

Schizopanacea

Is the simulator sick or not, given that he produces 'true' symptoms? Objectively, one cannot treat him as being either ill or not ill. (SS: 3)

Being young is like being like one of these malenky machines. (Burgess 2000: 140)

The extent to which the Ludovico technique reterritorialises Alex's schizes differs between Burgess and Kubrick.[4] The efficacy of the treatment is more pronounced at the end of the novel when Alex encounters his former gang member, Dim. Now a police officer, Dim is as violent as ever, but this violence is now endorsed by the State's crackdown on the nadsat. Dim can barely recall his former life, seems to have no memory of his former droogie, Pete, and upbraids Alex for his vestigial Nadsat: 'Not to speak like that. Not no more, droogie' (111). Driven insane by the Ludovico technique, Alex is welcomed by Alexander, ignorant of Alex's identity and planning to use his mania as an example of the State's imminent totalitarianism. 'You can be a very potent weapon,' he tells Alex, 'ensuring that this present evil and wicked Government is not returned in the forthcoming election [. . .] Before we know where we are we shall have the full apparatus of totalitarianism' (118). But when Alexander learns that Alex raped and murdered his wife, he tortures him with Beethoven. Unable to entertain thoughts of violence or sex, and unable to experience anything other than violent illness upon listening to his beloved music, Alex self-defenestrates. The 'deep hypnopaedia' (130) that returns Alex's Nadsat vocabulary and consciousness signals less a reclaiming of his former self than the extent to which the State can intervene into the unconscious. It is equally important, though, that Alex's experience of this is more corporeal than cerebral, occurring at the level of sensation rather than cognition: 'Like for instance I had this idea of my whole plott [flesh] or body being emptied of as it might be dirty water and then filled up again with clean' (127). Both Burgess and Kubrick have the Minister of the Interior apologise to Alex, returning him to his schizophrenic state to avoid public scandal. What interests us here is that, in this denouement, the previously antagonistic poles of the minor and major languages are in agreement. Rather, they enter a genial relationship. 'He speaks to me as a friend, don't you, son?' queries the Minister. 'I am everyone's friend,' Alex replies, 'except to my enemies,' and the Minister pats him on the shoulder and declares him a 'good good boy' (131–2). But a chance encounter with his former droogie, Pete, now a happily married bourgeoisie, is a revelation for Alex, who decides that 'youth must go' (140) and that he must redeem himself with marriage, children, employment and dutiful citizenship.

Omitting the (unconvincing and inconsistent) redemptive conclusion, Kubrick sees Alex returned to his schizophrenic mania, shaking the hand of the apologetic Minister (Anthony Sharp) while fantasising about new acts of sex and violence, telling us, 'I was cured all right.' This final scene is of particular significance for our focus on Deleuze, and for the Baudrillardian critique elaborated in the remaining chapters. Burgess ends with redemption, tracing a line from adolescence to maturity. But what if Kubrick's is less an ironic or subversive denouement, a victory for Alex, than a gesture that *reconciles schizophrenia with the sinister benevolence of the State*? The Minister of the Interior knows Alexander and the dissidents are a more palpable threat than Alex's schizophrenia. So, they incarcerate Alexander and nourish Alex's violent libido. The State saves face by presenting a smile to its enemies, Alex's contrite parents welcome him back into the home, and the psychiatrists applaud his renewed verve, his violent and sexual responses to images. Superegoic figures – State, family, psychiatrists – *no longer serve a prohibitory function*. Rather, the *injunction of the superego is obscene enjoyment*, a reversal of Freud propounded by Lacan (1992: 310) and adopted by Žižek (2009: 58) and Baudrillard (*S*: 24) which we shall examine in detail in subsequent chapters. Alex addresses the Minister in Nadsat as a droogie, who cuts up his food and feeds him like a child, because 'we always help our friends'. The State compensates Alex for the mania of the Ludovico technique with job security and a generous salary.

The new alliance proposed in the penultimate image, the cheerful schizo shaking hands with the munificent State, will be taken up in subsequent chapters.

Notes

1. Baudrillard considered Kubrick's film a 'dull splendour of banality [and] violence' (*SS*: 119), a sentiment developed in Chapter 3.
2. All page references to the novel are taken from the 2000 edition.
3. For the translation of Nadsat see Stanley E. Hyman (1963).
4. As is well known, Kubrick worked from the American edition of the novel, which omitted the redemptive final chapter.

Chronic S(t)imulation

We could almost speak of media harassment along the lines of sexual harassment. Alas! the problem always remains the same and it is insoluble: where does real violence begin, where does consenting violence end? (Baudrillard 1995: 74–5)

The mirror phase has given way to the video phase. (*A*: 37)

Beware of the other's dream, because if you are caught in the other's dream you are screwed. (Deleuze 2001: 103)

With the exception of *Crash*, no cyberpunk text has inspired more inquiry along Baudrillardian and Deleuzian lines than David Cronenberg's *Videodrome* (1983) which seems emphatically able to demonstrate and augment either theoretical position. Indeed, Cronenberg seems to be the director of choice for critics of both persuasions. In *Videodrome*, Max Renn (James Woods) is the President of CIVIC TV, a television station that broadcasts hardcore violence and softcore pornography. Pursuing new markets and new perversions, Max has Harlan (Peter Dvorsky) pirate signals, leading them to the enigmatic Videodrome: 'Just torture and murder. No plot, no characters, very, very realistic. I think it's what's next.' Attempting to decipher the origin of the signal, Max becomes sexually involved with the masochistic Nicki Brand (Deborah Harry), who quickly abandons the relationship to become a Videodrome 'contestant'. The carcinogenic signal inspires fantasies of torture, masochism and sadism that render indiscernible the distinction between reality, phantasy and simulacra, wherein bodies, machines and images interact in ecstatic, violent assemblages. Max finds his corporate interests, phantasies and bodily and psychic integrity at the centre of a 'battle for the mind of North America' waged between Barry Convex (Leslie Carlson) of Spectacular Optical – whose corporate slogan is 'Keeping An Eye On The World' – and the Cathode Ray Mission, presided over by McLuhanesque media prophet and creator of Videodrome Professor Brian O'Blivion (Jack Creley), who intended it to be 'a new organ, a new part of the brain', a catalyst for the next step in human evolution, the 'Video New Flesh'.

Spectacular Optical, a front for a systemic organisation, murdered O'Blivion and took control of Videodrome. O'Blivion now exists on thousands of pre-recorded videotapes, appearing 'on television, as television', and his daughter, Bianca (Sonja Smits), who presides over the Cathode Ray Mission, lives in fear of Videodrome agents. Against the O'Blivions' intentions, the 'New Flesh' agenda is revealed to be a mere pretext in a conspiracy to purge society of its violent and sexual addictions. As Harlan, who is in the service of Videodrome, explains to Max, 'we're entering savage new times, and we're going to have to be pure, and direct, and strong if we're going to survive.' Max learns that, rather than pirating the Videodrome signal, it was never broadcast, but rather narrowcasted directly at him, as part of Videodrome's moral purge, one he is now enjoined to perpetuate.

A Television is Being Beaten

This is not a phantasy, it is a program. (*TP*: 168)

From this description, one can see why *Videodrome* appeals to Baudrillardians and Deleuzians alike. Whilst the earliest Baudrillardian readings focus on simulation, critics have linked it to Deleuze's schizoanalysis. *Videodrome*, like *Crash*, is becoming-Deleuzian, since these interpretations share the same disavowal of Baudrillard. My own reading suggests two things: first, that the film stages the breakdown of the sensory-motor scheme and the opsigns and sonsigns of Deleuze's time-image; second, that both Deleuze's and Baudrillard's revisions of Freud, *Masochism* and *Seduction*, offer new interpretative and complementary strategies. But first, a selective survey and commentary on relevant scholarship will better highlight *Videodrome*'s central significance, and why it continues to occupy fiercely contested, shifting terrain.

As with all of Cronenberg's SF, ambivalence is at the very core of *Videodrome*'s narrative and aesthetics. By placing this ambiguity ahead of other interpretative foci, Jameson's analysis acquires its strength. While not explicitly evoked, Jameson's diagnosis bears the impress of Baudrillard's simulacrum as the implosion of social, political, sexual and economic spheres into the transpolitical, the intertwinement of capital, biology and representation that erodes the subject's psychic and physical ego boundaries:

It becomes impossible to say whether we are here dealing any longer with the specifically political, or with the cultural, or with the social, or with the economic – not to forget the sexual, the historical, the moral, and so on. But this conflation [. . .] uniquely intensifies the signifying power of this work that, rotated on its axis, can be said to comment on any of the above virtually inexhaustibly. (1992: 25–6)

And:

What is finally most interesting about this titanic political struggle between two vast and faceless conspiracies (in which the hapless Max is little more than a pawn) is that they are finally the same, the twin faces of our unconscious meditation on the inevitable mutations a now repressed history has in store for us: fear and hope alike, the loathing for the new beings we ourselves are bound to become in the shedding of the skins of our current values, intimately intertwined as in some DNA of the collective fantasy, with our quasi-religious longing for social transubstantiation into another flesh and another reality. (Ibid. 28–9)

Jameson's is the most authoritative analysis, but Bukatman's is, if not the paradigmatic reading, the Baudrillardian. He notes the mixture of verbatim McLuhan media theory with the hypostatisation of 'Baudrillard's most outrageous propositions' (1993: 85) where McLuhan's conservative technological utopianism is replaced by Baudrillard's equally technologically deterministic vision.[1] The television image is, for Baudrillard, that which, unlike cinema, 'suggests nothing, which mesmerises, which itself is nothing but a screen, not even that: a miniaturised terminal, that, in fact, is immediately located in your head – you are the screen, and the TV watches you – it transistorises all the neurons and passes through like a magnetic tape – a tape, not an image' (*SS*: 51). The strength of Bukatman's interpretation is that it locates the film's depiction of the 'failure of interpersonal communications [as] an integral part of an industry which privileges the spectacular over the intimate, and pseudo-satisfaction over genuine comprehension' (1993: 86) and argues that the 'subject of the Cronenberg film is hardly human action', but the 'structure of external power and control to which the individual (in body *and* soul) is subjected' (2003: 202–3). In this sense, the film develops a critique of the media, focusing on 'image addiction', 'high-tech alienation', simulation and media control, in the Baudrillardian vein of controlled desublimation:

It is the voluntarism of the television experience, the 'free choice' of the viewer, which permits the incursion of controlling forces [. . .] Images stand in for a lost social whole, the spectator's alienation is masked *via* the reified whole of the spectacle, the capitalist forces are thereby able to reproduce themselves at the expense of the worker/consumer/spectator. (1993: 89)

Bukatman misleads, however, when he announces that *Videodrome* 'moves beyond the classically political through its relentless physicality. The film's politics have less to do with economic control than with the uncontrolled immixture of simulation and reality' (ibid. 89). If the economic determinant in simulation is speculative or finance capital, itself unpresentable, then this relentless physicality is less a moving beyond the political than the structural ambience of a violent system rendered in somatic terms: *the subject becomes the genitalia of capital, enjoined to its circulation, so that the intense scenes of polymorphous fluctuation that occur under the sign of liberation are consonant with the corporation's ambitions.*

The film's appropriation of McLuhan is much more sophisticated than Bukatman suggests. Professor O'Blivion is a thinly veiled McLuhan; his technological pontification is verbatim McLuhan, but also not dissimilar to Baudrillard's own theoretical proximity to McLuhan, nor to Deleuze's own McLuhanesque maxims that the brain is a screen and the screen is a brain. For O'Blivion:

> The television screen is the retina of the mind's eye. Therefore, the television screen is part of the physical structure of the brain. Therefore, whatever appears on the television screen emerges as raw experience for those who watch it. Therefore, television is reality, and reality is less than television.

What goes unnoticed is the extent to which the film engages with McLuhan's religiosity. The Cathode Ray Mission (whose logo is the Sacred Heart) bears a triple function: an undertaking, a geographic location, and a television station – squalid, dilapidated and attracting 'derelicts' in droves. They are ushered into semi-private cubicles/confessionals and administered, in charitable, religious fashion, television. The hallmark of their alienation, or 'disease', for Bianca, is their 'lack of access to the cathode ray tube'. When Max presses her – 'you think a few doses of TV are going to help them?' – she replies, 'watching TV will help them patch back into the world's mixing board.' *Videodrome* seems to comment on and critique McLuhanism. First is the religiosity of McLuhan's global village, the most revealing sign of which lies not in the film's images, but in the subtle leitmotif of church bells that announce the presence of first O'Blivion and, later, Bianca, whose entry into the room is similarly foreshadowed by the superior tolling. But the film provides what McLuhan's own theory lacks: a critical vision of the political structures of access and control. Max and Bianca's first discussion takes place in an opulent room, replete with stained-glass window, overlooking the Mission's relief centre, the view of which is obscured by a plush curtain. When Max peeks through at the derelicts transfixed by their televisual charity, he 'love[s] the view'. While the scene spatialises the distribution of power in crude, top-down, split-level fashion, one can here see why Baudrillard and, ultimately, Deleuze rejected Foucault's panoptic model, hinged on the always-assumed presence of a disciplinary, despotic gaze. Here, the gaze is 'benevolent', yet all the more controlling.

What most vividly distinguishes the Deleuzian interpretation from the Baudrillardian is an almost ubiquitous relaxation of the depiction of corporate control and manipulation, some ejecting it altogether in favour of the immanence of becomings that elevate schizophrenia to a general principle unmoored from capital, more an aesthetic than a process. Barring this complacency, the emphasis changes from Baudrillard's emphasis on the body 'as a site of psychic and ideological invasion' (Kellner 1989b: 89) to the film's corporeal and psychotropic affects that co-problematise the nature of perception (objective, subjective, virtual, delusional) and embodiment (gendered, sexed, organic, machinic, virtual). They thus offer alternatives to Jameson's thesis that *Videodrome*'s 'corporeal revulsion [. . .] probably has the primary function of expressing fears about activity and passivity in the complexities of late capitalism, and is only secondarily invested with the level of gender itself' (1992: 31).

Anna Powell foregrounds the schizophrenic body without organs, extolling *Videodrome*'s capacity to 'undermine boundaries between inside and out'. Her suggestion that the 'narrative likelihood that they are all hallucinations does not reduce their affective force' (2005: 80) is correct, but, as I shall show below, for all the wrong reasons. For now, it is important that Powell rejects a Freudian reading in favour of the 'molecular plasticity' of a Deleuzian 'radical undermining of two fixed gender identities', whereby 'Max is becoming a more complex and fully alive person through the loss of subjective wholeness when his body incorporates extraneous matter'. This reading, Powell concedes, is ultimately compromised by other rigid boundaries that privilege 'violation' rather than the 'promising new interface' of becoming-machine (ibid. 81–2). The schizoanalytic attention to affect with regard to the spectator suffers from the absence of attention to capital as causal agent. For Powell, it is not the violence of reterritorialisation that leads the film down the path to wrack and ruin, but the psychoanalytic tropes of the horror film. Becoming is, in essence, the primacy of effect over cause, but schizoanalytic 'creativity' is but one term in the capitalism and schizophrenia assemblage, insofar as the two work together. This emphasis in Powell is deceptive: schizophrenia, elevated to an affirmative malady rather than as 'without lack, but definitely not without risk or peril' (*D*: 99), follows a line of obliteration, an all-too-hasty deterritorialisation that culminates not (just) as she ruefully concludes, at the point at which the horror narrative trajectory imposes its inevitable curtailing of transgression, but, rather, with the reimposition of the internal limits of capital. No surprise then that capital never surfaces in Powell's analysis, and the Sadean pleasure she confesses to derive from the film stems from Max's 'unmanning' (2005: 81), a suitable revenge given his pornographic business interests. 'Revenge' is clearly one of the film's points, but the ideological and narrative frame (unreliable though it may be) is spirited away: the Videodrome signal is ultimately in the service of a conservative, puritanical vision, and any resultant becomings are largely complementary, rather than adversarial. Instead of deriving any negative example from the film, Powell, like many who privilege gender, identity and affirmation over political economy, faults the film for not following through on its promises. The implication is that *the best one can hope to do is transform oneself, rather than transform the fundamental structures of political economy or reorient the diffuse media landscape in the interests of social change.*

Steven Shaviro situates *Videodrome* in relation to Deleuze and Foucault's schemata of desire and power as immanent and corporeal, reading the permeable, transmogrifying assemblages of human and machine as running the gamut of gender ambiguity and deconstructing phallic scopophilia. He announces that 'we have entered a new regime of the image, one in which vision is visceral and intensive instead of representational and extensive' (1993: 139):

> The brutally hilarious strategy of *Videodrome* is to take media theorists such as Marshall McLuhan and Jean Baudrillard completely at their word [. . .] But *Videodrome* [contrarily] suggests that [. . .] 'hyperreality' is hot, not cool. Far from being 'intangible,' it is gruesomely physical [. . .] The body is not erased or evacuated; it is rather so suffused with video technology that it mutates into new forms, and is pushed to new thresholds of intense, masochistic sensation [. . .] To abolish reference and to embrace 'virtual reality' is not, as Baudrillard imagines, to reduce desire to a series of weightless and indifferent equivalences. The more images are flattened

out and distanced from their representational sources, the more they are inscribed into our nerves, and flash across our synapses. (Ibid. 137–8)

Shaviro's conclusion, quite antithetical with the film's, is that 'Cronenberg leaves us [not] with a Baudrillardian vision of absolute, totalitarian entrapment', but rather that the emphasis 'falls on ambivalence and monstrosity', making us 'obsessively aware that it is cultural and political technology – and not natural necessity – that imposes the restricted economies of organicism, functionalism, and sexual representation' (ibid. 141–2). The identification of technological imposition is correct, but the ambivalence is at least double, since the capitalist investments of Spectacular Optical trigger Max's metamorphoses, and the equally ambiguous Cathode Ray Mission is user friendly in the most ambivalent and unpromising of ways. The ambivalence Shaviro identifies implies Deleuze's impersonal desire, trending either to paranoia/fascism or to schizophrenia. Ultimately, denouncing Baudrillard's negative theorisation of virtual reality/capitalist hyperreality in favour of lethal, delirious material affects seems a false distinction. Baudrillard's controlled desublimation seems the more likely explanation. *Videodrome* does blur and render psychosomatically a multitude of binaries – self/other, inside/outside, individual/institution, human/machine, male/female, masculine/feminine – but the schizo lines of flight are symptoms (enjoyable, traumatic) of a process *where control, rather than flux, is the privileged term, and the achieved objective.* Max's desire is programmed or, more so, *pre-programmed and pre-recorded* by the signal, realising Baudrillard's anticipation that desire would enter into simulation, and that power becomes 'dead power' when, in the guise of reciprocity and resistance, it 'no longer succeeds in producing the real, in reproducing itself as real, or in opening new spaces to the reality principle, and where it falls into the hyperreal and vanishes: *this is the end of power*' (*FF*: 77): the beginning of absolute control.

Rosi Braidotti, one of the most prominent contemporary Deleuzians, also essays an interpretation of *Videodrome*. Braidotti's stance is an admixture of Deleuze and Luce Irigaray, whereby the otherwise conflicting poles of difference and non-essentialist feminism are put to work under the sign of affirmation and creativity, dynamism and immanence. Two flawed claims arise. First is that the radical materialism of Deleuze (and Irigaray) is presently being 'ignored' or 'silenced' by post-Lacanian negativity, namely Žižek's, whilst she also bemoans the intensification of class inequality in the hyperreal (2002: 57, 245). Setting aside the highly questionable notion of this 'silencing' of Deleuze, the paradox is that Žižek and Baudrillard, as exemplars of Lacanian negativity, draw attention to this very intensification with greater force than Braidotti's delicate 'yearn[ing] for a more joyful and empowering concept of desire and for a political economy that foregrounds positivity, not gloom' (ibid. 57). But the political economy does not run on good intentions, and gloom is nevertheless the mode to which she resorts to critique gender inequality. Second, Braidotti labels Baudrillard a nihilist (hard to dispute) but also suggests that he engages in euphoric celebrations of virtual disembodiment (ibid. 181), the standard misreading of Baudrillard. The force of the film, for Braidotti, is its technological reconfiguring of gender stereotypes. On this count, *Videodrome* is commendable in its ability 'to domesticate the male body and to make it available, disposable, manipulatable, exactly as the female body has always been'. But the film refuses to follow through:

> The dislocation of the categories of otherness is enacted, but no genuine alternative emerges. All we get is a man violating himself as a woman, and masochism is the dominant theme [. . .] The becoming-woman of the Majority repeats the worst traits of the phallogocentric regime: it is an exercise in humiliation and an apprenticeship in self-mutilation. The man undergoes what women have had to suffer for centuries: this is the ultimate scenario of powerlessness and violation of one's own body and it making at best a generalised becoming-Sadean. (Ibid. 249)

Braidotti's position is already troubled by the uneasy theoretical collusion of female subjectivity (non-essentialist though it may be) and Deleuze, but any keen reader must surely grasp the inaccuracies of her invoking masochism and sadism, at least in Deleuze's terms.

The intransigence of the Baudrillardian position is its technological determinism and foreclosure of human agency, whilst its uncompromising negativity is shared by Jameson. Although *Videodrome*'s conclusion validates this pessimism, one can resist it to explore new readings. What is most dishonest about these Deleuzian interpretations is their revolutionary tenor that removes the fact that, as Kellner points out, 'the major villains [there are few 'heroes'] in Cronenberg's films are corporate executives, and throughout his films there is a sly sometimes strong critical commentary on corporate capitalism and hegemonic class formations' (1989b: 96). Max's metamorphoses become punishment for his mercantile hubris, itself altogether insignificant in the face of corporate control. The implication is that the intensity or availability of becoming is relative to one's affluence, and the desiring unconscious is misrecognised as the Lacanian superego's injunction to enjoy, right up to self-destruction: 'The Law becom[es] an injunction to pleasure after having been its interdiction. An effect of simulation inverted: it is when pleasure seeks openly to be autonomous, that it is truly a product of the Law' (*S*: 24). Having acknowledged where the film's political force lies, I will now expand on this in conjunction with the film's aesthetics and psychoanalytic dimensions.

The Retina of the Mind's Eye

In *Masochism*, Deleuze untangles Freud's conflation of two distinct disorders in the category of sadomasochism by exploring the male masochist's relation to the maternal figure instead of the father. In *Seduction*, Baudrillard reaches into psychoanalytic antiquity to recover the female hysteric as a counteragent to the libidinal economy, and a rejoinder to Deleuze's schizo. Against Freud's unity of opposites (that the difference between masochism and sadism is nothing more than a reversal of instincts) Deleuze posits masochism's specificity, supersensual affect, imagistic qualities, the hermaphroditic qualities of the masochist (rather than the androgyny of the sadist) and a configuration of the maternal figure, the oral mother. Cancelling the father in the symbolic, the mother becoming the Law, produces a secondary 'sexless' birth or parthenogenesis (1989: 61; see Studlar 1984). The psychoanalytic aspects of Baudrillard's formulation of seduction become apparent when supplemented by Jean Laplanche's retooling of Freud's hysteria, posthumously named seduction theory (Freud 1995: 96–111; Freud and Breuer 2004) before being abandoned in favour of the Oedipus complex: Baudrillard himself cites Jean Laplanche with approval (*S*: 55).[2] Laplanche replaces Freud's diagnosis of hysteria as resultant of (real or imagined) sexual assault visited upon the child by the parent (usually the father) with the general theory of seduction, whereby the (primarily female) parent's physical, visual and auditory contact with the child is itself a violent encounter with the unconscious of the other, a situation where there 'is *too much* perceived reality'. The other's attentions are 'seductive because they are opaque, because they convey something enigmatic' (Laplanche 1989: 94, 128). From Freud, Baudrillard retains the indiscernibility of real and fantasised repressed events, or that traumatic memories were in fact the result of Freud's own suggestion (Gleaves and Hernandez 1999: 331). Baudrillard's central claim is therefore that the 'hysteric combines the passion for seduction with that of simulation' (*S*: 119). The object/ other of desire stages, simulates and seduces – shocks, confronts, leads astray, reverses or repels – the subject. Despite Baudrillard's prescriptive intent to mount a counterargument to Deleuze, whereby the (feminine) hysteric opposes the (masculine) schizophrenic, I will argue for a homology between these two works, just as Laplanche conjoins seduction and masochism (1999: 201–17). The entry point for my discussion is Deleuze's cinema work, itself compared to Baudrillard's *Seduction* (Vaughan 2010; Trifonova 2003).

A Deleuzian analysis of *Videodrome* allows us to locate the crisis of the movement-image as one that affects both the spectator and the film's characters. Against celebratory evocations of the time-image, one should note that Deleuze is careful to situate its emergence as more or less contemporaneous with the transition from discipline to control (*TI*: 26–7). Cinematic consciousness relates to the formal composition of shots that divide and reunite perception. Actions belong to neither 'the spectator, nor the hero', but to the camera itself, variously assuming the position of the 'human, sometimes inhuman or superhuman' (2012a: 21) or, as O'Blivion puts it, 'a new organ, a new part of the brain'. What characterises the transition from the movement-image to the time-image is the substitution of narrative coherency for the singular intensities of becomings (*N*: 59) of which there are two consequences. First, the image is no longer realist, but composed of opsigns and sonsigns. Second, truthful or organic narration becomes 'crystalline narration', which 'ceases to be truthful, that is, to claim to be true, and becomes fundamentally falsifying' (*TI*: 127). Deleuze calls this power of the false, which Pisters describes as consonant with a culture which, on the one hand, 'has moved from considering images as "illusions of reality" to considering them as "realities of illusions" that operate directly on our brains and therefore as real agents in the world'. On the other, the power of the false calls into question 'truthful' systems of judgement (2012: 6, 95). Time-, crystal- and mental-images do not, Deleuze stresses, occur subjectively within a character's head. They are an unattributable objective illusion, whereby a 'character does not act without seeing himself acting, complicit viewer of the role he himself is playing' (*TI*: 6).

Videodrome dramatises this crisis, Max's exposure to the signal the catalyst. Although the features of the time-image characterise the film as a whole, one particular sequence illustrates this, also adjoining the film's masochistic and seductive valences. Under the pretence of diagnosing his brain tumour, Barry Convex must record and analyse Max's hallucinations. He affixes a machine, part viewfinder, part video recorder, part virtual-reality simulator, to Max's head. Pain, Convex says, opens new cerebrospinal receptors, allowing the signal to 'sink in', triggering hallucinations. Cut to Max's point of view of a grainy, poorly rendered image. Convex opens the visor and the rush of sensory data from the external world collides with Max's mental-image in a blinding light, causing him to yelp. One assumes this to be the necessary jolt of pain, which the viewer shares with Max, required to begin the hallucination. Max's mental-image slides into hallucination, becoming clearer as Nicki emerges, extending a whip to Max. Cut to Max, no longer wearing the device. Cut to a tight frame of Nicki, no longer an embodied subject, but a degraded image: 'What are you waiting for, baby?' she pouts, 'Let's perform. Let's open those neural floodgates.' Pan out to reveal a continuity shot that is in fact an establishing shot of Nicki's image circumscribed by a fleshy, sensuously pulsating and vascular television set, no longer in Spectacular Optical, but the Videodrome theatre. Camera tilt, and Max alone is in the frame, centred at eye level before the camera. He begins to whip not the television (although this is implied by the sensuous moans of pain and pleasure that resonate in the theatre) but the perspectival space occupied by the spectator. The whip licks and snaps against the lens in an exercise in punishment and, pursuing the film's masochistic theme and assuming consonance between the disembodied, cacophonous sonsigns, pleasuring and feminising the viewer, and Max's own view of himself.[3] What are we to make of this objective fantasy of masochism, sadism, seduction, simulation and technology?

Seduction/Masochism

> The worst thing being to turn desire into reality. (Baudrillard 2006a: 79)

In the opening pages of *Seduction*, Baudrillard infamously announces that 'Freud was right: there is but one sexuality, one libido – and it is masculine. Sexuality has a strong, discriminative structure centred on the phallus, castration, the Name-of-the-Father, and repression. There is none other. There is no use dreaming of some non-phallic, unlocked, unmarked sexuality' (*S*: 6). While this move has disappointed many readers (Kellner 1989a) and incensed others (Irigaray 1980 in Grace 2000), one should note that it is followed by a hostile critique of Freud's view of anatomy as destiny (thus he reproaches Irigaray for, in his view, retaining it) in favour of, like Lacan, sex and sexuality as symbolically constructed around the phallic signifier. Echoing Lacan, for Baudrillard, 'In the sexual bipartition masculine/feminine, an arbitrary and structural distinction on which the sexual reality (and repression) principle is based, "woman" thus defined is only ever man's imaginary', the product of 'an immense labour of phallic simulation' (SED: 133, 103). So, Baudrillard calls seduction feminine by 'the same convention that claims sexuality to be fundamentally masculine' (S: 7). Complementing this logic is what Baudrillard calls the 'phallus exchange standard', whereby the phallus becomes, like Marx's formulation of money as the universal equivalent, 'the absolute signifier around which all erogenous possibilities come to be measured, arranged, abstracted, and become equivalent' (SED: 114–16). Baudrillard thereby contends that 'the subversive privilege the body was given since it was always in a state of repression is now coming to an end in the process of emancipation' (SED: 117).

Baudrillard's logic is adjoined to pornography, and he places Deleuze's desiring-production under the phallic signifier and, thus, the phallic exchange standard, which reduces the object/other to a simulation of one's own desire. For Baudrillard, pornography is less a matter of content – the depiction of *sexual* acts – than of form – the *depiction* of (sexual) acts; a relationship between the perceiving subject and the perceived object. Obsessed with anatomical detail and the hyperbiological, pornography compensates for the subject's passivity (symbolic or literal impotence) so that the pleasure derived is not scopophilic, as Laura Mulvey (1989) famously theorised, but that of traversing mediation, the distance between subject and object, the object becoming transparent (withholding nothing) or obscene. Here Baudrillard is gesturing to the (primal) scene as either witnessed or fantasised, the 'ob' prefix bearing a double connotation of a simultaneous movement towards and away from the symbolic dimensions of phantasy. Traversing representation to become simulation, pornography offers up the truth (detail, reality) so much that sex 'merges with its own representation' at the expense of 'perspectival space, and therefore, that of the imaginary and of phantasy – end of the scene, end of an illusion' (S: 29). Baudrillard conjoins desire and the production of the hyperreal, so that one 'no longer partake[s] in the order of desire but in the order of the frenzy of the image [. . .]

Images have become our true sex object, the object of our desire'
(2012: 35).

CIVIC TV's corporate structure attests to Baudrillard's intertwining
of capital, desire and production as a masculine enterprise, since male
characters determine broadcast content. Indeed, it is what he called
'a "sexually affluent society." It can no more tolerate a scarcity of
sexual goods than of material goods' (*S*: 26). In the boardroom, Max,
Raphael (David Bolt) and Moses (Reiner Schwarz) consider a new
video, *Samurai Dreams*. Raphael declares its content – 'Oriental sex'
– 'unnatural' and, thus, lucrative, whilst Moses disapproves, declaring
it 'not tacky enough' to turn him on: 'Too much class, bad for sex.'
Martin Ham picks up on the significance of the names these two characters bear. He identifies in Moses the biblical figure, and its association
with prohibition, but also a mediator between the truth and the public,
and he associates Raphael with the Renaissance painter (2004: para
8). Max, however, wants something 'tough' that will 'break through'
to 'what's *really* going on under the sheets', not something 'naïve' and
'sweet'. In an inversion of the Platonic triad of the true, the good and
the beautiful, here, truth, prohibition and aesthetic merit are oriented
toward the production of appearances, of transparency.

From this vantage point, Max is able both to rationalise his
occupation and to maintain cynical distance from it. He declares in
private that 'the world's a shithole'. But when television presenter
Rena King (Lally Cadeau) queries CIVIC TV's programming and
its contribution to a violent and perverse society, he replies, 'It's a
matter of economics. We're small; in order to survive we have to give
people something they can't get anywhere else. I care enough to give
my viewers a harmless outlet for their fantasies and their frustrations.
As far as I'm concerned, that's a socially positive act.' There is truth
to Deleuze's mutual indictment of capitalism and psychoanalysis, for
this rationalises Max's actions:

> NICKI: I think we live in overstimulated times. We crave stimulation for its
> own sake. We gorge ourselves on it. We always want more, whether it's
> tactile, emotional or sexual, and I think that's bad.
> MAX: Then why did you wear that dress?
> NICKI: Sorry?
> MAX: That dress. It's very stimulating. It's red. You know what Freud
> would have said about that dress?
> NICKI: And he would have been right. I admit it. I live in a highly excited
> state of overstimulation.
> MAX: Listen, I'd really like to take you out to dinner tonight.

There are two things to note here. The first is when Max 'deciphers' the unconscious he puts it in the service of capital. Second, Max mistakes the projection of his desire for his mastery of the phallic order: he desires Nicki, accuses her of desiring him, and she capitulates. Max can claim no accountability for the biases of the libidinal economy, but can justify his role within it by highlighting the complicity of its detractors. The Freudian logic runs deeper, as does the film's combination of psychoanalytical and filmic projection, right down to Freud's earliest formulation of hysteria and seduction. Hysteria is an imitative logic whereby the object advertises what it fundamentally rejects (Perelberg 2005: 5) to simulate the subject's desire. Indeed, it soon becomes apparent that Nicki's sexual interests lie elsewhere and, later, that she herself is a trap for Max's desire. Max warns Nicki that his Videodrome tape, featuring a woman whose breasts are being flogged, is not 'exactly sex', to which Nicki responds, 'Says who?' Max goes to turn the tape off, but Nicki stops him, saying that she 'can take it', that it turns her on. When she asks Max to cut her, he awkwardly rebuffs. Undeterred, Nicki talks about how one might become a contestant and asks Max to 'try a few things' with her. The masochistic theatrics they then engage in show the inexperienced and disoriented Max sticking pins through Nicki's ears and sucking on the wounds, to Nicki's arousal. One should avoid the obvious penetrative analogy and, with Deleuze, focus instead on the masochist's rejection of end-pleasure as an interruption of desire and, second, on the reversal of Max's claim to mastery of the unconscious and decoder of Nicki's desire. Nicki does not desire Max, but masochism. Later, Nicki leaves the relationship to become a contestant. When Max angrily tells her not to audition, she responds by branding herself (Nicki Brand; later, a corporate brand) with a lit cigarette, and then offers it to Max, who gingerly accepts and scrutinises it. We note with Baudrillard that the phallus and the feminine are conjoined by simulation, and that as the desired object, the imitative logic of the hysteric's seduction is to 'use signs which are already simulators' and turn 'them into traps' (FF: 100). The point here is not the transferral of the symbolic phallus, as in Judith Butler (1993), but the masochist's abuse of it. Thus Max, who is often seen smoking, in a subsequent meeting with one of his suppliers, Marsha (Lynne Gorman), will regard her ignited cigarette with distrust.

This abuse of Max's symbolic mastery and seductive reversal recurs throughout the film. Max's obsession with Videodrome is both mercantile – 'there's almost no production costs!' – and psychosexual. When Convex confronts him, asking 'Why would anybody watch a scum show like Videodrome?', Max replies, 'Business reasons', invoking the mocking rejoinder, 'What about the other reasons? Why do you deny you get your kicks out of watching torture and murder?' – a question Max avoids. Max's primary psychological defence to scenes of masochism is disavowal, enacting Freud's tripartite elaboration in 'A Child is Being Beaten' (1922). The title of the essay is the third and final stage, rendering the witnessing of a beating impersonal, since neither the beater nor the beaten is identified. This scene begins with the sadistic pleasure derived from witnessing violence visited upon another, succeeded by the masochistic interval, where the witness assumes the subjectivity of the beaten. For Freud, this interval is both the most crucial and the most ambiguous, for it is repressed. However, like the primal scene, it is also what might have been fantasised. Nicki identifies with the masochistic interval, whilst Max oscillates between the first and final stages. It is also notable that these stages complement commercial imperatives: sadism that excites Max (and viewers) whilst the depersonalised performance disarms the threat of reality. As Max observes on his second viewing, 'You can't take your eyes off it, it's incredibly realistic. Where do they get actors who can do this?' The first time he sees Videodrome is, however, the determining instance. As he later learns from Harlan, it is at this precise moment that the signal was implanted. Max cannot understand Videodrome, but it arouses him, compels him to repeat (rewatch) and repress. It becomes his own personal complex, or 'my Videodrome problem'. They don't know from whence the signal comes; it is scrambled, its code constantly changing. At the same time, 'we never leave that room' – the Videodrome theatre – and its transmission is, as Deleuze says of masochism, a 'frozen, arrested, two-dimensional image', a fetishistic 'process of disavowal and suspension' (1989: 31–2). As a pornographer, Max's drives are organised and protected by phallic defences, which prefer the hyperreal. As Marsha warns him, 'What you see on that show, it's for real, it's not acting,' to which Max replies, 'I don't believe it. Why do it for real? It's easier and safer to fake it.'

When the masochistic phantasy returns, Max resorts to defence mechanisms. With Nicki's assurance that she was 'made for that show' running through his head, Max becomes increasingly unnerved and arms himself with a gun. Cronenberg arranges some overtly vaginal imagery, and Max opens a triangular case made of leather (tactile and fleshy) with a plush red lining, a gun ensconced in folds of fabric, and the zipper's interdigitation connotes dentition, which will later repeat itself in somatic terms. Max's incompetence is signalled by his inept handling of the weapon, and the magazine impotently topples out of its frame. The fetish object is not a disavowal of castration – the phallus is an introjected object possessed by the oral mother. In another scene, Max awakes from the hallucination in which he fantasises being whipped by himself, and the camera pans out to reveal that it is no longer Nicki's image/television body that is being beaten, but Marsha's. Max wakes, not at Spectacular Optical, but at home in bed, to find Marsha, bound, gagged, bleeding, and dead. He calls Harlan and demands that he photograph the body to prove the malicious hallucination. When Harlan inspects the bed, Marsha appears never to have been there. Max has previously disavowed, or claimed to be irresponsible for, the transparency he himself facilitates, but he now resorts to the distinction between phantasy and reality, convinced the image will serve as an index rather than as simulation. When this fails – he and the other pornographers have rendered it irretrievable – Max is convinced that his actions will have been documented by Harlan's record of the Videodrome signal. In the subsequent confrontation he learns of Harlan's subterfuge, that he is now a victim of his own enterprise.

The most obvious manifestation of the oral mother is the scene where Nicki's luscious red lips, pressing their way out of the television set, plead with Max to 'come in', and Max plunges head first into the spongy image. Unnerved by this encounter, Max returns to Bianca, telling her to beware Videodrome because 'it bites', to which she replies, 'What kind of teeth do you think it has?' Here we get the Freudian equation of the male masochist's fantasies of castration yielding feminine pleasure and, later, the vagina dentata signalled earlier. Max's body becomes unbearably receptive, with mind-controlling cassettes rapaciously inserted into his new vaginal orifice. When Max discovers the gaping aperture in his abdomen, his first instinct is to secrete his gun within it. When the unlikelihood of this registers, Max fumbles around for the missing firearm. But the evocation of castration is misleading. When he later withdraws the gun, it is fused to his arm, subordinating the castrating function of the phallus as something donned or affected to a unilateral signifier, eliding the symbolic phallus with the penis-as-organ. These are, as Baudrillard would have noted with Lacan, strictly male fantasies and, more to the point, the transformations, or becomings, are entirely subordinate to the whims of the Videodrome agents.

The properly hermaphroditic subject Deleuze supposes to be the triumph of masochism occurs only after a literal rebirth as the 'Video New Flesh'. Bianca becomes Deleuze's oral mother as both nurturing and deadly. As she says, 'I am my father's screen,' assuming the symbolic function of the Law. Rebirth occurs when Max goes to assassinate Bianca but ends up confronted with the fact that Nicki was murdered on Videodrome and, then, his own death and rebirth. The properly seductive and, by turn, masochistic moment of the film occurs here with the revelation that Nicki died on Videodrome. 'They used her image to seduce you,' Bianca tells him, 'but she was already dead.' Seduction, for Baudrillard, 'consists in letting the other subject believe himself to be the subject of his desire' (*S*: 86) and, here, the object of Max's sadistic Videodrome fantasies, which he believed to be alive and desiring subordination, turns out to be a pre-recorded lure. The revelation, affirming the premise of Deleuze's power of the false, is comparable to that in Hitchcock's *Vertigo* (1958) where the 'shock [. . .] is not that the original turns out to be merely a copy – a standard deception against which Platonism warns us all the time – but that (what we took to be) *the copy turns out to be the original*' (Žižek 2012a: 140). What Baudrillard shares with Lacan is that attaining or deciphering the truth of the desired object, the other, *is the traumatic moment where desire itself vanishes*.

When a biomorphic, phallic weapon emerges from the television screen, mirroring Max's own appendage, Lacan's mirror phase becomes Baudrillard's video phase. The weapon fires at Max, but a cut away from the shot of bullets entering him reveals that the trauma has registered on the screen from whence the discharge emanated, which has now become his chest. Max kneels before Bianca. 'That's better, so much better,' she says. 'It's always painful to remove the cassette, to change the programme, but now that we have, you'll see that you have become something quite different from what you were. You've become the video-word made flesh.' From here, in a Deleuzian schizophrenic movement, Max turns the previously subordinated hermaphroditic assemblage against the Videodrome agents. His vaginal chest opening feigns passivity, willingly opening up for Harlan at his request, and, in a castrating gesture, dismembers his arm. The biomechanical firearm then disposes of Convex, whose own body erupts with all manner of grotesquerie.

However, the conspiracy reaches far beyond its local agents, as

Nicki, appearing (possibly as a hallucination) before Max on a television screen, tells him:

> I've learned that death is not the end. I can help you [. . .] You've gone just about as far as you can go with the way things are. Videodrome still exists. It's very big, very complex. You've hurt them, but you haven't destroyed them. To do that, you have to go on to the next phase [. . .] Your body has already done a lot of changing, but that's only the beginning, the beginning of the New Flesh. You have to go all the way now. Total transformation [. . .] To become the New Flesh you must first kill the old flesh. Don't be afraid to let your body die.

Videodrome is an abstract signal, its human agents expendable components. To combat the machine, one must evacuate one's own body. Max is shown a video of his own suicide, which he then re-enacts, transcending the film's equation of bodily death with an image of an exploding television stuffed with organs and viscera, to a disembodied state where, like Nicki, he exists as a semi-autonomous image in the service of the Cathode Ray Mission. The quasi-religious fantasy of transubstantiation, noted by Jameson, might be something of an understatement, the film more gesturing to cerebral integration. The choice Max makes to side with the Cathode Ray Mission against Videodrome is not really a choice since both are dead ends. The notion of total body evacuation in favour of a virtual existence is surely the most un-Deleuzian proposition, and postmodernity's most miserable offering. If anything, the film enjoins us to hope, with Deleuze, that 'we no longer have much faith in being able to act upon situations, but it doesn't make us at all passive, it allows us to catch or reveal something intolerable' (N: 51). The implication is certainly not that a single heroic gesture is incapable of toppling the system but, even more pessimistically, the very real and disturbing notion that embodied subjectivity might no longer be the decisive terrain on which the media and, by extension, global capitalism can be conceived and, thus, challenged. In the next chapter, we will retreat from the disembodied, virtual fantasies of cyberpunk that inform this conclusion, yet retain a fascination with probing the boundaries between phantasy, technology and simulacra.

Notes

1. In many ways McLuhan preconditioned English-speaking critics to Baudrillard's and Deleuze's theories (Theall 2001). Cronenberg has discussed the influence of McLuhan (Grünberg 2006: 65–6).

2. Others have made this link between Baudrillard, Lacan and Laplanche (Thomas 1992; Poiana 2008; Weatherill 2000).
3. See Patricia MacCormack (2009) on Deleuze, cinema and masochism.

Seducing-Machines

It is clear that the car crash is seen as a fertilising rather than destructive experience, a liberation of sexual and machine libido. (Ballard 1990: 157)

We are all, in the framework of this system, survivors. Not even the instinct of self-preservation is fundamental: it is a social tolerance or a social imperative. When the system requires it, it cancels this instinct and people get excited about dying. (*PES*: 86)

Crash is *the* Baudrillardian novel. 'Anticipating Marshall McLuhan and Jean Baudrillard, Ballard demonstrated how encroaching advertising and mass consumer culture played on submerged desire, implanting new, artificial subjectivities to create a schizophrenic underclass' (Sellars and O'Hara 2012: xii). The primary focus in J. G. Ballard's *Crash* (1973) is 'a cult of bored, middle-class professionals who feel alive only after modifying their bodies via staged car crashes' (ibid 2012: xii).[1] Their leader, Vaughan, feeds on the neuroses of his followers, encouraging them with questionnaires to fantasise about dying in crashes with celebrities, developing comprehensive psychosexual profiles, while he himself obsesses over Elizabeth Taylor. In both Ballard and Cronenberg's 1996 film adaptation, the unexpected crash breaks people out of their neurasthenic yet promiscuous existences. Under Vaughan's leadership, they are introduced to a 'benevolent psychopathology' that enjoins them to the technological transformation of their bodies, and facilitates new, perverse sexual practices. Characters are no longer alienated from their surroundings or from each other, but physically and psychologically interconnected, their remodelled psychic apparatuses corresponding with their external world. James, the narrator, explains: 'I realised that the entire zone which defined the landscape of my life was now bounded by a continuous artificial horizon, formed by the raised parapets and embankments of the motorways and their access roads and interchanges' (53).[2] This artificial horizon is formed at the junction of the flows of the industrial landscape and communications technologies: a riot of celebrity mythologies, accumulated fictions, images and technoscientific planning and research bear down upon subjects in an oppressive, yet seductive, simulation. In Cronenberg, Vaughan travels from the city's high-rise apartments, hospitals and film studios to squalid outer suburbs and derelict racetracks, recruiting new test subjects. Ballard arranges a deranged economy of subjectivities, pitting those that have achieved 'optimum auto-death' – James Dean, Albert Camus, Jayne Mansfield, John Kennedy – against a litany of vestigial subjectivities: 'psychopaths', 'neurasthenic housewives returning from their VD clinics', 'excited schizophrenics', 'manic depressives', 'luckless paranoids', 'sadistic charge nurses', 'lesbian supermarket manageresses', 'autistic children' and 'mental defectives' (15). In between these two extreme poles are James (James Spader in the film), an advertising executive, his wife Catherine (Deborah Kara Unger), a pilot, Helen (Holly Hunter), a doctor, and Vaughan (Elias Koteas), a computer scientist and once-famous television producer.

Ballard's novel prompted a brief essay by Baudrillard in 1976 and his introduction to anglophone SF critics in a 1991 issue of *Science Fiction Studies*. Baudrillard's analysis is exceptional not only because it 'is the only text Baudrillard considers worthy of lengthy citation' (Luckhurst 1997: 124) but also because of his claim that *Crash* is 'the first great novel of the universe of simulation' (*SS*: 119) and thus intended to demonstrate his central claims. The affinities between Baudrillard and Ballard have long been noted, so much so that 'despite the fact that, unlike the most famous theoretical "pseudo-couple" of Deleuze and Guattari, they have not collaborated together, numerous points of exchange exist between them' (Noys 2008: para 1; see Cusset 2008: 67). Baudrillard and Ballard share the view that technology and consumerism usher in an entropic existence under capitalism, with the subject confronted by an increasingly unreal existence dominated by simulacra where, in Ballard's words, 'the human inhabitants of this technological landscape no longer provided its sharpest pointers, its keys to the border-zones of identity' (48–9). Nonetheless, the accuracy of Baudrillard's interpretation has been disputed, described as an outright 'hijacking' (Baxter 2009: 10). Key to these objections has been the rejection of Baudrillard in favour of Deleuze. More than *Videodrome*, *Crash* is becoming-Deleuzian. The stakes are significantly higher than those of *Videodrome*, for Baudrillard himself wrote on *Crash* and accorded it great significance. This trend towards Deleuze gained new validity when Cronenberg adapted Ballard's novel. 'Through an effect of ironic precession, the critical analysis of a film pre-existed the film itself':

> Cronenberg's *Crash* appeared, to the reader of Baudrillard's eponymous text, as the perfect but de-mined adaptation [. . .] of his critical model [. . .] *Crash*, understood here as a theoretical machine ruminating on the question of the simulacrum [. . . .] found itself realised, but retrospectively. (Thoret 2011: para 9)

Thoret gets the sentiment right, but in fact most of the scholarship on Cronenberg's *Crash* employs Deleuze rather than Baudrillard. This is unsurprising: one need not really know what a desiring-machine is to find it evocative of the film or the novel. But Roger Luckhurst keenly notes that *Crash* is remarkably pliable, accommodating numerous theoretical frames, with the novel 'not so much read as reiterated in a different register' (2005: 516). These frameworks 'can and do provide illuminating commentary. Yet it is surely significant that *Crash* can support so many self-sustaining yet entirely contradictory readings. It might be that the studied neutrality of the text cunningly reshapes itself to whatever theoretical approach is thrown at it' (ibid. 518). The aim of this chapter is to make careful distinctions between Deleuze and Baudrillard, to show their precise contributions, and why they gravitate to *Crash*.

Crash is exceptional in that theory seems to run away with the novel at Ballard's expense. Indeed, *Science Fiction Studies* critics accused Baudrillard of deliberately distorting his transparent intentions. But appealing to Ballard is much more problematic than assumed. The final paragraph of Ballard's preface is clear: 'Needless to say, the ultimate role of *Crash* is cautionary, a warning against that brutal, erotic and overlit realm that beckons more and more persuasively to us from the margins of the technological landscape' (6). Critics have appealed to Ballard's unambiguous intent, which is, unlike the novel, striking in its clarity. But the truth is that Ballard was rather flexible on this matter. In 1995 he said that 'in the final paragraph, which I have always regretted, I claimed that in *Crash* there is a moral indictment of the sinister marriage between sex and technology. Of course it isn't anything of the sort. *Crash* is not a cautionary tale. *Crash* is what it appears to be. It is a psychopathic hymn. But it is a psychopathic hymn which has a point' (quoted in Sellars and O'Hara 2012: 309). The following year, however, Ballard insisted that *Crash* 'has to be a cautionary tale. If not, it's a psychopathic statement' and that, in retrospect, he simply 'plays devil's advocate and completely adopts what seems to be an insane or perverse logic in order to make a larger point' (ibid. 329–30). In 1997, he added that while *Crash* was not moralising, it was nevertheless a cautionary elucidation on the eroticisation of technologised violence (ibid. 340–1).[3] Whether Baudrillard was deliberately unfaithful to Ballard's intentions ultimately benefits neither position. But Baudrillard was at least in agreement with Ballard on the subject of genre, for both were determined that *Crash* was *not* SF. Lamenting his earlier moral injunction, Ballard adds 'that the other way in which I went wrong was in all my talk about science fiction. Of course *Crash* is not science fiction' (ibid. 309–10). While this too has been subject to variation, Ballard earlier describing it as 'a kind of science fiction of the present' (ibid. 125), the technoscientific conditions present in the novel are consistent with our own, and calling it SF, for Ballard, detracts from this:

> I constantly see *Crash* referred to as an SF novel, and of course it isn't in any conceivable way. But by calling it SF, it's a way of distancing book from reader. It's a way of not facing up to what the book is trying to say. I think SF has probably come to an end, because it's in the air we breathe. (Ibid. 269)

What 'the book is trying to say' is not forthcoming, but clearly its force comes from this minimal separation of reality and fiction. Bukatman's description of it as 'high-tech porn' (1993: 6) is misleading: stripped of Ballard's technomedical prose, the underlying premise is primitive, so that estrangement derives not from technological plausibility, but from the novel's psycho(patho)logy. The classification of Cronenberg's film was rather different, revolving around whether it was suitable – or safe[4] – for mainstream distribution. It has varyingly been described as drama, thriller, pornography, 'quasi sci-fi' and 'hardcore fantasy reality' (Rodley 1997: 189). As Cronenberg explained, 'A lot of people think of *Crash* as a sci-fi book [. . .] It's the psychology of the characters. It's not a normal psychology, but it's presented as normal' (quoted in Wardle 1997: 29). Had the film been more generically associable with or marketed as SF, one has to imagine that the surrounding controversy would have been significantly diminished (Barker et al. 2001). The outrage the film provoked was not a result of it not being SF, but its depraved content certainly jarred with its unassuming form. Lacking sufficient distance between the real and its imaginary projection, the film takes this psychopathology as its zero-degree, elaborating it, and it is never questioned by the characters themselves. Ballard was prone to changing his position, but never wavered from Freud. He commented numerous times that his premise was Freud's distinction between latent and manifest content of dreams – between underlying meaning and apparent content – was less a psychological, introspective distinction than one that had to be made in external reality (Sellars and O'Hara 2012: 6, 342; Ballard 1990: 156). In a famous passage, Ballard is in agreement with Baudrillard's sense of McLuhan, claiming that reality appears to us as increasingly devoid of substance: 'Despite McLuhan's delight in high-speed information mosaics we are still reminded of Freud's profound pessimism [. . .] Voyeurism, self-disgust, the infantile basis of our dreams and longings – these diseases of the psyche have now culminated in the most terrifying casualty of the century: the death of affect' (1984: 96).

Hyperreality

> In my own way, I am very much a moralist. (Baudrillard 2004b: para 25)

Although references to SF are common in Baudrillard, 'Crash' and 'Simulacra and Science Fiction' constitute his only detailed textual analyses. Thus, they must have a central significance to our understanding of Baudrillard's approach to SF. Despite being frequently cited, Baudrillard's 'Crash' has never been read in detail, nor read closely alongside 'Simulacra and Science Fiction'. This lack of attention has meant that it has suffered from casual citations and misunderstandings that belie a complex and challenging argument. When Baudrillard declares that *Crash* is the first great novel of the universe of simulation, one is struck by the fact that the novel has nothing to do with the 'miniaturised cells, matrices, and memory banks, [and] models of control' (*SS*: 2) that Baudrillard claims to be characteristic of the hyperreal.[5] Before addressing this, we will have to work through the necessary contextual material, for lack of attention to this has impeded a proper understanding of Baudrillard's claims.

The arguments levelled at Baudrillard in *Science Fiction Studies* (hereafter *SFS*) concern his infidelity to Ballard's intentions and to the novel itself, the rejection of simulation as a totalising hypothesis, and the immoral celebration of technology and simulacra. While these objections will be addressed, one should immediately note that they were, at the time of writing, at a disadvantage. First, critics were called on to respond to two essays translated specifically for publication in the journal. While 'Crash' tells us much about Baudrillard, read in isolation, even with 'Simulacra and Science Fiction', it borders on incomprehensible and unrepresentative. Second, the responses neglect Baudrillard's invocations of Deleuze. Third, and compounding the first two, when these essays were published, little of Baudrillard was available in English. Since their publication was intended to bring Baudrillard to the attention of SF critics, this point deserves considerable attention. Only a handful of Baudrillard's books had been translated by 1991 (*CS*, *PES*, *MP*, *FF*, *S*, 1983a, 1983b, 2012[6]); most of these are incomprehensible without *Symbolic Exchange and Death*, which outlines Baudrillard's revised Marxism. For all his apocalypticism and hysterics, the moral tenor of Baudrillard's work, while progressively distrusting of any leftist progress or critique, and adhering to no orthodox position, is irretrievably moored in a dualistic view of political economy:

> All that capital asks of us is to receive it as rational *or* to combat it in the name of rationality, to receive it as moral *or* to combat it in the name of morality [. . .] Its instantaneous cruelty, its incomprehensible ferocity, its fundamental immorality – that is what is scandalous, unacceptable to the system of moral and economic equivalence [. . .] One imputes this thinking to the contract of capital, but it doesn't give a damn (*SS*: 15)

Before we scrutinise 'Crash', it will be worth revisiting the impress of these factors on Baudrillard's theses on SF. Unlike SF critics such as Jameson, Freedman and Suvin, Baudrillard splits utopia off from SF, but his accompanying argument that there are no more utopias, and no more SF, is effortlessly contradicted by empirical evidence (Milner 2012: 97). Baudrillard was neither an SF nor a literary critic, but he saw in *Crash* something that equalled in explanatory force his own concerns, and the three orders of simulacra that he overlays on to SF have a coherence that is more than suggestive. They proceed thus: operatic, naturalist simulacra; operative simulacra of production; operational, cybernetic simulacra of simulation. To each corresponds a representational mode: utopia, SF 'strictly speaking', and the science-fictional hyperreal (*SS*: 121). We must be careful not to disassociate simulacra from capital, since each has an economic determinant and cognate periodisation: pre-industrial society up to primitive accumulation, industrial capitalism, and late capitalism. Each order is not annulled by its successor, but absorbed, so that one will find in the second elements of the first, and so on, so that the empirical presence of a former instance – SF in this case – within a successive phase – hyperreality – disavows the hegemony of each successive phase.

Baudrillard emphasises this in 'Simulacra and Science Fiction', arguing that 'science fiction in this sense is no longer anywhere, and it is everywhere, in the circulation of models, here and now, in the very principle surrounding simulation.' It is not with reference to SF that he illustrates this, but to the organisation of labour in (then) East Germany, where 'factories-simulacra' 'reemploy all the unemployed to fill all the roles and all the posts of the traditional production process but that don't produce anything' (SS: 126). Baudrillard's examples, Disneyland and prisons, afford greater insight. Disneyland is an exceptional space of infantile regression, rampant consumerism, phantasmagoria and technological marvels, disavowing the presence of these very features beyond its walls; prisons serve to 'hide that it is the social in its entirety, in its banal omnipresence, that is carceral' (SS: 12). Whilst the consensual fictionalisation of a piece of reality conferring authenticity on what lies beyond is a Lacanian gesture, Baudrillard mistakes a discrete phenomenon for a totality. The question is not so much empirical but of psychological distance between the real and imaginary (although not in the Lacanian sense) as determined by capitalism. This hypothesis becomes clearer once distance is defined as the 'gap that leaves room for an ideal or critical projection' (SS: 122). In the first order, the gap is maximal and the imaginary utopia transcends the real.[7] The second order is marked by elaborations which project the productive technologies of the real into an imaginary. SF is thus 'an unbound projection of the real world of production, but it is not qualitatively different from it' (SS: 122). In the third order the thesis becomes more provocative: 'is there an imaginary that might correspond to this order? The most likely answer is that the good old imaginary of science fiction is dead and something else is in the process of emerging' (SS: 121).

At this point Baudrillard's representational distance appears untenable, but it can be supplemented by three interconnected points, the first relating to genre: 'Classical science fiction was that of an expanding universe, [. . .] counterparts to the more terrestrial forms of exploration and colonisation of the nineteenth and twentieth centuries' (SS: 123). This was linked to the utopian transcendence of alienation and social contradictions and to the intertwinement of technological advancement with social progress. The 'New Wave' SF that Baudrillard describes as comprising the third-order 'something else', that of Dick and Ballard, favours technological and social entropy over progress, and the movement's watchword, the paranoid psychoses of 'inner space', was directly opposed to technoscientific advances into 'outer space'. Neither the New Wave nor cyberpunk, Andrew Milner observes, 'represented anything like so decisive a break with tradition' as previous shifts in the genre, and are better understood as 'late moments within SF, just as Jameson's "late capitalism" is a late moment within capitalism' (2012: 96–7). But Baudrillard's misrecognising what is now a subgenre for SF in general has some merit since, like Jameson, who declared cyberpunk to be the literature of late capitalism, Baudrillard's 'something else' is indicative of a phenomenon beyond SF. Whether this is simulation or merely a transient symptom thereof will concern us here.

This is better understood through Baudrillard's own mutated psychoanalysis and a restricted sense of simulation as in the first instance an economic phenomenon. Formerly, the 'imaginary was the alibi of the real, in a world dominated by the reality principle' (*SS*: 122): the fetishised imaginary stands in and compensates for an absence in the real, giving rise to consensual reality. Today, Baudrillard argues, this process undergoes a reversion, so that 'it is the real that has become the alibi of the model, in a world controlled by simulation' (*SS*: 122): the fetishisation of the real stands in and compensates for the decline of the imaginary, which, unlike the real, does not disappear, but becomes 'reabsorbed', so that the real and the imaginary become the singular hyperreal, real and imaginary deprived of substance and difference. When Baudrillard says that 'paradoxically, it is the real that has become our true utopia', but a utopia with the substance of a 'lost object' (*SS*: 123), we should accord this its full psychoanalytic resonance as an object that, in Lacan, one relinquishes in order to enter the symbolic, but here relinquished in order to enter the hyperreal. The corollary is that simulation signals the foreclosure of utopian alternatives. The necessary alienation that gives rise to the apprehension of social contradictions is subsumed by the illusory freedom afforded by integration via communication technologies and an economy no longer moored in material production. The 'hell of simulation, which is no longer one of torture, but of the subtle, maleficent, elusive twisting of meaning' and the 'conjunction of the system and of its extreme alternative' will '*no doubt end up giving rise to socialism*', but 'it is from the death of social that socialism will emerge' (*SS*: 18, 26). While cinema at the time was nostalgically fetishising the past, as in Roman Polanski's *Chinatown* (1974), or rewriting history, as in Francis Ford Coppola's *Apocalypse Now* (1979) (*SS*: 43–8, 59–60), in (New Wave) SF:

One is from the start in a total simulation, without origin, immanent, without a past, without a future, a diffusion of all coordinates [. . .] It is a universe of simulation, which is [. . .] insuperable, unsurpassable, dull and flat, without exteriority – we will no longer even pass through to 'the other side of the mirror,' that was still the golden age of transcendence. (SS: 125)

As Milner suggests, utopias that abreact to second-order simulacra complicate Baudrillard's theorisation, but the discontinuity between first-order utopia and SF is nevertheless correct (2012: 97). The more thorny point is whether the shift from second-order SF to hyperreality entails the same discontinuity. 'Without a doubt,' Baudrillard writes, 'the most difficult thing today, in the complex universe of science fiction, is to unravel what still complies (and a large part still does) with the imaginary of the second order, of the productive/projective order, and what already comes from this vagueness of the imaginary, of this uncertainty proper to the third order of simulation' (SS: 126). The New Wave was an epiphenomenon, and if *Crash* is an exemplary case thereof, but also of simulation, the problem that emerges is whether the correspondence between the science-fictional hyperreal and simulation retains its force in the light of the historicisation of the New Wave. The bond between the science-fictional hyperreal and simulation proves relative, rather than Baudrillard's insistence on interchangeability. By this logic, simulation disappears with the New Wave, which reduces simulation to an aesthetic, or simulation has no homology with contemporary SF: unlike *The Matrix*, Ballard's *Crash* is one of the few SF examples that Baudrillard claims encapsulate his hypotheses. In truth, the problem is his nomination of *Crash* itself as the great novel of simulation: the car, and how characters interact with it, is more identifiable with 'the mechanical robot machines, characteristic of the second order' than the 'cybernetic machines' and biotechnologies of the third (SS: 126). Yet, the public and critical reactions to Cronenberg's *Crash*, which were infinitely more hostile and notable than the reception Baudrillard received in the comparatively small world of SF criticism, give new relevance to his hypothesis.

Baudrillard's introduction to SF criticism proper came in 1991, with the publication of a special issue of *SFS* entitled 'Science Fiction and Postmodernism'. The issue, for Csicsery-Ronay Jr in his introduction (1991a), was conceived in order to present Baudrillard's untranslated work on SF – specifically the essays 'Simulacra and Science Fiction' and 'Crash' from *Simulacra and Simulation* – to anglophone critics, and to invite SF critics to respond. The responses of two prominent SF critics, N. Katherine Hayles and Vivian Sobchack, will concern us here. In her response, 'The Borders of Madness', Hayles alludes to the science-fictional qualities of Baudrillard, but the crux of her response is that simulation is not a totalising phenomenon:

> Every existing simulation has boundaries that distinguish it from the sur-rounding environment [. . .] Virtual reality environments are limited by the length of the cables attaching the body apparatus to the computer. Only when these boundaries do not exist, or cease to signify that one has left the simulation and entered reality, does the dreamscape that Baudrillard evokes shimmer into existence [. . .] The borders separating simulations from reality are important because they remind us of the limits that make dreams of technological transcendence dangerous fanta-sies. (1991: 321–2)

Cables increasingly cease to impose such limitations, but Hayles's argument retains most of its force. 'The Iowa farmer', she stresses, 'will not be easily persuaded that he lives in a world where it is no longer possible to distinguish been simulation and reality' (ibid. 321).[8] True, simulation does not work as a spatial totality, neither geographically nor conceptually – this 'border' is, presumably, from where Baudrillard himself writes. But, like Ballard's Vaughan, he 'isn't interested in pedestrians' (150) or farmers, nor easily domesticated. Our farmer's experience of groundwater pollution by agrichemicals and use of synthetic hormones in livestock rearing constitutes a blurring of the formerly science-fictional speculation and the real. The worth of his grain is subject less to its quality than to wagers placed on its value, and there is more to be made in this pure exchange of capital without reference to the material commod-ity, which will happen whether or not he is convinced that this traded grain is real or simulated.

If Hayles sought to domesticate Baudrillard, Sobchack goes further by turning his reading back on to his own body, accusing him of being 'naively celebratory', that he 'jacks off (or in) contemplating "artificial invaginations"' (1991: 327–8). She ultimately reproaches Baudrillard for abstracting bodily experience entirely:

> Baudrillard's techno-body is a body that is *thought* always as an *object*, and never *lived* as a *subject* [. . .] One's own body resists the kind of affectless objectification that Baudrillard has *in mind* [. . .] Baudrillard is so into *thinking* the techno-body as without organs and full of orifices, so erotically seduced by the (very male?) confusions of sex and death [. . .]

that he reads Ballard's *Crash* obscenely [. . .] Getting the descriptions right, he gets the tone all wrong and thus, where Ballard is cautionary [. . .] Baudrillard is celebratory. (Ibid. 327–9)

Later, Sobchack adds that Baudrillard's 'alienated and highly fetishised fascination with the body-object' 'long[s] to escape the lived-body and its limitations', not unlike those 'obsessed with physical fitness'; his 'dizzying pro-technological rhetoric hides anti-technology desire and its self-deception promotes deadly, terminal confusions between meat and hardware' (1998: 316–19). Ardent though this is, the critique suffers on three counts. First, as she says of Baudrillard's Ballard, Sobchack gets the descriptions of Baudrillard right, but not the tone. Second, she attributes Deleuzian and Lacanian points to Baudrillard. Third, there is a lack of familiarity with Baudrillard's work on consumerism and capitalism.[9]

Hysteria-Machine

Having outlined Baudrillard's position on SF, and with these critiques in mind, we can now revisit 'Crash'. Baudrillard begins by opposing Ballard's technology in *Crash* to the 'functionalised visions' of Marx and McLuhan, who see technology as 'extension[s] of the human body' (*SS*: 111). This is true of McLuhan, less so of Marx, for whom technology has the capacity both to alienate and to liberate. Unlike McLuhan, the body in *Crash* is 'no longer a functional medium' and, unlike Marx, no longer the 'body as labour in the order of production', but 'dispersed [. . .] as an anagram in the order of mutilation' (*SS*: 111–12); no longer a body whose labour power is exchanged for capital, or a component of the machine, but symbolic, commutable material, 'confused with technology in its violating and violent dimension' (*SS*: 111). Baudrillard then introduces the first of several allusions to Deleuze. The body in *Crash* is 'a body without organs or pleasure of the organs, entirely subjected to the mark, to cutting, to the technical scar – under the shining sign of a sexuality without a referential and without limits' (*SS*: 111). The key allusion here is 'body without organs' as a compound noun and/or adjectival relation, which is translated as such in *Simulacra and Simulation*, as in Deleuze, from French *corps sans organes*. In Evans's translation for *SFS*, it reads as 'a body with neither organs nor organ pleasures' (Baudrillard 1991: 313) so that the emphasis falls on Freud's organ pleasure.[10] He claims that *Crash* is entirely superficial, possessing no psychological or psychoanalytic depth: 'No affect behind all that, no psychology, no flux or desire, no libido, no death drive [. . .] No repressed unconscious (affects or representations)'; to essay any psychoanalytical reading would be a 'secondary reading [. . .] reinject[ing] a forced meaning' (*SS*: 112).

Although rejecting flux, desire and affect, Baudrillard brushes up against anti-interpretative, anti-representational schizoanalysis in his traversal of Freud and Lacan. Whereas Deleuze and Guattari reject the foundations of psychoanalysis, Baudrillard, as noted in Chapter 2, accepts Freud's single, masculine libido. Similarly, *Crash* reinvents Freud's body economy, where 'organic and functional' genital sexuality directed towards end-pleasure is superseded by the 'possible metaphors of symbolic exchange'; symbolic not in Lacan's sense whereby sex 'is nothing but the inscription of a privileged signifier [the phallus] and some secondary [feminine] marks', nor sex as the 'rarefaction of a drive called desire on previously prepared zones' (*SS*: 115, 114).[11] Traumas are 'no longer metaphors for castration', but 'a semiurgy of contusions, scars, mutilations, wounds that are so many new sexual organs opened on the body' (*SS*: 113, 112). Distinguishing paranoia from schizophrenia, Deleuze writes that an 'abstract machine will be overcoding – it will overcode every assemblage with a signifier, with a subject, etc. – or else it will be mutant, mutational, and will discover behind every assemblage the point that undergoes the basic organisation, making the assemblage shoot off into a different one' (*D*: 118). It is this schizophrenia that Baudrillard identifies and gravitates toward. Indeed, he reads the car-machine along the lines of Deleuze and Guattari's *Kafka* and their reading of *In the Penal Colony*. The car-machine is:

> different from the Machine of *The Penal Colony*, where the body in its wounds is still only the support of a textual inscription. Thus one, Kafka's machine, is still puritan, repressive, 'a signifying machine' Deleuze would say, whereas the technology in *Crash* is shining, seductive, or dull and innocent. Seductive because denuded of meaning, and because it is the simple mirror of torn-up bodies. (*SS*: 113)

This passage merits further explanation, because it is uncharacteristically approving of Deleuze, and thus complicates Baudrillard's reading. In Kafka's *In the Penal Colony*, a harrow carves the sentence conferred by the Law on to the flesh of a condemned prisoner. The prisoner is ignorant of his sentence, but as the harrow carves the sentence for hours on end, he learns, in a moment of transcendence, its meaning: 'You see it in the eyes. From there it starts to spread. A sight that might seduce one to take one's place under the harrow as well [. . .] The man begins to decipher the script [. . .] It's not easy to decipher the script with one's eyes; our man deciphers it with his wounds' (Kafka 2007: 160). This machine is one example Deleuze and Guattari use to illustrate impersonal desire, 'nonpossessive' and 'nonpossessed', requiring 'no precise knowledge of political economy'; rather, it is 'the business of the unconscious libido'. When converted into individual interests, interrupted or possessed, desire can be made to desire its own repression (*AO*: 346). Deleuze and Guattari suggest that the harrow-machine is 'too mechanical, still too connected to overly Oedipal coordinates' (*K*: 39) since the officer administers the Law with reverence to the former commandant. In the thrall of the commandant-father, and the Name of the Father as represented by the harrow's inscription, the officer seeks the transcendent, subservient experience of the condemned. The machine, however, malfunctions, and kills him: 'There was no trace of the promised transfiguration; the thing that all the others had found in the machine, the officer himself had failed to find' (Kafka 2007: 178).

It is the fate of Kafka's officer that Baudrillard projects on to *Crash*. Hitherto, Baudrillard's reading is celebratory and, as I have noted, Deleuzian in inspiration. But it changes gear when Baudrillard adds that all this promissory eroticism 'would be nothing without hyperreal disconnection', its obsession with photographs and video recordings. The image is 'not a medium nor is it of the order of representation [. . .] simultaneous in a universe where the anticipation of the event coincides with its reproduction, indeed, with its "real" production' (*SS*: 117). *Crash* thus resonates with what Baudrillard calls a 'culture of premature ejaculation' (*S*: 38) where 'everything becomes a hole to offer itself to the [masculine] discharge reflex' (*SS*: 112) resulting from the loss of the imaginary, flattened out with the real. The fetishised image takes the place of the real object, and the technological obscene takes the place of the imaginary scene, eliminating the symbolic:

> Pleasure (whether perverse or not) was always mediated by a technical apparatus, by a mechanism of real objects but more often of phantasms – it always implies an intermediary manipulation of scenes or gadgets. Here, pleasure is only orgasm, that is to say, confused on the same wave length with the violence of the technical apparatus. (*SS*: 116)

This is why any promise is eventually undercut by the hyperfunctional and the hyperreal. Important here is Baudrillard's placing

Crash in 'the same universe as that of the hypermarket, where the commodity becomes the "hypercommodity"' (*SS*: 118), referring us to 'Hypermarket and Hypercommodity' (*SS*: 75–8): consumers no longer satisfy their needs, but are tested and interrogated by objects (rather than commodities) to reproduce the code of consumption, 'beyond the factory and traditional institutions of capital, the model of all future forms of controlled socialisation' (*SS*: 76).[12] This returns us to the economic reasoning of simulation: the logic of *Crash* is, for Baudrillard, that of the market; the commutability of bodily and technological forms is the schizophrenic experience thereof. The novel 'devours its own rationality', it 'reaches its paradoxical limits and burns them', so that *Crash* is a 'violently sexed world, but one without desire, full of violated and violent bodies [. . .] but one void of sensuality' (*SS*: 118–19): its promissory eroticism is a symptom of simulation rather than a challenge. Rejecting Ballard's preface, Baudrillard suggests that *Crash* is beyond the moral gaze, beyond 'critical negativity', a 'dull splendour of banality or of violence' that is neither good nor bad, but 'simply fascinating' (*SS*: 119). There is nothing perverse, subversive or, indeed, immoral about *Crash*: the trauma of the accident divorced from contingency becomes 'the Rule', part of an administered simulation pact. The unexpected accident, the crash, 'the residual bricolage of the death drive for the new leisure classes', is 'no longer the exception to a triumphal rationality' nor 'the order of the neurotic, the repressed, the residual or the transgressive' (*SS*: 113). *It is not celebration that ultimately characterises Baudrillard's 'Crash', but appalled fascination.*

What Ballard and Baudrillard ultimately share – although not in these exact terms – is the notion that schizophrenia is subject to general promotion in a society with neither prohibition nor restraint, what Ballard described as the 'normalisation of psychopathology', 'the way in which formerly aberrant or psychopathic behaviour is annexed into the area of the acceptable' (quoted in Sellars and O'Hara 2012: 254, 343). Baudrillard's (mannerly) distaste for *Crash* lies in its lack of sensuality, which has been replaced with techno-sexual violence, which resonates with (at least one of) Ballard's comments on the novel that 'there's *only* sex there. The realm of the affections has been obliterated. That's what the book is about: the transcendence of affection and the emotions, which is what I see as the main achievement of technology (ibid. 205).[13] Baudrillard's Lacano-Marxian insight, against Deleuze's 'strategy of desire', is that capital conjoins the id and the superego, enjoining them to a managed liberation of the pleasure principle 'entirely controlled by production and planning' (*PES*: 85). Baudrillard is in fact closer to Lacan's conception of the obstacle or prohibition as that which sustains desire, rather than occludes it (Lacan 1998: 185). In the hyperreal, where everything is disclosed, the phantasy or minimal illusion that sustains desire and props up reality bottoms out, and all that remains is a brute fascination with the obscene: 'Sex can be perfectly liberated, perfectly transparent, without desire and without pleasure (it still functions)' (*FS*: 85).

Organs, Drives and Orifices

Deleuzian interventions into *Crash* follow the pattern of those in the previous chapter: technology and simulacra are not the oppressive, dehumanising forces Baudrillard supposes, but generate a host of new deterritorialisations. Most deduce Deleuze's desiring-machines and bodies without organs from the characters' interactions with technology. Christian Bök hastily and injudiciously draws together Ballard, Baudrillard and Deleuze under the sign of the desiring-machine to promote a 'cyborgonic schizonoia' (2002: 54) that is figurative rather than evaluative. Michel Delville stops short of an analysis, but proposes that in Ballard's *Crash*, sex, violence, technology and politics 'are necessarily intertwined' and thus a counterpart to Deleuze and Guattari (1998: 6). For Justin Clemens and Dominic Pettman, '*Crash* is essentially a meditation on what happens to desire when we factor the environment into the equation (which is, of course, something we should do in the age of machinic assemblages)' (2004: 41). Andrzej Gasiorek quickly bypasses Baudrillard to argue that Ballard provides the technological and historical determinants absent in Deleuze, who nevertheless illustrates how desire is assembled in a technological landscape. The emphasis in Ballard nonetheless falls on 'the power of independent logics to mould [the] individual' (2005: 86). For Matthew Holtmeier, the characters 'construct Bodies without Organs as they allow themselves to find pleasure in new relationships', but he draws on Deleuze and Guattari's qualification that assembling a body without organs is not to be undertaken lightly, that it can be fatal. So, when Holtmeier asks 'is this where Baudrillard is headed with his forgetting the danger of death and valorising the simulacra?' (2009: 4, 8), the question, besides ignoring Deleuze's simulacrum, pertains equally to the role of Deleuze in Baudrillard. Deleuzian readings extend to Cronenberg's film, independent of or in conjunction with Ballard. Sara Eddleman suggests that the 'scenes where Cronenberg takes apart or marks the body or intentionally blurs the boundaries between bodies, or between bodies and technology [. . .] can be read as attempts to create bodies without organs' (2009: 3). The argument extends to film form, where Cronenberg's style, which 'favours surface over depth (for another important concept for the BwO is the *surface*) and an often-elaborate framing/re-framing of body-images, further serves to visually represent the process of creating the BwO' (ibid. 3). The rejection of depth in favour of the surface event is true to Deleuze, and differs from Cronenberg scholarship that gives Freudian explanations. Championing wounds that create 'the potential for creating discontinuity and difference' (ibid. 8) rejects biological pre-assignations, but also discounts the trauma to which other critics have drawn attention, which here becomes a secondary consideration to the pure positivity of Deleuze's difference. Whether this is more promising than Baudrillard's reduction of the body to a sign system of marginal differences, ensnared in commodity logic, is left unchallenged.

The most implausible reading thus far is Darrell Varga's, the central claim of which is that '*Crash* can be seen as more than a simple affirmation of the loss of meaning on the part of the social and individual body, as is the case in some strains of Baudrillard-influenced postmodernist thinking' (2003: 264) and that Deleuze can retrieve the film from Baudrillard's purview. Without citing Baudrillard, Varga announces that 'Ballard's novel (and I would add Cronenberg's film) is by no means a Baudrillardian neo-conservative celebration of the disavowal of the body but instead explores desire in bodily transformation while at the same time articulating the limits and losses accompanying transformation' (ibid. 263). Varga then proceeds to sabotage his own argument, first by relying on Sobchack's expanded reading of Baudrillard, the inaccuracies of which we have seen, and, second, by misreading Sobchack herself. Varga cites with approval and optimism Sobchack's definition of a body without organs as 'a techno-body that has no sympathy for human suffering, cannot understand human pleasure, and since it has no conception of death, cannot possibly value life' (ibid. 263).[14] This body without organs/techno-body is precisely what Sobchack took Baudrillard to celebrate, denouncing its pursuit of immortality on its trajectory towards technological transcendence. Chronically disabling his argument, Varga mistakes Sobchack's body without organs for Deleuze's, and proposes that this critical perspective helps us to distinguish between the usefulness of Deleuze and Guattari's thinking and the nihilism of Baudrillard's later writings in which there is no possibility of liberation or transgression. Deleuze and Guattari's thinking is not the same as Baudrillard's techno-fetishism, which, as Sobchack points out, obscures his anti-technological desires. (Ibid. 263)[15]

Varga infers bodies without organs and desiring-machines from the commingling of technology and the body, and though 'articulat[ing] an urge to transcend alienation in the expression of desire at the limit of the flesh', the film is 'unable to transcend homosocial conventions' (ibid. 268). Even if we excuse the misreadings compounding the mis-appropriations, the substitution of Deleuze for Baudrillard neither resolves nor explains this deadlock.

If Varga's incomprehensible substitution of Deleuze for Baudrillard and the Deleuzian renovations above shadow Baudrillard's sup-posed celebratory reading, Braidotti turns *Crash* into a posthuman manifesto. Sobchack is again summoned to set the moral compass, guaranteeing that 'the ethical issue is crucial to the whole discussion of non-unitary subjects, of bodies without organs and organs dis-engaged from bodies' (Braidotti 2002: 224). Sobchack might claim that, 'prosthetically enabled, I am, nonetheless, not a cyborg' (1998: 319), but for Braidotti she is mistaken, since she 'literally brings us back to our senses by reminding us of the pain of actually becoming a cyborg' (2002: 224). Unwittingly rehearsing Baudrillard, Braidotti says that in Ballard, 'every scar is consequently a border that can be trespassed [. . .] a borderline zone, object of admiration and aberra-tion, irresistibly attractive' amongst the 'molecular promiscuity of bodies with organic and inorganic others'. *Crash* promises 'a qualita-tive leap over the last doubts and hesitations that hold humans back from the concerted actualisation of new virtual embodiments, which contemporary technologies make possible' (ibid. 238). If Baudrillard was naively celebratory, then Braidotti is rhapsodical in her claim that *Crash* points to 'an ethics of neo-realist appraisals of risks and fears' that displace 'grandiose meta-discourses such as Marxism and psychoanalysis' (ibid. 262). Braidotti reads the final scene in Cronenberg thus: James, having run his wife, Catherine, off the road, rushes to her side, and asks her, 'Did you come?':

The female of the species, however, sadly remains contained within the confines of her skin-clad bodily organism. Not so much because of her biology, but of what was made of her biology by the phallic signifier, she has to admit, defeated, that no, she did not come. And then, in what I can only describe as an act of sublime love, her husband strokes her ever-so-tenderly and promises: 'Maybe the next time.' There is hope yet. Not the nostalgically-founded hope of old-fashioned humanism, not the perverse hope of a psychoanalytically-phrased polymorphous perversity: just the hope for a qualitative transmutation of the human body into a post-human organism [. . .] Breaking out of the straight-jacket of normal literally means breaking out of one's skin, ripping open the envelope [. . .] Change hurts, transformations are no mere metaphors. (Ibid. 237)

Braidotti has misquoted the scene, for James actually asks 'Are you hurt?', to which Catherine replies, 'I think I'm all right.' Her 'defeat' is not her inability to climax, but her inability to succumb to the apparently necessary trauma; the promise of another attempt implies that the couple will continue until she does. It is the women of *Crash*, then, that struggle to accept the will to technological transformation. The text 'propels humans out of the last vestiges of postmodern nostalgia for humanistic wholeness, or melancholia due to its loss', but the female characters are caught somewhere between stubbornly resisting 'becom[ing]-minoritarian' and the 'far superior power of attraction and hence the competition of the machine [. . .] and the subject-positions it enables' (ibid. 238).

By overemphasising its more subversive themes, Braidotti's Deleuzo-feminism and Deleuzian readings avoid many of *Crash*'s thornier points. For one, genital mutilation is central to the fantasies of Vaughan and his followers. Vaughan imagines the piercing of Taylor's uterus coinciding with his own car-crash orgasm, and he creates collages which perfect her imminent mutilation with clippings from medical textbooks and the Road Research Laboratory. It is hard to endorse promiscuous and polymorphous readings of Ballard when the overriding sentiment is irretrievably masculine, if not misogynist. Most of Vaughan's test subjects are prostitutes, invariably described as unintelligent 'whores' selected for their likeness to Taylor and for the way their skin tone matches the car's interior (171). Descriptions of female anatomy range from clichéd evocations of vulvas as 'wet flower[s]' (53) and clitorises as 'inert nub[s]' (178) to the repulsed description of Catherine masturbating, her 'fingers grovelling at her pubis as if rolling to death some small venereal snot' (180).

The most confronting scene in both Ballard and Cronenberg is the sex act between James and Gabrielle (Rosanna Arquette in the film), a cyborgic panoply of sexual possibilities and BDSM prostheses that support her spine and legs. Gabrielle is the most perversely equipped of all the characters, most notably for the distal, corrugated and trench-like scar on her thigh that James prefers to her vagina for its erotic possibilities. After penetrating it, James sets about 'irrigating' (179) it and her other injuries and mechanical support structures with his semen. Cutting through Ballard's generative prose, James is simply ejaculating on Gabrielle in dull and pornographic fashion. Their encounter sparks his imagination further, and he fantasises about Catherine's 'mouth and face destroyed, and a new and exciting orifice opened in her perineum by the splintering steering column, neither vagina nor rectum, an orifice we could dress with all our deepest affection' (179–80), heralding less a new eroticism than an intensification of male fantasies of female sexual utility. Ultimately, the body that grounds Braidotti's analysis is a souvenir rather than an ethical horizon. Braidotti can make *Crash* do anything (and in this she is not alone) except serve as an admonitory tale of violent technoeroticism or a negative, albeit ambivalent, critique. The only thing more wearisome and uncritical than Baudrillard's reduction of everything to simulation is this laborious task of sifting through the wreckage to salvage some shred of positivity, whereby degenerative impulses and infantile regression move in the same direction as a technological quasi-transcendence, and 'a joyless, superegoic command to keep on fucking' (Botting and Wilson 1998: 187).

Cracks in the Simulacrum

> What does it mean to disarticulate, to cease to be an organism? [. . .] You don't do it with a sledgehammer, you use a very fine file. You invent self-destructions that have nothing to do with the death drive. (*TP*: 177)

Baudrillard is correct when he says that *Crash* is a 'model of science fiction that is no longer one', it is '*our* world, nothing in it is "invented"' (*SS*: 125). There is no projection of the real world into an imagined space, no fantastic machines or technoscientific extrapolation of the second-order type. Returning to Suvin's definition of SF, there is no novum as he intended. However, as we saw in Chapter 1, an expanded conception of the novum here presents itself as psychopathology. This is better explained, along with Baudrillard and Deleuze, by Freud's theses on trauma and Laplanche's seduction theory. For it is the desires of these characters, what compels them to do what they do, that constitutes the novum per se; whether these are overdetermined by the exterior world or whether they arise from the unconscious, or a combination thereof, is what is truly sinister and exciting about the novel and the film.[16]

Crash seduces Deleuzians because it draws together technology and desire. But their invoking the body without organs and desiring-machines remains superficial, and does little to explain the novel or the film in depth, whereas the nature of desire and simulacra remains unexplored. Short of venturing an analysis, Luckhurst speculates on the insights of a Deleuzian reading of Ballard's *Crash* that opposes his simulacrum to Baudrillard's (1997: 127–8). Indeed, the psychoanalytical motivations of *Crash* resonate with Deleuze's simulacrum, which is derived in equal parts from philosophy and psychoanalysis, specifically, Plato's philosophy of representation and Freud's death drive. Where Freud struggled to reconcile repetition with the libido, Deleuze uncovered the affirmation of simulacra and difference as emerging from repetition. In Freud, each actor manifest in a phantasy is ascribed a latent pre-assigned role in a formal logic of representation and interpretation (things and people stand in for mothers, fathers, etc.). For Deleuze, this logic is reductive: rather than 'unmasking' manifest content, Deleuze suggests that these appearances are not to be reduced to a role, but understood as difference in and for itself. Latent content is not reality waiting to be discovered or interpreted. Rather, 'simulacra are the letter of repetition itself. Difference is included in repetition by way of disguise' (*DR*: 19). The death drive produces an 'other death' whereby simulacra are not reducible to the imposed forms of a psychoanalytically predetermined ego (*DR*: 138). Plato, for Deleuze, erects a 'moral vision of the world' (*DR*: 155) by positing an ideal, transcendent identity that distinguishes not only the good and the bad copy, but the copy and the simulacrum that appeals both to external appearance and to interior essence. An appeal to an essence is a moral ideal to be rejected in favour of a 'surface typology' of 'impersonal, preindividual nomadic singularities' (*LS*: 126). Deleuze characterises the stage preceding the formation of the ego and superego as one of schizophrenia and simulacra (rather than Melanie Klein's paranoid-schizoid splitting of good and bad partial objects) to which corresponds the body without organs (*LS*: 215–16). Whence derives the complementarity between sexual drives and simulacra, creating new erogenous zones, objects and images (*LS*: 227–8) and simulacra that are 'flush with the real', schizo desiring-machines 'identical with the production of the real' (*AO*: 87).

The relations Deleuze establishes between desire, simulacra and repetition emerge after the trauma of the crash. Cronenberg begins with three consecutive scenes of rear-entry sex, not necessarily constitutive of an active-masculine/passive-feminine binary. But as it relates to film form, this implies detachment and depersonalisation, establishing a rhythm whereby pleasure is prematurely and abruptly denied with a cut, only to begin anew somewhere else. The opening scene begins with Catherine pressing her exposed breast to a plane fuselage, tucking it back into the cup of her bra when the hand of her anonymous male partner attempts to fondle it. As her unseen partner rouses her from behind, Catherine brushes her mouth against her reflection, before pressing her face to it and caressing her reflected cheek. The following scene is a mirror image of Catherine's encounter, the focus now on James and an anonymous woman face down and prostrate on a desk in a camera room. Later, at their apartment, Catherine leans against a rail, looking outward over the motorways, and hitches up her dress for James. James asks whether Catherine orgasmed in her encounter, to which she replies that she did not, whilst James admits that his own encounter was equally unsatisfying. This scene effects a failed synthesis of the previous two, Catherine repeating the phrase 'maybe the next one', whilst James penetrates her from behind, before the film cuts away from another anti-orgasm. Ballard's characters' alienation is much more symptomatic of their technological environment. For Catherine, James is an 'emotional cassette' (37); for him, she is 'as inert and emotionless as a sexual exercise doll fitted with a neoprene vagina' (51). There are lengthy descriptions of James comparing Catherine to a 'demonstration model', and of him inspecting and probing her ears, vagina and anus for erstwhile secretions. Besides feigning ignorance over each other's affairs, their only source of arousal is masturbating each other while watching television footage of student riots, wars, natural disasters and police brutality, 'violence experienced at so many removes [that] had become intimately associated with [their] sex acts' (37).

This affectless existence, with the minimal psychological investment of a partner – present in body but not really 'there' – is essentially autoeroticism, sex without the intervention of an other, or minimal level of mediation. The insistence that the crash releases repressed desires (Ruddick 1992; Hayles 1991) is dubious, since this must surely depend on a repressive mechanism nowhere apparent. The traumatic scenario is better explained through different psychoanalytic avenues. Despite Ballard's Freudianism, *Crash* is better read with Laplanche's revision of Freud. After his crash with Helen, James becomes an infant, as everything around him becomes simultaneously enigmatic and erotic. In passages that recall Laplanche's seduction theory, his entire surroundings become sexualised; he draws no distinction between the bodies of the nurses that care for him and the technological prosthesis and equipment that envelop him. Nurses attend 'only to [his] most infantile zones' (33), adjust his orthopaedic braces, replace the tubes that drain his wounds, work his bowels, and clean his orifices. He immediately feels isolated from the reality of the accident, fictionalising it, and begins to resymbolise the trauma in sexual terms. The crash with Helen is imagined as 'a model of some ultimate and yet undreamt sexual union' (40) and the foundation of an erotic connection. Vulnerable in this revitalised world, James begins a sexual relationship with Helen where he imagines she resuscitates or revives him. The affections of women become maternal, yet also sexual as he imagines that the female X-ray operator sees him as a sex doll replete with 'every conceivable orifice and pain response' (40). Catherine assumes responsibility for his sexual gratification, absentmindedly masturbating him while voyeuristically describing his crash, her affections compared to those of the nurses. Behind these resymbolisations of trauma is the primary seduction phantasy, a blockage that becomes acceptable to James once it undergoes technological renovation:

> I visualised the body of my own mother, at various stages of her life, injured in a succession of accidents, fitted with orifices of ever greater abstraction and ingenuity, so that my incest with her might become more and more cerebral, allowing me at last to come to terms with her embraces and postures. (180)

The crash violently introduces the heretofore absent gap or mediator between the imaginary and the real, between people, narcissistic autoeroticism and the other.[17] In Cronenberg, the first real, head-on – missionary, if you like – encounter is the crash between James and Helen immediately following the balcony scene. Against the languid camera and aestheticised stupor of preceding scenes, there is a rare moment of agitated cutting, with James struggling to control his car, which careers into oncoming traffic and into a head-on collision with Helen and her husband. Helen's husband crashes through both his windscreen and James's. The silent encounter between Helen and James is shot in a revelatory manner, each holding the other's gaze through shattered windscreens. The intrusion of the real – trauma that brings the psyche into confrontation with one's own body and the unconscious of the other (Kittler 1999: 16; Laplanche 2001) – ruptures the narcissistic envelope in which James has heretofore existed, symbolised by the piercing of the car's protective shell, and visually asserted through the cracks in perception suggested by the shattered windscreen. The accident signals a transformative moment that ruptures Baudrillard's simulacrum:

> After the commonplaces of everyday life, with their muffled dramas, all my organic expertise for dealing with physical injury had long been blunted or forgotten. The crash was the only real experience I had been through for years. For the first time I was in physical confrontation with my own body, an inexhaustible encyclopaedia of pains and discharges [. . .] After being bombarded endlessly by road-safety propaganda it was almost a relief to find myself in an actual accident. Like everyone else bludgeoned by these billboard harangues and television films of imaginary accidents, I had felt a vague sense of unease that a gruesome climax of my life was being rehearsed years in advance, and would take place on some highway or road junction known only to the makers of these films. (39)

Cronenberg and Ballard take this intrusion of the real beyond contingency, and develop a psychopathology founded on repetition. Here we can draw together Freud's death drive, Laplanche's seduction theory and the simulacrum. Unable to reconcile the repetition of trauma with the pleasure principle, Freud theorised that repetition afforded mastery over the traumatic event, substituting an active role where there once was only passivity, and cultivated the anxiety and anticipation absent in the original trauma. Where the trauma involves physiological injury, narcissistic hypercathexes on the injured organ bind excess sexual excitation (Freud 1995: 600, 609–10). Laplanche's model differs in that seduction is bound to trauma: the psychic and physiological effraction constitutes the ego, but the resultant sexual excitation is itself traumatic, rather than bodily injury alone (Laplanche 2001), and to resymbolise sexual excitation is to master trauma.[18] The same drives of mastery, perfectibility and reassertion inform Baudrillard's simulacrum, defined as 'a repeat performance of the first, but its repetition *as something more real*' (A: 42).

Efforts to resymbolise sexual trauma and reinvest reality with meaning become highly cathected fields of production. At the film studio where James works, he details the hours spent simulating wounds and bruises so that Taylor will look like a real crash victim. The film will cut to her, already posed in a wreckage, whilst Seagrave (whose phantasy is that actors will be forced to crash their own stunt cars), made up to resemble Taylor, will perform the actual crash – 'potent fusions of fiction and reality' (111). Later, James, Vaughan and Helen attend an open day at the Road Research Laboratory, where they watch in real time, and then in slow motion, scientists test their hypotheses against simulated crashes, anticipating injuries and traumas with crash-test dummies. According to Vaughan's perverse logic, these trials are performed to increase the number of road accidents, foreshadowing the technological reproduction of reality. 'The technology of accident simulation at the R.R.L. is remarkably advanced,' he enthuses while working his groin. 'Using this set-up they could duplicate the Mansfield and Camus crashes – even Kennedy's – indefinitely' (123). After watching the simulated crash, they then rewatch a recording of it in slow motion on video monitors:

> As we watched, our own ghostly images stood silently in the background, hands and faces unmoving while this slow-motion collision was re-enacted. The dream-like reversal of roles made us seem less real than the mannequins in the car. I looked down at the silk-suited wife of a Ministry official standing beside me. Her eyes watched the film with a rapt gaze, as if she were seeing herself and her daughters dismembered in the crash. (128)

The film studio and the Road Research Laboratory give privileged access to the spectacle, which is not the event itself, but how the pseudo-event is meticulously manufactured, revealing the labour behind and psychological investment in simulation. Rather than the event being demystified, the spectators leave the studio agitated, their endeavours to resymbolise their own trauma falling short of the death drive's aim to unbind psychological and physiological tension. In the second instance, an illustration of the mirror-video phase, the crowd can only watch passively, becoming less real than mannequins, nar-cissistically invested in a rehearsal of their own deaths. The passion for mastery and to reinvest the traumatic real with meaning makes reality itself less authentic, so that, as Deleuze wrote of Platonism, albeit in a different tenor, 'behind every cave there is another, even deeper; and beyond that another still. There is a vaster, stranger, richer world beneath the surface, an abyss underlying every foundation' (*LS*: 146–7). But the abyss signals the death of affect, and the event becomes an epiphenomenon. Observing a minor crash from his balcony, James observes that they '*are* rather like rehearsals. When we've all rehearsed our separate parts the real thing will begin' (50).

While destinies become irretrievably intertwined with a techno-logical death, Ballard simultaneously takes James through the three phases of Freud's narcissism, from the polymorphous perversity, autoeroticism and seductive invasiveness he experiences when con-valescing, to the secondary narcissistic displacement of the ego on to an ego-ideal, primarily in imagistic scenarios (Freud 1995: 545–62) – namely when James drives through a car wash while Vaughan and Catherine have sex on the back seat. In both Ballard and Cronenberg, James, Catherine and Vaughan form a psychosexual triangle, Vaughan becoming a phantasmal figure who mediates and animates their sex lives, especially Catherine's. She becomes unable to climax without recounting elaborate fantasies that involve Vaughan, nor without interrogating James about Vaughan's penis, anus and semen, requiring him to describe a homosexual act with Vaughan. She ultimately displaces James altogether: 'Catherine had taken over the fantasy. Whom did she see lying beside Vaughan, herself or me?' (118). James reconciles the phantasmal intrusion by identifying with Vaughan narcissistically. In the car wash, whilst James watches in his rear-view mirror, Vaughan puts Catherine through contortions resembling car-crash victims, before penetrating her. James's impo-tence is supplemented by the voyeuristic pleasure derived from the scene, but also from seeing Vaughan, his ego-ideal and her phantasy, satisfying his wife in a way he himself cannot. The scene reconfig-ures and reverses the physical and psychic incapacitation and erotic attention James received from Catherine while in hospital, the sluic-ing of the soap analogous to James's passive and Vaughan's active ejaculations, the battering of the rollers in accord with Vaughan's treatment of Catherine's body. Vaughan leaves Catherine's skin and genitals bruised, to which James devotes all his affections, 'loving [Catherine] for the blows Vaughan had struck her body' (166). The third and final phase of narcissism is the integration of the ego with the ego-ideal. Against any 'subversive' reading, we retain some sense of Ballard's Freudianism, which bears the impress of Freud's early theorisation of homosexuality as narcissistic identification. James becomes convinced that Vaughan is a projection of his own fantasies and thrice describes the eventual 'sodomy' that occurs between them, with James the dominant partner, as devoid of sexuality, performed only for its aestheticised, photographic fidelity to acts already imag-ined and planned. Without Vaughan photographing him having sex in cars, without his superegoic approval, James finds orgasm either impossible or unsatisfactory.

The tragic seriousness of Vaughan's obsession to die in a crash with Taylor only becomes truly apparent at the moment of shameful failure, the moment at which Baudrillard's simulacrum as an operational totality becomes vulnerable to Deleuze's subversive simulacrum. James and Vaughan speed to a crash in which Taylor is reported to have been killed. Incensed that Taylor has died in a genuine accident rather than one designed by himself, Vaughan discovers something much more disturbing. Seagrave, prompted by Vaughan's questionnaires and calculations, and addled by drugs and an untreated concussion, has taken it upon himself to simulate Taylor's death. Wearing a wig and Taylor's clothing from the film set, Seagrave has fatally crashed his car into that of a television presenter. Seagrave deprives Vaughan of his phantasy, realising it in a crash of his own making, real in its occurrence, but amateurish and intrusive in its unexpected arrival outside of Vaughan's meticulous rehearsals. It is not the dissimilitude between Vaughan's fantasies and this crash that distresses him, but that the psychic support structure of the simulacrum is exposed as insufficient, prey to the real. His pretences to mastery of technology and desire become subject to irruption, to cracks in the simulacrum, emerging not as a more perfect, more real, repetition, as is Baudrillard's simulacrum, but a traumatic anticipation. The accident then occupies the space originally reserved for the event, and the only way Vaughan can recover from this trauma is to resymbolise and repeat it:

> I realised what had most upset Vaughan. This was not Seagrave's death [. . .] Seagrave had pre-empted that real death which Vaughan had reserved for himself. In his mind, from that accident onwards, the film actress had already died. All that remained now for Vaughan was to constitute the formalities of time and place, the entrances of her flesh to a wedding with himself already celebrated across the bloody altar of Seagrave's car. (187)

The analogous scene in Cronenberg is shot in more bathetic fashion. Seagrave's (Peter MacNeill) balding head, hairy chest, blotchy face and bloated body are in disjunction with Mansfield's blonde wig, gaudy pink coat, dishevelled bra and celebrity-accessory toy dog. Both exasperated by and admiring the scene before him, Vaughan admonishes the dead Seagrave – 'You couldn't wait for me! You did the Jayne Mansfield crash without me!' – while photographing the scene both for posterity and to fictionalise it. Unable to resymbolise or traverse the phantasy, Vaughan becomes depressed and ever more deranged, self-injuring and reopening healed wounds. The photos Vaughan keeps on the walls of his apartment – those that document his successful television career – 'fix his identity by marking it upon some external event' (168) whilst, in a revision of Oscar Wilde's *Dorian Gray* (1890) where technological simulacra replace representational painting, his own body becomes 'a collection of loosely coupled planes. The elements of his musculature and personality were suspended a few millimetres apart, floating beside me in this pressure-free zone like the contents of an astronaut's capsule' (198).

Eventually, the novel's circular narrative returns to where it began, with Vaughan's death. His innumerable rehearsals and careful planning are all for naught: he drives his car off an airport flyover, aiming for Taylor's limousine, and misses it entirely to crash through the roof of an airport bus loaded with skybound passengers. For James, the scene 'seemed to parody the photographs of crash injuries that covered the walls of his apartment', yet it constitutes 'his only true accident' (9, 7). For Durham, Ballard's is a quasi-utopian and darkly 'comic dénouement':

> If a utopian content is to be found in the spectacle, it is revealed here [. . .] Vaughan's trajectory toward the event that would once and for all propel him into the image-sphere [. . .] is clearly meant to satirise the unhappy consciousness of the consumer who, in aiming to propel his body into the mythic space of the spectacle, only succeeds in rejoining the other members of the audience. (1998: 71)

And it is this perverse sense of utopia, with its unhappy consumers and audiences-cum-spectacle addicts, that will occupy us in the following chapter. For Hayles, by contrast, the significance of Vaughan's death rests in the very 'riot of signification' (1991: 323) evoked by the airport and planes overhead, as though Vaughan were attempting to transcend his psychopathology and technological environment. This is immediately undone by the fact that Vaughan inadvertently kills a busload of passengers destined for the airport. Moreover, this transcendental impulse must refer to some type of spirit or essence, which is nowhere present in the novel. Rather, we should read literally, with the transcendent metaphor hitting the bitumen along with Vaughan: *there is no one on that plane*. Rather than transcendence, Cronenberg and Ballard end with narcissistic transference. In Ballard, James prepares for his own fatal crash, assuming Vaughan's subjectivity and narrative trajectory. At the climax of Cronenberg, James commandeers Vaughan's car, repeatedly ramming it into Catherine's until she loses control, and it veers off the road and rolls over. Catherine, who had unbuckled her seatbelt in expectation, is thrown from the car, but is nonetheless uninjured. James's subsequent line, 'Maybe the next one,' returns them to their psychosexual deadlock, with the violence of their predetermined deaths, like Kafka's harrow, now woven into the very logic from which the crash delivered them.

Notes

1. Ballard's *Crash*, as Bould ably puts it, contains 'everything you need to know about sex, technology and commodity fetishism' (2009: 250) and Ballard was an important source of inspiration for cyberpunk (Pasquinelli 2008).
2. All page references to the novel are taken from the 1995 edition.
3. A statement he would contradict again in 1999 with reference to Jean-Luc Godard's *Weekend* (1967): 'He sees the car as the symbol of American capitalism, and the car crash as one of the wounds inflicted by capitalism on the docile purchasers of motor cars; people whose lives are completely modified by Wall Street. Whose sex lives are reduced to the kind of banal banter that you get in advertising commercials. I thought: "That's the *wrong* approach." He's missed the point. He doesn't see that the car is, in fact, a powerful force for good in its perverse way [. . .] I knew Godard didn't get it – because he saw the car crash in rather old-fashioned Marxist political terms' (quoted in Sellars and O'Hara 2012: 366–7). Ballard discredits the most common interpretation of *Weekend* (Silverman and Farocki 1998: 83–111).
4. At the behest of the British Board of Film Classification, psychiatrists weighed in on whether it might provoke imitations and whether the characters might be adopted as role models (Luckhust 2005).
5. Baudrillard might have revised this declaration in light of Michel Houellebecq's *Atomised* (1998), with the author acknowledging Baudrillard's influence.
6. I have used the most recent edition here, but *The Ecstasy of Communication* (1987) was first translated in 1988.
7. One infers from Baudrillard citing the 'island of utopia' the socio-political utopian tradition of Thomas More's *Utopia* (1516).
8. Said farmer would probably find the figures Hayles describes in *How We Became Posthuman* (1999) equally unconvincing, seeing no need to reprioritise embodied subjectivity within a virtual environment.
9. These points are better explored by closely reading Baudrillard, but it is worth pointing out that his *Consumer Society*, which was available in English, devotes a chapter to Sobchack's point about the fetishisation

of the body, where 'sexuality is *once and for all part of the unlimited process of production and marginal differentiation*, because it is the very logic of that system which has "liberated" it as *erotic system* and individual and collective consumption' (*CS*: 144). Sobchack is more or less correct: Baudrillard's is not a lived body, but one trapped in a semiological system, its gestures, expressions and investments producing marginal differences and sign-values intimating, rather than constituting, difference. Moreover, it is hard to imagine one whose 'anti-technology desires' were so self-evident as Baudrillard's, and we might as well add that the only thing more legendary than Baudrillard's dislike of technology was his technological incompetence (Cusset 2008: 249).

10. Sobchack incorrectly attributes this to Baudrillard, claiming that hers is 'definitely *not* a thigh "without organs"' (1991: 328). She was herself recovering from surgery that resulted in amputation.

11. Sobchack reads this as Baudrillard's point (1991: 328), rather than his evoking Lacan, and Constable alone has noticed this (2011: 144).

12. Moreover, Baudrillard elides consumers and commuters, adding that the 'hypermarket cannot be separated from the highways that surround and feed it, [. . .] from the whole town as a functional screen of activities' (*SS*: 76).

13. Barbara Creed notes that despite sex, violence and traffic accidents, the film is 'unexpectedly detached, sombre, even pensive' (1998: 175).

14. The full quotation, uncited by Varga, begins: 'Without my lived-body to live it, the prosthetic exists as part of a body without organs – a techno-body' (Sobchack 1998: 319), without which Varga misrepresents Sobchack's position.

15. Varga's subsequent points, that the pornography in *Crash* lies 'in the invasive practices of the mass media in their reduction of private gesture to commodity within the mediascape and the routinisation of expression', and that the film 'makes explicit the linkage of work, commodity-image production, and casual sex' (2003: 265, 270), have nothing to do with Deleuze, but everything to do with Baudrillard.

16. Baudrillard only once commented on Cronenberg's *Crash*: 'All risk situations, which were once man's natural lot, are today re-created artificially in a form of nostalgia for extremes, survival and death. A technical simulation of pain and sacrifice [. . .] Handicaps, mutilations, prostheses, sexual fascination with accidents and lethal technologies' (2011b: 66–7). Deleuze wrote neither on Ballard nor on Cronenberg, but suggested that the freeway is a unique example of control, with 'the unique goal that people can turn into infinity without ever enclosing everything yet are completely controlled. This is our future' (2001: 105–6).

17. Thus Laplanche, revising Freud, sees sexuality as beyond Eros and as

inherently traumatic, just as Žižek, following Laplanche and Lacan, insists on an element of harassment, or a mediating, intrusive gaze, without which sex becomes mechanical fucking (Laplanche 2001; Lacan 1998: 172; Žižek 2000: 285–6).

18. Little wonder then that Laplanche calls Cronenberg's *Crash* an 'extreme illustration' of his hypothesis (2001: n. 4).

4

Remote-Control Society

Consensus as the degree zero of democracy and information as the degree zero of opinion are in total affinity: the New World Order will be both consensual and televisual. (Baudrillard 1995: 85)

Capitalism is profoundly illiterate. (*AO*: 240)

Ray Bradbury's *Fahrenheit 451* (1953) is the American answer to the English dystopias of Aldous Huxley's *Brave New World* (1932) and George Orwell's *Nineteen Eighty-Four* (1949). The novel is famous for depicting a society in which firemen do not extinguish fires but start them. The title, we are told, is the temperature at which paper ignites, for the firemen burn books, which are prohibited to own or read. Instead, the public immerse themselves in wall-to-wall television circuits, where they converse with their 'parlour family', recreate social life by performing in interactive, televised plays, and engross themselves in radio transmissions broadcast to their inner-ear Seashells. In François Truffaut's 1966 film treatment, the interactive communications network is called The Family, and each of its users is a Cousin, whose social horizon consists of statistics about books destroyed daily (by their poundage rather than content or number), broadcast commercials, instructional films and Family plays. Bradbury and Truffaut follow a fireman, Montag (Oskar Werner in the film), whose disillusion with society, inspired by his neighbour, Clarisse (Julie Christie), imperils both his domestic and his professional life, represented by his wife, Mildred (renamed Linda in the film, also played by Julie Christie), and Captain Beatty (simply called The Captain, played by Cyril Cusack). *Fahrenheit 451* imagines a society where minority pressure groups and mass communications technology have evolved into a concordance between masses and the State. Culturally and historically depthless, the fragile texture of a society governed by technology and simulacra is regulated not by an authoritarian State, but by the public themselves – what Baudrillard calls the simulation pact.

Received wisdom tells us that *Fahrenheit 451* is a dystopia. For

Raymond Williams, what made Bradbury's 'powerful social fiction' was its crystalised 'pattern taken from contemporary society' (2010: 45) – that of post-war America and mass society. The tenor of the novel very clearly comes from the vilification of mass society compared to Leavisite minority culture. But, for Williams, both book burning and televisions are distractions from the 'actual and developed world' which the story captures, 'rather than in the given, unconnected future' (ibid. 16–17). Keynesianism is undoubtedly the economic milieu in which Bradbury's (and Truffaut's) texts were composed. But, if *Fahrenheit 451* demands our attention today, it is because there has been a rift in its mutual implication of socio-economic models and speculative technoscience, so that the latter is hegemonic in contemporary society. Its *immediate relevance* lies in the speculative interactive technology that then prefigured, but now intersects with, contemporary communications technologies, and the dialectic it establishes between technology and cultural politics now less emergent than dominant in contemporary society. This chapter will argue that *Fahrenheit 451*'s vision of the future has traversed the dystopian model, particularly that of Orwell's *Nineteen Eighty-Four*, to become an inversive utopia, and that its forms of subjectivity can be explained through Deleuze and Guattari's account of fascism.

Easy-Does-It Apocalypse[1]

The '80s began in 1983, with the publication of Jean Baudrillard's *Simulations*, which propelled a kind of weightless nebula into culture just before a charge of Orwellian paranoia took over: Would *1984* keep its appointment? The answer was no. The society of the spectacle had already become a society of spectators, and Foucault's panopticon a Möbius strip. Everyone was waiting for George Orwell, but Baudrillard arrived instead. (Lotringer 2003: 194)

Baudrillard was neither a literary nor an SF critic, so there is an unavoidable unease when he is forced to enter into dialogue with SF criticism, especially on the subject of utopia and dystopia. In fact, his vision of contemporary society is frequently described as dystopian and, erroneously, Orwellian. But comparisons with Orwell are suggestive and not made to locate him within a particular tradition. As we saw in the previous chapter, Baudrillard's determinism – technological, economic, crypto-Lacanian, techno-Freudian – posits socialism without the social, an inability to distinguish between the real and the imaginary, and a hollow utopia, so that where one once subscribed to the social contract, one now enters the simulation pact (S: 163). That it is a *pact* is crucial: against the determinism that characterises most of Baudrillard's thought, simulation society requires of its vestigial subjects substantial consensual cognitive labour to maintain its operational illusion. If this is utopia, then it is *inversive utopia*: dialectics are replaced by the transpolitical, contradictions cancel each other rather than synthesise, political messages are neutralised and no longer compete with each other, everything is disclosed, but lacks the hard kernel of reality. I now want to elaborate this perverse utopia with reference to Baudrillard's most prolonged engagement with utopia, his theoretical travelogue *America*.

One of Baudrillard's most scandalous proclamations is that America is 'utopia achieved', which conforms to no received use of the concept, and is empirically unpersuasive. But Baudrillard's perversion of the term captures what he finds distinctive about America. The nuance to this broadside is the suggestion that America has no history, and by history Baudrillard means European history in general, and Marxian dialectical history in particular. For Baudrillard, the American Revolution created a zero-degree utopia, a quasi-idealist utopia distinct from any European conception:

> America was created in the hope of escaping from history, of building a utopia sheltered from history, and it has in part succeeded in that project [. . .] The concept of history as the transcending of a social and political rationality, as a dialectical, conflictual vision of societies, is not theirs [. . .] Europe invented a certain kind of feudalism, aristocracy, bourgeoisie, ideology, and revolution: all this had meaning for us, but at bottom it had no meaning elsewhere. (A: 87)

America is hyperreal, inauthentic, wilfully uncultured and places a premium on individual liberation rather than societal freedom; its genius is its *'irrepressible development of equality, banality, and indifference'* (A: 97) and its spectacular but substanceless politics; it is liberal but not transgressive, it is pornographic but not sensual, its sovereignty is conformism; it is 'vulgar but "easy"' (A: 102). America's technocapitalism, like nothing before it, 'doesn't play by the rules of critique, the true game of history. It eludes the dialectic' (A: 86). America's banality and 'unculture' is 'utopian and pragmatic' whereas European revolutions were 'ideological and revolutionary' (A: 98). Baudrillard is not blind to his abuse of the concept. Rather, he conceives of European utopianism as the unresolved dialectic between utopian and scientific socialism, between the ideal and its materialisation, and American utopianism as a spontaneous hyperreal utopia:

> Ours is a crisis of historical ideals facing up to the impossibility of their realisation. Theirs is the crisis of an achieved utopia, confronted with the problem of its duration and permanence [. . .] We shall remain nostalgic utopians, agonising over our ideals, but baulking, ultimately, at their realisation, professing that everything is possible, but never that everything has been achieved. Yet that is what America asserts [. . .] We live in negativity and contradiction; they live in paradox (for realised utopia is a paradoxical idea). (*A*: 83–5)

And:

> *Utopia has been achieved here and anti-utopia is being achieved*: the anti-utopia of unreason, of deterritorialisation [. . .] of the neutralisation of all values, of the death of culture. America is turning all this into reality and it is going about it in an uncontrolled, empirical way. (*A*: 106)

It is this utopia achieved, this inversive utopia, and the Deleuzian connotation that I want to refine and pursue with *Fahrenheit 451*, arguing that its relevance lies in this paradox.[2] But there is already some disagreement as to what mode of political organisation *Fahrenheit 451* renders dystopian. Brian Baker (2005) argues that a critique of Nazism is Bradbury's agenda. Images of book burning, which prompted Bradbury to write the novel, are obviously redolent of the Nazis, as are Truffaut's SS-style costumes and variation of the Nazi salute.[3] Against this, Bould stresses Bradbury's immediate political environment and generic continuities, detecting an 'exaggerated Cold War suburbia [. . .] Utopian and dystopian traditions in SF have often focused on centred cities, but in *Fahrenheit 451* and other 1950s SF the centrifugal suburb becomes the key location' (2005: 103). The audacity of Baudrillard's utopia achieved is its positing of an alternative to the dialectical conception of history. This is not the case in Bradbury or Truffaut, who provide dialectical historicisations, but in both there is Jameson's waning of history, evidenced by the schizophrenic Cousins, who live in a perpetually stimulating present, but also by the predominance of historical revisionism. By their own dogma, the firemen were established 'to burn English-influenced books in the Colonies' in 1790 (thereby supplanting the first State of the Union address) by Benjamin Franklin, not 'the first American', but the first fireman. Baker's insight is to locate Bradbury's novel in what Jameson has called the anti-utopia and, more narrowly, the Cold War dystopia, of which Orwell is a representative, as an 'entirely mass-cultural and ideological phenomenon' with an aversion to utopia as a 'perfect system that always had to be imposed by force on its imperfect and reluctant subject', practically associated with Stalinism (Jameson 2007: 200, xi). For Baker:

> The reaction against the Utopia of technological wonder and World States, a reaction manifest in Huxley, Orwell and *Fahrenheit 451* (despite Bradbury's small-town, communitarian impulses), was partly produced by the drift away from the politics of the Communist-influenced left towards a centralist and 'liberal' consensus [. . .] [Bradbury's] world is suburban and middle class, corresponding to social criticism of the time of the corporate and consumerist culture of the American 1950s. (2005: 491–3)

Societies of control, coextensive with simulation, theorise how technology, power and the unconscious together produce a particular social machine. What distinguishes the society of control in *Fahrenheit 451* from Orwell's disciplinary society is the absence of State surveillance, effected in Orwell by the panoptic telescreens. Foucault's panopticon and Baudrillard's rejection of it both amount to the subject's internalisation of authority, but differ in their conceptions of whence authority proceeds. Before biopolitics and neoliberalism, Foucault's panopticon presupposed a point from which to survey the whole and a despotic gaze. Against *Discipline and Punish*, Baudrillard argues that communications technologies, particularly television, eliminate the authoritative source of the gaze: the consequences are the same, but the processes different. For Baudrillard, when surveillance is replaced by a generalised system of deterrence, people become more efficient regulators of their own and others' behaviour than any centralised, observational mechanism. The binaries on which the panopticon relies – active/passive, observer/observed, public/private – lose their specificity: 'There is no longer any imperative of submission to the model, or the gaze'; rather, the system assures us that '"YOU are the model!" "YOU are the majority!"' (*SS*: 29). The social realises control independent of supervising authority, and the interactivity of communications technologies 'reveals the fact that the (Orwellian) myth of *Big Brother*, that of the total policing of visibility, *has now been taken over by the public itself*, mobilised as both witness and judge. The public itself has become *Big Brother*' (2008b: 38, emphasis added).

Baudrillard's primary insight relates not to *surveillance*, but to *communication*. One of the earliest Marxian attempts to bring the

Orwellian dystopian model into relief with communications technologies is Hans Magnus Enzensberger's *The Consciousness Industry*. Mass media are said to be 'making possible mass participation in a social and socialised productive process, the practical means of which are in the hands of the masses themselves', but production and distribution is controlled in such a way that television 'does not serve communication but prevents it. It allows no reciprocal action between transmitter and receiver [. . .] [and] reduces feedback to the lowest point compatible with the system' (1974: 97). Orwell is rejected as undialectical and technically implausible, since 'blanket supervision would demand a monitor that was bigger than the system itself' (ibid. 99). Baudrillard rejects Marxian optimism that mass media afford social participation, and the concept of totalitarian control, for the 'mystique of the socialist predestination of the media is opposite but complementary to the Orwellian myth of their terroristic manipulation by authority' (*PES*: 172). With and against Enzensberger, Baudrillard rejects both socialist and Orwellian models of State and police control for two reasons, although form unites them. First, the medium is a predetermined system to which one must adapt rather than adapt to one's own ends: the form of one's response is always a given. The extreme hypothesis is that media fabricate 'non-communication', where a question or transmission 'answers itself via the simulated detour of a response', because what is transmitted is always returned in the same form (*PES*: 70). While this underscores the immutability of the communicative structure inversely proportional to variable content, the conclusion is unpersuasive. The point to be extracted is that the medium is accorded greater significance than content, so that what is truly promoted is the *act* of transmission rather than its *meaning*. The second hypothesis discredits the socialising effect of mass media and Orwell's model:

> By virtue of its mere presence, [television] is a social control in itself. There is no need to imagine it as a state periscope [. . .] The situation as it stands is more efficient than that: it is the *certainty that people are no longer speaking to each other*, that they are definitively lost in the face of a speech without response. (*PES*: 172)

Cutting through the hyperbole, a premium is placed on social *interaction* or exchange, considered to be more authentic than technologically mediated *communication*. Media and information 'act in two directions: outwardly they produce more of the social' through opinion polls, statistics, media coverage and technologically

mediated interactivity, but 'inwardly they neutralise the social relations and the social itself' (Baudrillard 1983a: 66). When centralisa-
tion, discipline and the passivity of the masses become ineffective and
inefficient modes of control, the system 'reverses its strategies: from
passivity to participation, from silence to speech [. . .] Everywhere
the masses are encouraged to speak, they are urged to live socially,
electorally, organisationally, sexually, in participation, in festival, in
free speech' (ibid. 23).

Deleuze is no technological determinist, but he shares Baudrillard's
view of television. For Deleuze, television is not characterised by its
mediation of experience, but by its immediate presence and mass
distribution: 'It's direct social engineering, leaving no gap between
itself and social sphere, it's social engineering in its purest form [. . .]
the form in which the new powers of "control" become immediate
and direct' (N: 74–5). Like Baudrillard, Deleuze senses that repression and oppression are inefficient compared to mass participation:

> We sometimes go on as though people can't express themselves. In fact
> they're always expressing themselves [. . .] Radio and television have
> spread this spirit everywhere, and we're riddled with pointless talk, insane
> quantities of words and images. Stupidity's never blind or mute. So it's
> not a problem of getting people to express themselves but of providing
> little gaps of solitude or silence in which they might eventually find some-
> thing to say. Repressive forces don't stop people expressing themselves
> but rather force them to express themselves [. . .] We don't suffer these
> days from any lack of communication, but rather from all the forces
> making us say things when we've nothing much to say. (N: 129, 137)

Deleuze values the aesthetic functions of cinema and literature
over the (anti)social function of television. But what appears as
personal distaste is secondary to the higher principle that 'machines
don't explain anything' (N: 175) because they are components in
an assemblage of technical and social machines. Machines 'express
those social forms capable of generating them and using them'
(PSC: 6). Television is accorded special attention by Deleuze and
Guattari in explaining technological subjectification. SF in general
and Bradbury's *Fahrenheit 451* in particular show how two distinct
relations between subjects and technology – machinic enslavement
and subjection – can coincide (*TP*: 640 n. 57). Machinic enslavement entails the subordination of the subject to technology. The
subject forms an assemblage with the machine, but its affects invest
in a higher authority. Subjection differs from enslavement because
the authority over the assemblage decouples the machine from the

subject, so that the machine is an external object, the subject a worker or user of the machine, whose capacity to affect the machine is attenuated: 'He or she is subjected *to* the machine and no longer enslaved *by* the machine' (*TP*: 504). A technical machine does not enslave by integration, but from a distance subjects its user to its pure functionality. Control societies do not intensify repression or ideology, but conjoin machinic enslavement and subjection, where 'normalisation, modulation, modelling, and information [. . .] bear on language, perception, desire, [and] movement', through 'microassemblages' of mass communication technologies (*TP*: 506). These microassemblages direct the subject to overestimate their level of agency, reducing them subject to a conduit in the flow of information.[4]

Tolerating Utopia

> The enjoyment of TV [. . .] is experienced as 'true' freedom; no one experiences these things as an alienation. Only an intellectual can say such a thing, from the depths of his moralising idealism. (*CS*: 73)

> The naïve utopias of the 1960s must be revised: 'Imagination in power!' – 'Take your dreams for reality!' – 'No limits to pleasure!' All of these slogans were realised (or hyperrealised) in the development of the system. (Baudrillard 2010b: 47)

Bradbury's depiction of a technologised society is far from complimentary, but its vision of technology itself is not deterministic. Although cluttered with casual technological conveniences, the novel goes to great lengths to place technology and society into a resolved dialectic. Beatty, the most learned of all, but also cunning and untrustworthy, traces a line from the beginning of the twentieth century through to image and communications technologies, accelerated technological development, increases in population and density and consumerism. All of a sudden, 'things began to have *mass*', and in a passage that recalls Horkheimer and Adorno's excoriation of the culture industry, its liquidation of the idea into technological effect (2002: 94–136), Beatty explains:

> Because they had mass, they became simpler [. . .] Once, books appealed to a few people, here, there, everywhere. They could afford to be different. The world was roomy. But then the world got full of eyes and elbows and mouths. Double, triple, quadruple population. Films and radios, magazines, books levelled down to a sort of past pudding norm

[. . .] In the twentieth century, speed up your camera. Books cut shorter. Condensations. Digests. Tabloids [. . .] Politics? One column, two sentences, a headline! Then, in mid-air, all vanishes! (61–2)[5]

Even Faber, his academic career made redundant, chastises as 'hopeless[ly] romantic' Montag's belief in an intangible and unnameable 'something' in books missing from his media-saturated environment. Faber reveals that media are not determined by form but, as Williams said of television and Deleuze of machines in general, respond to certain social needs: 'It's not books you need, it's some of the things that once were in books. The same things *could* be in the "parlour families" today. The same infinite detail and awareness could be projected through the radios and televisors, but are not' (90). Yet, in hyperreality, the very notion of meaningful communication evaporates:

You can't argue with the four-wall televisor. Why? The televisor is 'real'. It is immediate, it has dimension. It tells you what to think and blasts it in. It *must* be right. It *seems* so right. It rushes you on so quickly to its own conclusions your mind hasn't time to protest [. . .] It is an environment as real as the world. It *becomes* and *is* the truth. (92)

When form and content are no longer in dialectical relation, but inversely proportional, form overdetermines content and deprives the spectator of a scene coextensive with agency and communication.[6] It is *mass* – mass appeal, mass reproduction, mass consumption and mass civilisation – that Bradbury, with Leavisite resentment, privileges above other determinants. And once it reaches a certain level of saturation and acceleration, the situation will be irreversible.

Despite its dialectic between technology and society, in Bradbury there has ceased to be any contradiction between the desires of the masses and the State. The Captain, Faber tells us, 'belongs to the most dangerous enemy of truth and freedom, the solid unmoving cattle of the majority' (116). The social contradiction is, now more than ever, at its deepest on the global stage. But wilful ignorance of the global war that quietly rages is maintained by the simulation pact: 'The public ultimately consents to be frightened, and to be gently terrorised [. . .] even while it preserves a fairly profound indifference to war' (Baudrillard 1995: 50). Aggressive social inclusion is the primary way characters ward off the violence of the world, including the imminent apocalypse. The Seashells broadcast fragments of information that never amount to a complete picture: 'War may be declared at any hour. This country stands ready to defend its –' (40);

'"We have mobilised a million men. Quick victory is ours if the war comes . . ." Music flooded over the voice and it was quickly gone' (100). The impression instilled is of a distant, zero-casualty war (on their side, naturally) and one of Mildred's friends is unconcerned when her husband is enlisted: 'The Army called Pete yesterday. He'll be back next week. The Army said so. Quick war. Forty-eight hours they said, and everyone home. That's what the Army said. Quick war.' Besides, 'it's always someone else's husband dies, they say.' Mildred agrees: 'I've heard that, too. I've never known any dead man killed in a war. Killed jumping off buildings, yes, like Gloria's husband last week, but from wars? No' (102–3). Military planes, which occasionally rumble the house's foundations at the start of the novel, become an hourly occurrence, *but the nature of the simulation pact is such that the war must undergo psychic disavowal.*[7] In a moment of utter despair, Montag rages at Mildred's wilful compliance and desperate ignorance:

> Why doesn't someone want to talk about it? We've started and won two atomic wars since 1960. Is it because we're having so much fun at home we've forgotten the world? Is it because we're so rich and the rest of the world's so poor and we just don't care if they are? I've heard rumours; the world is starving, but we're well fed. Is it true, the world works hard and we play? (81)

The film's primary departure from the novel is its excision of the overactive technology and casual suburban violence that, like the war, also excised, is experienced indirectly, only revealed in Mildred's idle gossip or in Clarisse's existential musings. The development of communications technologies coevolved with expanding transport networks. Roadside billboards had to be extended from twenty feet in length to two hundred so that motorists could take note, and commuters are 'pounded into submission' (87) by advertising, tapping their feet and humming along to jingles broadcast on trains. These messages and acquired behaviours enter the private sphere, twice-fictionalised amidst wall-to-wall television circuits. The televisions 'do not initiate a making public of the private so much as a privatisation of the public: the whole world unfolds right at home, without one's having to leave the TV screen. This gives private persons a very special role in the system: a role of *application*, and no longer implication' (*AO*: 251). Mildred and her friends prattle about fashion and cars in the same breath as about their divorces, abortions, unwanted children and the most recent friend to commit suicide, all of which retreat into the background of chattering parlour families, rigged plays and advertisements. The banality and empty communication of the parlour families is coextensive with a similar devolution of passions. Bored firemen have their own technologised version of coursing, placing bets on the Mechanical Hound's killing of rats and cats they find on the streets. There is a high youth mortality rate from thrill killing or road accidents. But much of the violence is corporate sponsored, so that kids 'break window panes at the Window Smasher place and wreck cars in the Car Wrecker place', and the police tolerate suburban car races since everyone has insurance.

Against the thematic and aesthetic analogues to totalitarian governments – Nazi or Stalinist – or Bradbury's own immediate McCarthyite political environment, the novel's contemporary relevance rests *not in its paranoid foreshadowing of dystopia*, as in Orwell, *but in its homology with the sinister benevolence of inversive utopia*. Looming over *Fahrenheit 451* is the notion of repressive desublimation, the liberation or, rather, liberalisation of deviant behaviours conjoined to the commodification of transgressive behaviour. The public are permitted to rejoice in 'clubs and parties', buy and crash 'jet cars [and] motorcycle helicopters', indulge in 'sex and heroin, [and] more of everything to do with automatic reflex' (68). Here then is the aftermath of a crisis in the inability to represent the social totality politically and aesthetically. Here is Beatty's explanation:

> Now let's take up the minorities in our civilisation, shall we? Bigger the population the more minorities. Don't step on the toes of the dog-lovers, the cat-lovers, doctors, lawyers, merchants, chiefs, Mormons, Baptists, Unitarians, second-generation Chinese, Swedes, Italians, Germans, Texans, Brooklynites, Irishmen, people from Oregon or Mexico. The people in this book, this play, this TV serial are not meant to represent any actual painters, cartographers, mechanics anywhere. The bigger your market, Montag, the less you handle controversy, remember that! All the minor minor minorities with their navels to be kept clean. (64)

Beatty's facetious tenor and indiscriminate net should not be dismissed too brusquely. First and foremost, the emphasis is satirical, for few of these would for us constitute a legitimate minority. Moreover, it equates lifestyle choices with national identities, professions with religions, and, as a kind of social index, the inability of fiction to represent each of these differences. And this is Baudrillard's fundamental point about capitalism: *the market tolerates everything – indeed, that is how it proliferates – but at the expense of constitu-*

tive differences themselves, which must be rendered equivalent and exchangeable, so that each sacrifices its authenticity in order to be commutable: *banal equivalence stands in the place of meaningful antagonism.* In *Fahrenheit 451,* the crisis is resolved in a double movement that progressively rendered each minority, no matter how trivial, politically equivalent, simultaneously liquidating antagonism. It was not a misguided Enlightenment that rendered society thus, but rather inversive utopian tendencies. 'We must all be alike,' says Beatty. 'Not everyone born free and equal, as the Constitution says, but everyone *made* equal. Each man the image of every other; then all are happy' and spared 'our understandable and rightful dread of being inferior' (65–6). He continues:

> Our civilisation is so vast that we can't have our minorities upset [. . .] Coloured people don't like *Little Black Sambo.* Burn it. White people don't feel good about *Uncle Tom's Cabin.* Burn it. Someone's written a book on tobacco and cancer of the lungs? The cigarette people are weeping? Burn the book. Serenity [. . .] If you don't want a man to be unhappy politically, don't give him two sides to a question to worry him; give him one. Better yet, give him none. Let him forget there is such a thing as war [. . .] Cram them full of non-combustible data, chock them so damned full of 'facts' they feel stuffed, but absolutely 'brilliant' with information. Then they'll feel like they're thinking, they'll get a *sense* of motion without moving. (68)

The conceit here is the reduction of politics to tolerance, or political correctness, so that the affirmation of differences is coextensive with their sanitisation. Žižek, like Baudrillard (CS: 173), describes this as neoliberal utopianism, the affirmation of difference and recognition of 'otherness' deceitfully complemented by 'the obsessive fear of harassment – in short, the Other is okay insofar as its presence is not intrusive [. . .] This is emerging as the central "human right" [. . .] *the right not to be harassed,* to be kept at a safe distance from others' (2004: 508).[8] The Cousins' *ultimate freedom is freedom from politics.* In the ultimate perversion of the Orwellian dystopian model, this society is not the product of a despotic regime: it evolved naturally under the sign of laissez-faire governmentality, and the public willed it into existence:

> The public, knowing what it wanted, spinning happily, let the comic-books survive. And the three-dimensional sex-magazines, of course [. . .] It didn't come from the Government down. There was no dictum, no declaration, no censorship [. . .] Technology, mass exploitation and minority pressure carried the trick. (65)

The purest expression of the efficiency of this simulation society is in the extent to which disciplinary power is no longer required. Truffaut's Cousin Claudette gently reminds the viewing Cousins, 'do remember to tolerate your friends, however alien and peculiar they may seem to you. Don't despise minorities.' The firemen exist as a simulacral vestige of dead power, less a constant threat, and more a contingency plan that, as Baudrillard says, 'reinject[s] the real and the referential', 'to persuade us of the reality of the social'. 'To this end,' he continues, power 'prefers the discourse of crisis, but also, why not? that of desire. "Take your desires for reality!" can be understood as the ultimate slogan of power since in a nonreferential world, even the confusion of the reality principle and the principle of desire is less dangerous than contagious hyperreality' (*SS*: 22). Thus, Faber explains to Montag that 'the firemen are rarely necessary. The public itself stopped reading of its own accord. You firemen provide a circus now and then at which buildings are set off and crowds gather for the pretty blaze, but it's a small sideshow indeed, and hardly necessary to keep things in line' (95). As we shall see, Faber underestimates the efficacy of the spectacle, particularly when broadcast. And while Baudrillard's dismissal of Deleuze, and the suspicion with which he regards desire's capacity to endorse its own repression and oppression (*SS*: 18), is too casual, his assessment is nevertheless illuminating: while the firemen will, from time to time, provide a public spectacle, burning books and, if need be, a book reader, this should not deter us from recognising that although the firemen are a conspicuous extension of the State apparatus, *the State apparatus itself is entirely missing*. If the force of Orwell lies in its cautioning not just against communism or fascism, but against any type of centralised economy (Orwell 2000: 564), then *Fahrenheit 451*'s force emanates from the opposite direction: a State so decentralised and gaseous is the determining structure nonetheless. The efficiency with which this society regulates itself without the violence of the firemen is more sinister and more artful than Orwell's cruel Ministry of Love: the disciplinary, panoptic telescreens are replaced by *a gaze that comes not from despotic Big Brother, but from the masses themselves*. The Proles' subordination is more bearable, their occasional complicity more piteous than the enthusiasm with which the Cousins buy into the simulation pact, for all are accomplices – dutiful *informants* rather than duplicitous *informers* in Truffaut – devoid of symbolic alienation. Such is the nature of the simulation pact: 'Communication [i]s the functioning of the social within a closed circuit [. . .] The social contract becomes a "simulation pact" sealed by the media and the news' (*S*: 163). The Cousins no longer offer up a piece of liberty in exchange for domination, but disavow reality to maintain the collective artifice of the simulated social. And, like any fetishistic disavowal, *the simulation pact must be repeated so as to spirit away with each recurrence any intrusion of the real.*

Microfascisms

> We admire the earlier neurotics, the hysterics or obsessionals, who either got on with their business or did it in the family: the modern depressive types are, on the contrary, particularly vampiric or poisonous. (*D*: 83)

> Overwhelming versatility of desire in Deleuze, an enigmatic reversal that brings desire 'revolutionary in itself, and as if involuntarily, wanting what it wants,' to desire its own repression and to invest in paranoid and fascist systems? A malign torsion that returns this revolution of desire to the same fundamental ambiguity as the other, the historical revolution. (*SS*: 18)

One of the most challenging aspects of *Capitalism and Schizophrenia* is its account of fascism. It asks: 'Why do men fight *for* their servitude as stubbornly as though it were their salvation? [. . .] Why do people still tolerate being humiliated and enslaved, to such a point, indeed, that they *actually want* humiliation and slavery not only for others but for themselves?' (*AO*: 29). The anti-ideological answer is that even fascism is desired. 'There is no need to define fascism by a concept of its own devising' (*TP*: 236). Fascism refers not to a totalitarian State, but to molar organisations and to the molecular, the 'little neighbourhood policemen', 'the couple, family, school, and office': 'What makes fascism dangerous is its molecular or micropolitical power, for it is a mass movement: a cancerous body rather than a totalitarian organism' (*TP*: 236). Fascism does not trick or mystify, nor ideologically repress or lure, but grasps the body and its intensities and investments. Fascism is one of the paths desire can take, and though most conspicuous at the level of the State, its affects register and emanate from microfascisms, in both the totalitarian State and capitalism: 'The truth is that sexuality is everywhere: the way the bureaucrat fondles his records, a judge administers justice, a businessman causes money to circulate; the way the bourgeoisie fucks the proletariat [. . .] Hitler got the fascists sexually aroused. Flags, nations, armies, banks get a lot of people aroused' (*AO*: 293).

The composition of Truffaut's opening sequence tells us how to understand transitions from molar structures to microintensities. Seventeen consecutive shots capture at a distance television anten- nae. The camera then focuses in on the complex structure to isolate a mechanical feature, joint, wire or protrusion that occupies the frame. Each shot distinguishes itself by its exploded view of a singu- lar element of the mechanical structure, the speed of delivery (some are arrived at by smash zoom, others are approached at a measured pace), and its palette: intensities of orange, green, blue, pink, red and purple; the lustrous filters offsetting dull metals and plastics. Movement shrinks the amount of visual data, from saturation (complex geometries) to rarefaction (a single element), abstracting context to deliver detail. The repetition and minimal variation illus- trates how televisual mediation literally colours, skews and serialises perception. A voice-over supplies information usually conveyed by credits – like the inhabitants of the film, we are not readers: studio, cast, title, co-stars, screenwriters, source novel, composer (Bernard Herrmann), director of photography, colour by Technicolor, art director, production and design consultant, editor, associate pro- ducer, producer and director.

The immediate question is whether we afford this the dignity of Brechtian defamiliarisation. The film lays bare its compositional devices with jump cuts, protracted dolly zooms, double exposures and reverse-motion sequences that dissolve the fidelity between audible speech and facial movement. These ruptures are admired by others (Whalen 2007) but the film accomplishes much of this defa- miliarisation and artifice independently of them. The laboured meta- phors are so transparent they cease to create any functional depth: readers snack on knowledge-bearing apples, their illuminated minds ingeniously secrete books in lamp shades. Depthlessness is the point: the public's moronisation inoculates them against irony, and it is up to the viewer to suffer this deprivation to ensure they do not wind up like the characters – the overwhelming artifice guarantees that one is never under the impression that one is *not* watching a film.[9]

The exception to this is the reverse-motion sequence where Montag's protective gear is simultaneously divested and added piece by piece to and from his body, put to use when he sets his flame- thrower on the confiscated books, and shed once the film's motion returns to fidelity. The body and the State form a closed circuit of cyclical fragmentations and restorations, the body a tool that can be added to and subtracted from, put into motion and reversed, its gestures pre-recorded and replayable. In Bradbury, burning itself is for Montag the orgasmic discharge absent in his sexless marriage: 'It was a pleasure to burn. It was a special pleasure to see things eaten, to see things blackened and *changed*. With the brass nozzle in his fist, with the great python spitting its venomous kerosene upon the world, the blood pounded in his head' (11). Montag's job is less about maintaining the status quo than, in a reversal of the distinction between permissiveness enjoyed in private and conservatism adopted in public, providing an outlet for his pent-up frustrations.

Returning to television, Bradbury's consumer is twice rewarded and ultimately congratulated for their purchase with social inclusion, visibility and personalised participation dispensed as a supplementary reward. Mildred gets a role in a television play by sending in proof-of-purchase box tops, and a script is delivered to her door the very next day. Unlike Truffaut's, Bradbury's citizens retain their literacy, yet employ it selectively in accord with approved written material.[10] Plays are broadcast on the televisions – mundane domestic dramas that thrill Mildred. The play requires the viewer's affirmation of the lines, which are not only predetermined, but propel the drama onwards to no definite conclusion, a constant flow proceeding without finality:

> This is a play [that] comes on the wall-to-wall circuit [. . .] They mailed me my part this morning [. . .] They write a script with one part missing. It's a new idea. The home-maker, that's me, is the missing part. When it comes time for the missing lines, they all look at me out of the three walls and I say the lines. Here, for instance, the man says, 'What do you think of this whole idea, Helen?' And he looks at me sitting here centre stage, see? And I say, I say [. . .] 'I think that's fine!' (27–8)

Prescribed interactivity rather than spontaneous social relations is 'authentic' and socially commendable. The Montags only have three of their walls converted into interactive televisions, which is, for Mildred, a blight on her cultural capital and a social impediment. Inclusion and participation do not come cheap, and a wall conversion costs a third of Montag's annual salary. Such financial matters are absent from Mildred's reasoning, and she takes Montag's inadequate salary as a personal affront:

> It's really fun. It'll be even more fun when we can afford to have a fourth wall installed. How long you figure before we save up and get the fourth wall torn out and fourth wall-TV put in [. . .] If we had a fourth wall, why it'd be just like this room wasn't ours at all, but all kinds of exotic people's rooms. (28)

Bradbury describes the rationale of the plays, but Truffaut acts them out. Here, Linda is personally selected for the role, receiving a call from The Family that very day. Roused by an alarm announcing her impending contribution, she blusters to the television where the kaleidoscopic display transitions to Cousin Claudette, host of the drama: 'For Cousins everywhere, our family theatre. Come, play with us [. . .] So, will you come play with us? You will?! Good! I thought you would. Come in Cousins. Be one of The Family.' The drama unfolds midway, no context provided, two actors deliberating over seating arrangements for a social gathering – who should be seated next to whom, where the children should play . . . Unable to resolve the crisis, one of the actors turns to the camera, which zooms in on his stern expression. He addresses Linda directly: 'What do you think, Linda?' In a moment of Pavlovian conditioning, a light next to the screen flashes and bleeps, indicating it is her turn to contribute. Linda falters, and misses her chance. Untrammelled, the play assumes her consent: 'You see, Linda agrees with me.' Humiliated but not defeated, Linda gets the next two right. Another question is posed, the camera zooms in, and the light bleeps and flashes: 'It's Madeline, isn't it, Linda?' – 'Absolutely!' – 'Well if Linda thinks it's alright then it must be'; 'Do you have the answer, Linda?' – 'In the blue room' – 'Linda, you're right! She's right! Linda, you're absolutely fantastic.' 'You saw it, didn't you?' she beams at Montag. 'I gave all the right answers. Wasn't it wonderful? I could have been an actress, don't you think so?' The conceit of the play, as Montag later quips, is that there was nothing personal about Linda's selection – it was the *name* that was selected. Thus Linda, and 200,000 other Lindas, contributed lines that evening. Even if this is true, Linda prefers not to know, since she only cares that her friends saw her participate, and she turns on her bedside television, puts in her headphones and downs a tranquilliser. The inauthenticity of her selection and contribution does not tarnish the flattering and personalised invitation, nor inauthenticate the opportunity to be one of The Family.[11] What truly makes this an illustration of the simulation pact is the caveat provided by Cousin Claudette at the outset: 'Naturally, in what you are about to see, any similarity with the truth or with real life would be purely coincidental. Do bear that in mind.' This does not matter for Linda, nor does it matter that the play progresses with or without her 'active' input, or that she has no genuine capacity to determine its course: she happily sacrifices isolating reality and individual accountability for the simulated proximity and managed inclusivity of The Family.

Mildred's schizophrenia is defined by variations in intensities and speeds that act directly on her body and her unconscious. She rarely leaves the house, but whenever she does she enjoys the sensations of careering along the roads, always delighted by killing dogs. The majority of her time is spent in the lounge, watching television or conversing with the parlour family, who have coevolved with the concept of the family. Expanding on McLuhan, for Baudrillard the '"message" of TV is not the images it transmits, but the new modes of relating and perceiving it imposes, the alterations to traditional family and group structures' (CS: 123). Mildred and others with disposable income can purchase an attachment that personalises all televisual broadcasts which include microsegments of silence that can be occupied by the subscriber's name: a 'special spot-wavex-scrambler [. . .] caused [the] televised image, in the area immediately about [the] lips, to mouth the vowels and consonants beautifully' (71). The idea of having children horrifies Mildred and her friends, and those that do have them have no affection for them, and will only tolerate them in the house three days a month. Each of Mildred's friends has had dozens of abortions and their children are exclusively delivered via caesarean. This is not a moral point but a socio-technological one: people reproduce (or not) much as they make war: conveniently, with surgical precision, and with as few consequences and responsibilities as possible.

Mildred craves more family members, each one a further step from the nuclear conception of a family – everyone is an uncle, an aunt, a nephew or niece whose proximity is not diminished by technological mediation, but enhanced: 'My "family" is people. They tell me things; *I* laugh, they *laugh*! And the colours!' (80). This is in contrast to the forced intimacy in Orwell, where everyone is a 'comrade' (and a 'brother' or 'sister' of the Inner and Outer Parties in Michael Radford's 1984 treatment of Orwell). The familial alliance is generalised and strengthened in Truffaut, where everyone is a Cousin in The Family, and Linda becomes agitated without her 'kitchen family fix'. One thinks of how contemporary social media by default promotes everyone to the status of 'friend', everyone 'likes' everything you do so you are induced to return the favour, a casual interest in someone turns you into their 'follower', and those that observe without subscribing or contributing are 'lurkers'. As in Huxley, privacy and solitude become taboo, so much so that Clarisse, who enjoys naïve and unrehearsed activities (although her infantile enthusiasm and the paternalistic fascination these hold for Montag is rather cloying), is under State psychiatric observation, determined to rationalise and stratify her deviant sociality. In Truffaut, neighbours are wary of her and her family because they do not have an aerial, and she lives with her biological uncle rather than the Cousins.[12] In Bradbury, everyone is either permanently distracted by televisions or soothed to sleep by Seashells, transistor radio ear buds, so that Mildred mainly communicates with Montag by gesture or lip-reading during the day and, at night, 'an electronic ocean of sounds, of music and talk and music and talk coming in, coming in on the shore of her unsleeping mind' (20).

Technology, the speed, immediacy and intensity at which life flashes across screens, roadways and sensory organs, is counterbalanced by characters who constantly self-medicate, their bodies in perpetual flux. Mildred is addicted to tranquillisers and Montag comes home to find she has overdosed after unintentionally taking an entire bottle of thirty tablets. She lives in a perpetual present, refusing to believe that she overdosed and preferring a fiction about overindulging at a party. Nor can she recall that her third wall screen is a recent addition. When Montag wonders where Clarisse has gone, Mildred indistinctly recalls that she was hit by a car and killed, the implication being that Mildred was driving. Although she craves social interaction, her relationships are a sequence of singularities forgotten and replaced in an uninterrupted flow:

> And the uncles, aunts, the cousins, the nieces, the nephews, that lived in those walls, the gibbering pack of tree-apes that said nothing, nothing, nothing and said it loud, loud, loud [. . .] No matter when he came in, the walls were always talking [. . .] What was it all about? Mildred couldn't say. (51–2)

Truffaut internalises the contradiction between the corporeal rush of technological affects and psychic stupors with Linda addicted to both sedatives and stimulants. But even this attempt to reconcile conflicting intensities with pharmaceutical homeostasis buckles under the weight of internal contradiction: Linda overdoses, but the stimulants are harmless – sedatives, and, by implication, any attempt to disengage momentarily, disturbed her equilibrium.

Guattari speaks of the 'microfascism of one's own body, of one's organs', and how this is learned through television and the family, and maintained by specialised institutions (2009: 278). What is striking about *Fahrenheit 451* is that it contains all these elements. Communication technologies, recreational medications and their users form an uninterrupted flow, and voluntary disengagement or pharmaceutical escapism short-circuits the terminal: either one is shunned by society or the organs fail. To excuse oneself from The Family is a sign of disequilibrium, because it 'is forbidden to unplug yourself' from the simulation pact; the technosocial 'network principle carries with it the absolute moral obligation to remain plugged in' (Baudrillard 2003a: 197).[13] Readers are removed from society, placed in asylums, prisons or burnt alive, but social burnouts are recoupled to the technical machines of the televisions and the social machine of The Family. When Montag calls an ambulance for Mildred, maintenance workers, rather than doctors, arrive. Two machines revive her: one pumps her stomach, another exsanguinates and injects fresh blood and artificial serum. The casual invasiveness of the procedure repulses Montag as much as the machines, perversely equipped with cameras that transmit images of their 'slush[ing] up the emptiness' of her organs, while the 'impersonal operator of the machine could, by wearing a special optical helmet, gaze into the soul of the person whom he was pumping out'. 'Got to clean 'em out both ways,' the maintenance workers tell him. 'No use getting the stomach if you don't clean the blood. Leave that stuff in the blood and the blood hits the brain like a mallet, bang, a couple of thousand times and the brain just gives up, just quits' (22). Mildred is one of nine or ten evening 'blood jobs' of which there are around fifty a day: 'Got so many, starting a few years ago, we had the special machines built. With the optical lens, of course, that was new [. . .] You don't need an MD, case like this; all you need is two handymen, clean up the problem in half an hour' (23).

Her insides restored to equilibrium, Mildred is primed for reintegration with a contra-sedative, and wakes up famished. Truffaut accords a libidinal intensity to her revitalisation. 'Mind you,' the blood technician says with a cheeky wink, 'she'll have an appetite for all sorts of things' when she wakes up. 'She'll be starving, you'll find out.' True enough, Linda wakes and gorges herself before entering a libidinous catatonia, surprising Montag with her sexual appetite. The composition of this scene is especially important, because it demonstrates the intertwining of desire and State control. Earlier, Linda watches an instructional broadcast that teaches women how to subdue a male attacker. The programme shows in slow motion how to topple an opponent by kicking their legs out from under them. Linda now uses the same tactic in the bedroom on Montag, and the manoeuvre is captured in the same slow-motion, demonstrative fashion. The act is neither conscious nor planned, but an unconscious acting out of State *doxa* in sexual terms, with the television assembling and animating desire.

Truffaut again links desire and State control in an arrangement of scenes that begin with authorities harassing a long-haired youth on the streets. Cut to Linda, whose face occupies the entire frame, revealing that the scene is actually a television broadcast, which she is watching intently. Cut back to the broadcast, where the announcer praises the 'mop-up squad' who sheer off the youth's hair. 'It all goes to show', the announcer continues, that 'law enforcement can be fun', and the footage captures a group of onlookers delighted by the youth's humiliation. The next scene takes place at the end of the day, with Montag returning home on the train, on which passengers are absentmindedly caressing their bodies: a man draws his arm across his face, brushing his mouth against the hair of his arm; a woman tentatively strokes her coat, and runs her hands over her body and down her legs; another tenderly fondles and presses her cheek against her pelt; another tentatively runs her fingertips around her mouth and chin. The film then cuts to Linda, standing before a mirror, cupping and massaging her breast, admiring her gestures reflected back to her. The public simultaneously disavows and desires authoritarian violence with a fetish, literally compensating for the castrating act of hair removal with a direct substitute – their own hair or the fibres of their clothes. Linda, however, gazes lovingly into the mirror as she did the television, caught in a masturbatory and narcissistic feedback loop, savouring her hairless skin, with the affective force of castration cathected directly on to her body. *Microfascist fetishisation of the State apparatus rather than deprivation of literature emerges as the means of control.* When Clarisse presses Montag as to why people break the law by reading, his answer is *not* that they crave enlightenment, but *because it is forbidden*. The Captain correctly describes readers as perverts: to derive any satisfaction or symbolic value from their subversion, the pervert requires the power of the authority undermined to be absolute. The authoritarian apparatus is sustained not by the allure of the books, the prohibited objects, but by desire for *the prohibition itself*, fetishised in the process. The insight of the film is its presentation of microfascism, desire working against itself, the affects and intensities of desire and power working directly on the body.

Beautiful Souls

To flee, but in fleeing to seek a weapon. (*D*: 136)

Only in the cheapest generic Science Fiction does the revolution triumph, sweeping the conspiratorial present away, or on the contrary bringing to power those very conspiracies, thereby opening up an uninformed dystopia of geological duration. (Jameson 1992: 32)

But is this really what an achieved utopia looks like? Is this a successful revolution? Yes indeed! What do you expect a 'successful' revolution to look like? It is paradise [. . .] Mournful, monotonous, and superficial though it may be, it is paradise. (*A*: 107)

Montag's dissatisfaction with society and his bringing books into the home threatens his wife's capacity to integrate into society. She is shamed before her friends by his outbursts and attempts at reading aloud, and she ultimately informs on him. But before he is apprehended, Montag and Faber form a plan: Faber will rally dissidents with a printing press, and Montag will plant books in the homes of the firemen and report them. Truffaut has no Faber character, but his Montag will also frame and inform on the firemen so that 'the system will eat itself'. One can hardly imagine that this subterfuge would chronically disable the State apparatus. As Faber reminds Montag, the firemen are rarely called upon to exercise authority. The objective is to discredit and humiliate, to plant the seeds of corruption. On the one hand, there is a genuine attempt here to challenge the system on its own terms, staging a crime, making involuntary dissidents of the system's most ardent admirers to reveal the inauthenticity of the system itself. Although Bradbury's Montag is betrayed before the plan can be effected, that the engorged system will inevitably collapse under the weight of its own logic is guaranteed in apocalyptic terms when the disavowed war ruptures the fabric of the hyperreal.[14] On the other hand, the plan reveals an imaginative failure in revolutionary consciousness, since it is by simulation and deception that the State achieves its own victory over dissidents. Using the Seashells and televisions, the State mobilises the public to apprehend Montag. Viewers and listeners become extensions of the State's non-existent powers of observation and are told to mob the streets. Even the microfascist in Montag, victim and celebrity, desires the spectacle of his capture, in which he could objectively witness his own extermination:

> If he wished, Montag might rise, walk to the window, lean out, look back, and see himself dramatised, described, made over, standing there, limned in the bright small television screen from outside, a drama to be watched objectively, knowing that in other parlours he was large as life, in full colour, dimensionally perfect! And if he kept his eye peeled quickly he would see himself, an instant before oblivion, being punctured for the benefit of how many civilian parlour-sitters. (142)

The collective participation of the social is a conceit. Although he is pursued by helicopters and the venomous Mechanical Hound, the tangible threat to Montag is the thrill-killing youths who attempt to run him over, not because he is a fugitive, but because he is a pedestrian. The *real* pursuit unfolds on live television, interrupted only by 'necessary commercials' (142), to an audience of thirty million. The outcome is never in doubt: the audience is assured that the Hound never fails, and Montag's escape is less a threat to the preservation of social equilibrium than it risks exhausting the audience's attention. The State simply ambushes and executes an unwitting substitute whose facial features they scramble, using the same technology that simulates personalised address for the live broadcast:

> They know they can hold their audience only so long. The show's got to have a snap ending, quick! If they started searching the whole damn river it might take all night. So they're sniffing for a scapegoat to end things with a bang [. . .] See how our camera is coming in? Building the scene. Suspense. Long shot. (156)

There is some underlying validity to Montag and Faber's plan: the authoritarian apparatus is vulnerable at the level of the simulation that sustains it; the fact that cracks in its operational surface – cracks in the simulacrum – are quickly glossed over testifies as much. Nowhere is there an attempt to co-opt the medium itself, even though it is shown to be an effective force of collective mobilisation. The implication is that society is irretrievable, doomed to apocalypse in Bradbury and beyond redemption in Truffaut.

Montag flees, following the train tracks to their terminus, delineating the limit of technological society. Here he joins the nomadic book people, societal drop-outs, fugitives and dissenters, each of whom has relinquished identity and, in a horribly laboured metaphor, 'become' a book, assuming its title, and committing its content to memory. I can only cringe as they introduce themselves as *David Copperfield* and other works of the canon, but it has its value: the harmony of the State was sustained by televisual consensus, self-regulating and self-medicating Cousins, and ethnic, political, religious and cultural differences were 'preserved' by their elimination. Here, the book people are of various races and speak different languages. 'The organisation is flexible, very loose and fragmentary' (160), arose spontaneously, and its desubjectified nomads exist in packs, with none of the city's hollow camaraderie and non-communication.

No longer suffocated by technology, and ceasing to be Cousins in The Family, the nomads are confronted with the horizon of being outside the system, existing on the fringes of its territory. Although Bradbury's is a dialectical vision of technology and society, a gulf separates the imminent apocalypse and any sense of agency that might bring forth societal transformation. Sowing the seeds of discontent through re-education would do nothing more than 'nibble the edges. The whole culture's shot through.' Against any faith in organised resistance, Faber quells Montag's frustration with a resigned prediction: 'Patience, Montag. Let the war turn off the "families". Our civilisation is flinging itself to pieces' (95). The nomads have made peace with 'inevitability': 'Right now we have a horrible job: we're waiting for the war to begin and, as quickly, end. It's not pleasant, but then we're not in control, we're the odd minority crying out in the wilderness' (160). The nomadic enterprise is couched in a humility afforded by the sacrifice of the ego for a civilisation to come: 'The most important single thing we had to pound into ourselves was that we were not important, we mustn't be pedants: we were not to feel superior to anyone else in the world [. . .] You're not important. You're not anything' (160, 171). The apocalypse is, improbably, the very thing that lends credibility to this stoicism, acquiring an eschatological and theodicean dimension asserted by Montag's becoming the Bible, the novel ending with a reading from Revelation: the nomads will, after the nuclear fallout, return and rebuild.

Worried that his philosophy of difference would collapse into an apolitical novelty – and many argue it has[15] – Deleuze wrote that 'the philosophy of difference must be wary of turning into the discourse of beautiful souls: differences, nothing but differences, in a peaceful coexistence in the Idea of social places and functions . . . but the name of Marx is sufficient to save it from this danger' (*DR*: 259). It was arguably this very discourse that set in motion the societal transformation from which the nomads either were expelled or voluntarily fled, but here, in the wilderness, it is even more palpable. Writing on utopia in general, Jameson suggests that the:

vision of freshening our own stale and fallen universe, of a utopian revitalisation of the tired goods and services all around us, their projection
into some genuinely Jeffersonian commonwealth beyond the bomb [. . .]
compensat[es] for what we would otherwise have to see as an ideological
imbalance [. . .] an idealistic overemphasis on language and art in the
place of political action. (2007: 362)

Against this, Nicholas Harrison reproves Truffaut's denouement,
which:

starts to appear less contestatory, hinging as it does on a sympathetic
representation of the bookpeople as a highly literate and incorruptible
minority who are sufficiently mentally alert to benefit from books, and
who are isolated from, and superior to, unthinking masses [. . .] This
image is indistinguishable from that historically implicit in and integral to
the discourse of the censor, an image that could be described in identical
terms. (2001: 60)

For Harrison the book people resemble the State, but the film's
real political weakness is its stripping from the narrative war and
apocalypse, which makes its ending a pastoral fantasy. Unlike
Orwell, there is no prohibition against thoughtcrime. It thus becomes
a real problem that Truffaut's nomads destroy the books (burning
them, no less) they themselves have become, for this could very
easily have been accomplished without the nomadic flight from
power, forced exile for Montag but renunciation for most. It is not
awareness of society's misery they find, but *relief* from it. Indeed,
their willingness to subvert society from within makes them the
necessary contradiction. Absenting themselves means they remove
the dialectical contradiction necessary for change.[16] Little wonder
then that the State does not bother to exterminate them – they pose
no threat whatsoever. There might be something charming about
the multiracial polyglots, each abandoning their identity to 'become'
a book, quaintly reciting themselves ad infinitum in the unspoiled
countryside. Yet Herrmann's unbearably maudlin score and the
nomadic *littérateurs* are nothing more than the same 'mindless good
taste' in outlawed books, nomadically dispersed, but void of political
utility. That the serenity of the forest transitions into an inhospitable,
snow-covered landscape heralds the futility of their gesture, for this is
the complacent serenity of the beautiful soul, bowing out long before
the apocalypse becomes inevitable, dystopia deferred, not utopia
achieved.

Notes

1. *A*: 39.
2. Burroughs writes that 'the technocratic control apparatus [. . .] has at its fingertips new techniques which if fully exploited could make Orwell's *1984* seem like a benevolent utopia' (1998: 339).
3. Images of burning books are powerful, yet historically overvalued. Kittler shows that the production of print media remained relatively autonomous in Nazi Germany, considered by Hitler and Goebbels to be a 'completely ineffective medium', whereas visual and aural media were entirely in the service of the State (2012: 214).
4. Deleuze and Guattari explain that 'one is subjected to TV insofar as one uses and consumes it, in the very particular situation of a subject of the statement that more or less mistakes itself for a subject of enunciation ("you, dear television viewers, who make TV what it is . . ."); the technical machine is the medium between two subjects. But one is enslaved by TV as a human machine insofar as the television viewers are no longer consumers or users, nor even subjects who supposedly "make" it, but intrinsic component pieces, "input" and "output," feedback or recurrences that are no longer connected to the machine in such a way as to produce or use it. In machinic enslavement, there is nothing but transformations and exchanges of information' (*TP*: 506).
5. Marx: 'All that is solid melts into air.' Has Bradbury done his homework? All page references to the novel are taken from the 2004 edition.
6. Truffaut agreed, saying that in 'our society, books are not burnt by Hitler or the Holy inquisition, they are rendered useless, drowned in a flood of images' (quoted in Crisp 1972: 82).
7. Baudrillard writes that 'all bombs are clean: their only pollution is the system of security and of control they radiate *as long as they don't explode*' (*SS*: 42 n. 9).
8. Marcuse called this repressive tolerance. In a passage recalling Beatty's, he writes: 'Within the affluent democracy [. . .] all points of view can be heard: the Communist and the Fascist, the Left and the Right [. . .] In endlessly dragging debates over the media, the stupid opinion is treated with the same respect as the intelligent one, the misinformed may talk as long as the informed, and propaganda rides along with education, truth with falsehood. This pure tolerance of sense and nonsense is justified by the democratic argument that nobody, neither group nor individual, is in possession of the truth and capable of defining what is right and wrong, good and bad' (1969: 95). That the Orwellian model has been traversed by this inversive utopia is registered indirectly by Jameson: 'At the very moment in which the official dystopian imagination – in novels and films – has abandoned its older *1984*-type nightmare paradigms of the repressive Stalinist political state for new

"near future" nightmares of pollution and overpopulation, corporate control on a galactic scale, and the breakdown of civilisation [. . .] why do now old-fashioned *1984* fantasies return in the realm of political ideologies as the terror of some repression of Difference?' (2009: 213).

9. Added to this is Werner's stilted delivery, Cusack's camp performance, Christie as the cloying ingénue Clarisse, and breathless and gushing as Linda, all of which guarantee that the film comes off as SF soap opera. Those who praise its realism compared to Bradbury (Gonzalez 2010 and Harrison 2001: 56) are misguided: Bradbury's technological extrapolations are simply replaced by the equally unnatural TV-serial *mise en scène* and kitsch aesthetic of the 1960s suburban lounge. The film is not totally devoid of subtlety, but its dominant superficiality subsumes the work of defamiliarisation rather than grounding any formalist departures.

10. The genius of Truffaut's film is that it is a purely verbal and imagistic affair, with personnel files consisting only of photographs, and the newspaper a textless comic strip.

11. There is truth to Deleuze's observation that televised participation has 'nothing to do with beauty or thought, it's about being in contact with the technology, touching the machinery' (N: 73).

12. Is this not the same suspicion that accompanied the horror of recent mass murders committed in the US by James Holmes and Adam Lanza? So much was made of the fact that they lacked Facebook accounts, as though this was a vital clue, or a determining factor in their psychopathy.

13. Drawing on Cronenberg, Gibson and Jameson, Fisher underscores 'the mismatch between a post-literate "New Flesh" that is "too wired to concentrate" and the confining, concentrational logics of decaying disciplinary systems. To be bored simply means to be removed from the communicative sensation-stimulus matrix of texting, YouTube, fast food; to be denied, for a moment, the constant flow of sugary gratification on demand' (2009: 24).

14. See note 28 of the Introduction to this book.

15. Pisters summarises arguments that 'the twenty-first century has indeed become Deleuzian, as Foucault famously predicted, but only in the worst possible sense [. . .] In our globalised age people have locked themselves up in radical differences (ethnic, sexual, and religious) and the world has consequently turned into a fragmented nightmare of minishelters, catering to microidentities [. . .] conscious only of their own individual islands, living in ignorance of each other and connecting only in opposition through threats and terror' (2012: 243).

16. Hardt and Negri, following Deleuze, champion 'desertion, exodus, and nomadism. Whereas in the disciplinary era *sabotage* was the fundamental notion of resistance, in the era of imperial control [. . .] desertion

and exodus are a powerful form of class struggle' (2001: 212–13). Zygmunt Bauman is less optimistic: 'Escape is the opposite of utopia, yet psychologically it turns out to be the only substitute for it available today: one might say that it is utopia's new, up-to-date interpretation, adapted to the demands of our deregulated, individualised society of consumers' (2011: 25).

Contagion

5

Biocapitalism and Schizophrenia

All we are saying is that animals are packs, and that packs form, develop, and are transformed by contagion. (*TP*: 267)

Cloning is itself a form of epidemic, of metastasis of the species – of a species in the clutches of identical reproduction and infinite proliferation, beyond sex and death. (Baudrillard 2002: 196–7)

Deleuze and Guattari's plateau '1730: Becoming-Intense, Becoming-Animal, Becoming-Imperceptible . . .' invokes a range of SF texts. Even more than the preface to *Difference and Repetition*, where Deleuze adjoins philosophy to SF, in *A Thousand Plateaus* the genre is accorded great significance: 'Science fiction has gone through a whole evolution taking it from animal, vegetable, and mineral becomings to becomings of bacteria, viruses, molecules, and things imperceptible' (*TP*: 274). What interests Deleuze and Guattari about SF is its *figures of contagion*. They draw on a range of literature and film: Melville and Kafka are read alongside Lovecraft and Borges; the faces of Doctor Moreau's leopard men return (*TP*: 189, 273) and Scott Carey from Matheson's *The Shrinking Man* (1956) replaces Carroll's Alice (*TP*: 308), who preoccupied Deleuze throughout *The Logic of Sense*. The nonhuman animal, its viruses, bacteria, genes, deterritorialisations, nomadism, affects and intensities – that is, its capacity for contagion – is one of the most powerful figures in *Capitalism and Schizophrenia*. Deleuze and Guattari's animal is one of the specific concepts that attracted Baudrillard's critical attention. His 'The Animals: Territory and Metamorphoses' developed a sustained critique of their position.[1] This chapter will focus on Deleuze and Guattari's becomings-animal. It will take seriously their thesis that there are three animals, Oedipal, State and demonic, and far from being a general taxonomy, they are ontological categories defined by the intertwinement of desire, technoscientific experimentation and investments of capital. This chapter will establish the organising theme contagion. In so doing, it will seek to show how Deleuze and Guattari, Baudrillard and SF acquire a new relevance in biocapitalism.

To trace the line from control to contagion, we turn to the first SF text (Aldiss 2001), Mary Shelley's *Frankenstein* (1818), and the Oedipal animal, Frankenstein's monster. Thence we will look at the State animals in H. G. Wells's *The Island of Doctor Moreau* (1896) and Erle C. Kenton's *Island of Lost Souls* (1932). Finally, we will examine the demonic animal, the schizophrenic product of biocapitalism in Vincenzo Natali's film *Splice* (2009). The abstract machine that overcodes these assemblages is the *Frankenstein* myth, which tells us more about nonhuman animals than about the cyberpunk posthuman, which is the dominant account. It is essential that we not understand Frankenstein's monster as human, but as a becoming-animal. Hayles considers the demise of the liberal humanist subject, and the subsequent instantiation of the posthuman, an opportunity to return to postmodernism 'the flesh that continues to be erased' (1999: 5). Yet the posthuman can only be understood in relation to the human and, as Julie Clarke's *The Paradox of the Posthuman* (2009) suggests, the posthuman extrapolates beyond but nevertheless endorses humanism. If the posthuman is bound to slip back into humanism, and to conflate humanism with modernism (Latour 1993: 13), then it is necessary for posthumanism to emphasise those values it denies. A discourse founded on what humanism-modernism actively negates, according to Cary Wolfe, requires the nonhuman animal, since posthumanist posthumanism 'has to do with understanding – and understanding the consequences of – the very redefinition of what humanistic knowledge is after the disciplinary subjectivity as its core [is reconceptualised], the notion of the human that it "gives to itself"' (2010: 126). Although he mentions them overleaf, Deleuze and Guattari are not included in Wolfe's theoretical mapping (which includes, among others, Latour and Haraway) of posthumanist posthumanism (ibid. 125–6). Like Wolfe, Deleuze and Guattari oppose the 'anthropological dogma' (ibid. xiv–xv) of humanism that insists on the repression of the nonhuman animal (the term 'nonhuman animal' highlighting the animality of the human) and therefore also emphasise material existence.

At stake here is what George Slusser terms the 'Frankenstein barrier'. In Shelley, Victor Frankenstein denies the monster's demand for a companion and the means to procreate. Citing *Frankenstein* as the foundational SF text, Slusser takes this move as emblematic of the point at which the future possibilities of SF fold back upon one another through the denial of futurity, accompanied, as we shall see, by regression into Oedipal relations. While the denial of futurity

is Frankenstein's as much as the monster's, the barrier is nevertheless anthropocentric, for 'Victor seeks through reason to transform
animal nature, [and] that same animality [. . .] stands as a thing
unmoving in the path of not only Frankenstein's but all our dreams
of the future' (Slusser 1992: 51). For Slusser, the Frankenstein barrier
is the logic informing SF, and cyberpunk the means to overcome it
(ibid. 52). We have been preoccupied with the control assemblages
of cyberpunk; we now turn to biopunk, *and it is biopunk rather than
cyberpunk that will break the Frankenstein barrier, transforming it
from an apparatus of capture to one of contagion.* The *Frankenstein*
myth proceeds thus: it is established by Shelley; Wells and Kenton
formalise the latency of the nonhuman animal into an axiom; *Splice*
realises the ambitions of both. By analysing and contrasting Shelley,
Wells and Kenton's myths for modernity, and Natali's *Splice*, I
will argue that attention to the nonhuman animal provides a way
to reconceptualise this barrier in the twenty-first century, because
the *Frankenstein* myth has increasingly come to incorporate and
be identified with nonhuman animals. Using Latour's modernist
hybrid, I will show that *Frankenstein* and *Moreau* are paradigmati-
cally modern in their approach to nonhuman animals, and that this
enables us to understand the technoscientific and Oedipal relations
through Deleuze and Guattari's Oedipal and State animals. The
nonhuman animal in *Splice* is, by contrast, a product of postmodern, technoscientific biocapitalism, a very different type of hybrid
that gives rise to new technoscientific and Oedipal relations. The
contrast is contingent upon a more pronounced affinity with Deleuze
and Guattari's becoming-animal, the demonic animal, which makes
Splice more than just a recent example of the nonhuman animal
injected into the *Frankenstein* myth. Rather, it is a significant addition because it is the nonhuman animal that breaks the Frankenstein
barrier.

Two factors inform this change from human to nonhuman animal.
First, the bodies that concern me are defined by mythopoetical narrative conventions of genre and their technoscientific conditions. I thus
ascribe to becomings-animal a narrative function coterminous with
both modern metanarratives and their supposed lack of purchase in
postmodernism. For Haraway, Deleuze and Guattari's is a 'philosophy of the sublime, not the earthly, not the mud; becoming-animal
is not an autre-mondialisation' (2007: 28). On the contrary, Deleuze
and Guattari's becomings-animal, and the statuses of the nonhuman animal hybrids they produce, are grounded in and contingent

upon material technoscientific conditions and cultural attitudes. Indeed, it is the intersections of power relations – of technoscience and the family – that make it worthwhile to follow Deleuze and Guattari. The contrast between becomings-animal as they appear in *Frankenstein*, *Moreau* and *Splice* will allow us to reconceptualise the Frankenstein barrier. Second, the psychoanalytical valences at work shape conceptions of the nonhuman animal and, more specifically, the nonhuman animal hybrid, and these too are reconfigured by technoscientific conditions.

Deleuze and Guattari's becomings-animal illuminate the '*zone of proximity or copresence*' (*TP*: 301) between two molar forms over-coded by psychoanalysis and humanist modernity. Žižek summarises that 'becoming means transcending the context of historical conditions out of which a phenomenon emerges' (2012a: 13). Becomings are escapist and offer possibilities outside of overcoded cultural, social and political thinking, and also outside of myth. Deleuze and Guattari suppose we:

> know nothing about a body until we know what it can do [. . .] what its affects are, how they can or cannot enter into composition with other affects, with the affects of another body, either to destroy that body or to be destroyed by it, either to exchange actions and passions with it or to join with it in composing a more powerful body. (*TP*: 284)

Hybrids, creatures, Frankenmonsters and variations thereof are always already in some way nonhuman and understood as, or made to conform to, different understandings of the nonhuman animal. Wolfe's sense of posthumanism 'requires us to attend to that thing called "the human" with *greater* specificity, *greater* attention to its embodiment, embeddedness, and materiality, and how these in turn shape and are shaped by consciousness, mind, and so on' (2010: 120). With regard to Deleuze and Guattari's becomings-animal, the impulse to rethink the human is evident in studies of SF and Cronenberg (Melehy 1995), but both these and Wolfe miss the opportunity to focus not on the human, but on the nonhuman. This is also true of Slusser's Frankenstein barrier. With this change in perspective, the question might well be asked: can a nonhuman animal participate in a becoming-animal? Deleuze and Guattari leave the question unresolved, save to state 'I cannot become dog without the dog itself becoming something else' (*TP*: 285). There seems to be an avoidance of the nonhuman in the interest of accounting for the human – an approach nevertheless implicit in Wolfe's assertion – that echoes Haraway's critique. Wolfe later suggests that, for 'biopolitical theory, the animality of the human becomes a central problem – perhaps *the* central problem – to be produced, controlled, or regulated for politics in its distinctly modern form' (2010: 100). I am not interested in the becomings-animal of the human, for the distinctly modern and human-centric nature of the Frankenstein barrier renders them problematic. I will look at where the becoming-animal of the nonhuman goes, and how it reworks the Frankenstein barrier.

A Filthy Type of Yours

An operation worthy of Doctor Moreau: horrible and magnificent. (*TP*: 189)

Shelley subtitled *Frankenstein* 'The Modern Prometheus' and, although the novel was first published on the cusp of Romanticism and in the spirit of the Age of Enlightenment, John Turney is right to say that the novel is 'the governing myth of modern biology' and a 'myth of modernity' (1998: 3, 8). It is in this sense of modernity that the hybrid Frankenstein creates is intelligible through Bruno Latour's conception of modernism. He argues that modernism is characterised by two impulses: the creation of 'new types of beings, hybrids of nature and culture', and the 'purification' of these forces into distinct zones of human (culture) and nonhuman (nature):

> So long as we consider these two practices [. . .] separately, we are truly modern – that is, we willingly subscribe to the critical project, even though that project is developed only through the proliferation of hybrids down below. As soon as we direct our attention simultaneously to the work of purification and the work of hybridisation, we immediately stop being wholly modern. (1993: 10–11)

The hybrid thrives when and where it is most suppressed and effaced. In this sense, hybrids are endemic to modernism, proliferating and interbreeding in substrata, yet effaced by modernism's tendency to create binaries between human and nonhuman, between 'what happens "above" and what happens "below"', and between nature and culture (ibid. 12–13). To extrapolate Latour's binaries, we find the division between 'masculine' transcendence, arising from the Cartesian *cogito* operating in the culture sphere, and embodied 'feminine' subjectivity, aligned with nature and the distinction between human and nonhuman animals.

Frankenstein is both Prometheus *pyrphoros*, the Titan who stole fire from the gods and delivered it to humans, and Prometheus *plasticator*, 'said to have created or recreated mankind', often with the same fire, 'by animating a figure made of clay' (Joseph 1998: vi). Less frequently is Prometheus – and, by extension, Frankenstein – considered in relation to nonhuman animals. Vint observes that in 'some versions of the legend, Prometheus is contrasted with his foolish brother Epimetheus, who is given the task of distributing positive traits to the animals. Lacking foresight, Epimetheus has run out of gifts when he reaches humans; in compensation Prometheus steals fire for humanity.' Thus we might 'acknowledge Prometheus's compensatory gift of technology as that which has created the human-animal boundary' (2010a: 182). It is the ad hoc and consolatory Prometheus, and the humanist repression of animality and the desire for transcendence described by Wolfe (2010: xv), that is characteristic of modernity:

> For what made the *grand récits* of modernity master narratives if not the fact that they were all narratives of mastery, of men seeking his telos in the conquest of nature? What function did these narratives play other than to legitimise Western man's self-appointed mission of transforming the entire planet in his own image? (Owens 1998: 75)

Frankenstein's 'fervent longing to penetrate the secrets of nature' (39)[2] and to bring them under his control is the impulse of modernity, and its use of the consolatory gift of technology affects perceptions of nonhuman hybrids. Susan Squier suggests that Frankenstein's monster is 'an interspecies hybrid', functioning 'as a point of origin for the negative literary image of xenogenic desire' (1998: 366). The monster is metonymically animalised by Frankenstein, who calls him 'daemon', 'wretch' and 'vile insect' (99), and assembled in a 'workshop of filthy creation' with materials furnished from the 'dissecting room and the slaughter-house' (55). Frankenstein's manipulation of these materials makes him a 'distinctly modern hero who embodies the deepest impulses of modernity to control nature, perfect social existence, and produce new forms of life' (Best and Kellner 2001: 159).

Becomings are always opposed to these metanarratives. This is not to say they are absent from narratives, since Deleuze and Guattari develop their theory with reference to Melville's *Moby-Dick* (1851) and Kafka's *Metamorphosis* (1915). Metanarratives strive for certainty and resolution, which is antithetical to escapist becomings. In structuralism, myths are understood by binarism and invariance and 'it is always possible to try to explain these *blocks of becoming* by a correspondence between two relations, but to do so most certainly impoverishes the phenomenon under study' (*TP*: 262). More specifically, becomings often resolve themselves into molar identities. They can be arrested and recoded as necessary transgressions that create illusory ideological openness. Thus 'myth recapitulates them in its own terms in order to curb them [. . .] Societies [. . .] have always appropriated these becomings in order to break them, reduce them to relations of totemic or symbolic correspondence' (*TP*: 262, 273). Becomings are therefore 'more like fragments of tales' (*TP*: 262) than narratives, although their arrest and resolution into or affirmation of the fixity of the molar is the stuff of metanarratives.

The becoming-animal of Frankenstein's monster in the narrative is instructive. For Slusser:

> To place *Frankenstein* at the beginning of the SF genre is to erect what I call the Frankenstein barrier. If SF is distinguished from other literary forms by the fact that science is given a free hand there to construct things to come, then Victor is the first SF protagonist. And he actually makes, for the first time in a literary work, a true thing of future possibility. But that future thing, perhaps because it is a thing of fiction as well, seems destined to collapse back on itself [. . .] Shelley's novel opens SF's epistemological futures only to subject them to a particularly stringent law of inverse proportionality. (1992: 48–9)

Slusser identifies an essential quality of the *Frankenstein* myth: the interconnectedness between the denial of futurity and the Oedipal relationship between creature and creator; Victor's refusal forces 'the future back on itself so that it is now the future itself that blocks the future, in the form of a thing destructively *present* at each of Victor's junctures of futurity – family, friendship, marriage' (ibid. 48). Returning to Latour, we can identify the double movement of modernity at work, since Frankenstein, a figure of the social, takes nature as his object in order to 'purify' it of indeterminacy (1993: 62) yet the result is a nonhuman animal hybrid whose potential for proliferation causes the utmost anxiety.

As in the schizoanalytic critique of Freud, Frankenstein's monster 'get[s] bogged down and fall[s] back to the Oedipal family animal' (*TP*: 276). Just as the denial of futurity retards the narrative for Slusser, so too 'one allows oneself to be re-Oedipalised not by guilt but by fatigue, by lack of invention' (*K*: 33). *Frankenstein* is (inadvertently) summarised by Deleuze and Guattari:

The old-time theologians drew a clear distinction between two kinds of curses against sexuality. The first concerns sexuality as a process of filiation transmitting the original sin. But the second concerns it as a power of alliance inspiring illicit unions or abominable loves. This differs significantly from the first in that it tends to prevent procreation; since the demon does not himself have the ability to procreate, he must adopt indirect means. (*TP*: 271)

Frankenstein's Promethean transgression restages original sin, and his monster must indeed adopt indirect means to procreate, entreating Frankenstein to make him a female counterpart. The biblical analogues and allusions to Milton's *Paradise Lost* are well documented (Milner 2005). Yet it is not the mythopoetical dimensions of the monster, or its self-identification with the biblical Adam and Milton's Satan, which evoke terror. Rather, it is the monster's *ontological status*, 'his immanent embeddedness in the life-world' (Csicsery-Ronay Jr 2008: 154), that is repellent. Janet Staiger notes that in 'botany and zoology, the function of hybridisation is to produce invigorated offspring by crossbreeding, but the offspring may be sterile. So, too, the hybridised literary text [. . .] may create a strong effect, but the hybrid itself does not generate a new family' (2003: 195). *Frankenstein*, however, has produced offspring in the form of innumerable adaptations, and Frankenstein's terror at the thought of the monster's fecundity implies he is not sterile either. His unhappy trajectory can be understood as the arresting of a line of flight characteristic of a botched becoming.

The monster of the Frankenstein barrier is Deleuze and Guattari's domesticated and sentimental Oedipal animal, those that 'invite us to regress, draw us into a narcissistic contemplation, and they are the only kind of animal psychoanalysis understands' (*TP*: 265). The daddy-mummy-animal triangle Deleuze and Guattari suppose characteristic of the Oedipal animal is evident. Frankenstein is incestuous not because Elizabeth is his sister, but because of his conflation of her with his mother. When he dreams of Elizabeth, she decays and transmogrifies into his dead mother and he wakes to find the monster hovering over him. The monster is the 'unnatural' offspring of a repressed sexual attraction for his mother and a manifestation of Oedipal anxiety. This anxiety is accentuated by the psychoanalytical figure of the *Doppelgänger* because the 'Oedipalised animal as psychoanalysis sees it [is] the image of the father' (*TP*: 269). The monster becomes Frankenstein's *Doppelgänger*, his 'own spirit let loose' (77), who claims, 'my form is a filthy type of yours, more horrid even from the very resemblance' (130). Frankenstein's refusal to create another monster is his wresting back of patrilineal control, but the monster, enraged by the denial of sexual reproduction, says, 'I shall be with you on your wedding-night' (168), evoking the primal scene. The monster, assuming the early stage of a child's psycho-sexual development, interprets it as violence visited upon the mother, and murders Elizabeth.

The Hand that Makes

> With ingenuity, one thus discovers, like a new and unexplored *scientific* field, the psychic life of the animal as soon as he is revealed to be mala-dapted to the death one is preparing for him [. . .] The prisoner needs liberty, sexuality, 'normalcy' to withstand prison, just as industrially bred animals need a certain 'quality of life' to die within the norm. And nothing about this is contradictory. The worker also needs responsibility, self-management in order to better respond to the imperative of produc-tion. (*SS*: 132)

At the end of Shelley's tale, the monster perishes in the Arctic snow, but innumerable reworkings testify that he is hardly dead. Though he returns to a state of Oedipal repression, restagings of the arti-ficial creation and manipulation of life cannot be told without some acknowledgement of *Frankenstein* 'because, like stories from the Bible, it has passed into general and universal mythol-ogy' (Reichardt 1994: 136). Indeed, for Paul O'Flinn, 'There is no such thing as *Frankenstein* [. . .] There are only *Frankensteins*, as the text is ceaselessly written, reproduced, refilmed and rede-signed' (2005: 22).[3] Wells's *The Island of Doctor Moreau* is an important elaboration of the *Frankenstein* myth, not only because Wells himself credited Shelley as its inspiration, but also because it replaces her ambiguous hybrid with nonhuman animals. In so doing, it significantly recasts the myth, introducing new techno-scientific axioms and metaphysical codes that reorient the relation between creator and created, and, as will become clear, introduces new axioms to the Frankenmyth. In Wells's novel, the seafaring Prendick is stranded on an island where the disgraced Doctor Moreau, through a mix of religious instruction and vivisection, creates new creatures called Beast People. Where Frankenstein's monster's ability to procreate goes unrealised, Moreau's Beast People can procreate with limited success: their 'part waste sexual emotion' (77)[4] yields offspring, although most die of physiological

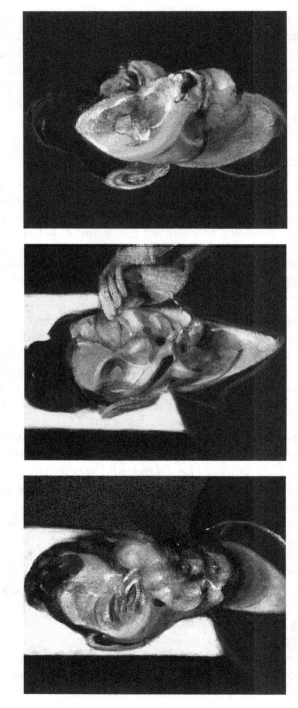

Figure 5.1 Francis Bacon, *Three Studies for Portrait of Lucian Freud*, 1964. © The Estate of Francis Bacon. All rights reserved. DACS/Licensed by Viscopy, 2015. Photo: Prudence Cuming Associates Ltd.

deficiency, or are cannibalised. But none can maintain their molecular form and they revert to nonhuman animals.

Moreau embodies modernist, humanist science and the privileging of transcendence established by the objectification of nonhuman animals, and it is the paradox of the novel that he humanises them in order to demonstrate their nonhumanness. The Beast People are Deleuze and Guattari's animal of the second kind, which has two interrelated characteristics: it is scientifically classifiable as an animal species, and it is made to participate in 'great divine myths, in such a way as to extract from them series or structures, archetypes or models' (*TP*: 265). Scientific practices coerce the nonhuman animal into objectification by making it conform to an anthropocentric worldview. They are animals of the State's 'bio-ideology' (Gomel 2000), which means, in the discourse of modernism, that any 'hybrid that threatens to transgress the border [. . .] is reclassified and ascribed to *either* the human *or* the non-human sphere' (Lykke 1996: 16). Physiologically, Moreau's Beast People are chimeras born of quasi-xenotransplantation rather than hybrids. The former are a non-genetic 'combination between two different species', rather than a 'product of breeding two different species' (Seyfer 2004 in Ferreira 2008: 224), though both are 'caught in the unacknowledged space that exists between the clear distinctions between human and animal' (Ferreira 2008: 232). Moreau's experiments allow him to transcend the nonhuman animal by reaffirming its anthropocentric impoverishment, and his cruelty towards the Beast People borders on indifference. The Beast People are Cartesian animals, devoid of a soul, their minds too nonhuman to be lastingly manipulated.

The aesthetic correlate of Wells's rhetoric of indefinition is Deleuze's analysis of becomings-animal in the paintings of Francis Bacon.[5] For Prendick, the interstitial physiognomy of the Beast People intimates a 'generalised animalism' (122) attributable neither to humans nor to nonhuman animals. Similarly, for Deleuze, Bacon's faces are assemblages of 'asignifying traits': 'Sometimes the human head is replaced by an animal; but it is not the animal as a form, but rather the animal as a *trait*' (*FB*: 16). Prendick describes the face of a Beast Man thus:

> I had never beheld such a repulsive and extraordinary face before, and yet
> – if the contradiction is credible – I experienced at the same time an odd
> feeling that in some way I *had* already encountered exactly the features
> and gestures that now amazed me. (12)

Rather than evoking the uncanny registers of psychoanalysis, the simultaneous presence of *Heimliche* and *Unheimliche*, the face here is a *'zone of indiscernibility or undecidability* between man and animal [. . .] It is never a combination of forms, but rather the common fact: the common fact of man and animal' (*FB*: 16). Prendick seeks to eliminate this indiscernibility through restorative violence, to make mythically overcoded flesh of the Beast People. Prendick's attacks seek the face's total erasure, to restore it to signification. The features of the 'flayed child' (52) are rendered unrecognisable to his satisfaction: 'I cut it over, gashed down its ugly face with the nail in my stick' (60). Prendick easily erases the offending visage, shooting the grovelling Beast Person in the woods in the face, and treats the Puma Woman similarly: '[I] fired again point-blank into its ugly face. I saw its features vanish in a flash. Its face was driven in' (102). Effaced, the Beast People are reterritorialised as animals of the State, overcoded as dead animal flesh that affirms the certainty of the human body. The line of flight constituting the Beast People's becoming-animal is arrested in the form of the dead nonhuman animal, as codified by State bio-ideology.

For Vint, 'like Frankenstein, Moreau turns against his created beings when their material reality does not match his aspirations' (2010a: 190). But this is not the case, since Moreau expects no transcendence from his Beast People: he might pretend to 'burn out the animal' (76) with pain, but he truly aims for the 'ideal' yet unattainable human form (71). Moreau affirms the nonhumanness of the Beast People by recapitulating their inability to become human. Thus, 'pain becomes a just punishment for the ability to feel pain. Similarly, the scars and mutilations of the vivisection function as an after-the-fact legitimisation for inflicting them, for nobody so ugly could possibly deserve any better' (Gomel 2000: 418). The Beast People become Deleuze and Guattari's second animal, subject to a binary logic by which 'channels of transmission are preestablished: the arborescent system preexists the individual who is integrated into it' (*TP*: 18).

Moreau's vivisection and scientific manipulation of the material sphere provide a veneer for his transcendence. While Frankenstein's experiment augments the 'material horizon of the organism' (Milburn 2005: 283), Moreau confirms its ontological and spiritual limits, though it is he who polices them. For Moreau, pain divides the material nonhuman animal from the transcendent human; pain is, 'for us, only so long as we wriggle in the dust' (72). He chastises Prendick for his materialism: 'So long as visible or audible pain turns you sick, so

long as your pain drives you, so long as pain underlies your propositions about sin, so long, I tell you, you are an animal, thinking a little
less obscurely what an animal feels' (71). Moreau thus 'reinforces a
metaphysics of subjectivity derived from the human-animal boundary' (Vint 2010a: 190). Moreau's vivisection and Prendick's violence
arrest the molecular becomings of the Beast People to affirm their
own molar states in opposition to nonhuman animals: 'You will be
organised, you will be an organism, you will articulate your body
– otherwise you're just depraved' (*TP*: 159). The Beast People are
made to aspire to the molar human:

> Not to go on all-Fours; *that* is the Law. Are we not Men?
> Not to suck up Drink; *that* is the Law. Are we not Men?
> Not to eat Flesh nor Fish; *that* is the Law. Are we not Men?
> Not to claw Bark of Trees; *that* is the Law. Are we not Men?
> Not to chase other Men; *that* is the Law. Are we not Men? (57)

The monster's superior physiology makes *Frankenstein* the ur-text
of cyberpunk narratives (Hollinger 2010: 192; Economides 2009;
Haraway 1991: 151) and Frankenstein's psyche undergoes a Freudian
Oedipal split, with the monster as his displaced unconscious. Moreau
is, by contrast, a classical humanist, entrenched in the 'notion of the
self as an ahistorical given, whose timeless essence and nature is that
of a rational human mind, ontologically distinct from its body' (Best
and Kellner 2001: 195). He is a consummate Cartesian, unflinchingly
driving a knife into his leg to demonstrate the epiphenomenal nature
of his body and his mastery over it. For Moreau, the body is abject
material, the nonhuman animal, and, in death, he achieves transcendence as his conflation of science and myth persists in the Law.
Science and myth are thereby interconnected, as transgressors are
punished by Moreau, the transcendental scientist, and by Prendick:

> *His* is the House of Pain.
> *His* is the Hand that makes.
> *His* is the Hand that wounds.
> *His* is the Hand that heals. (57)

The Beast People's status as State animals draws us closer to the
social status of genetically engineered hybrids, whose futures are
determined by the expectations and interests of their creator. *Moreau*
is undoubtedly an 'uncanny anticipation of xenotransplantation and
genetic engineering' (Best and Kellner 2001: 170), but its depiction of
nonhuman animals strives towards mythology.

In the most sophisticated film treatment of Wells, Kenton's *Island of Lost Souls*, the Beast People are genetic hybrids rather than chimeras. As Moreau, Charles Laughton employs vivisection and plastic surgery, but also new technologies, 'ray baths' and genetic manipulation, and biohacks the nonhuman animal's germplasm. The film thereby engages nascent speculation into genetic manipulation, even though DNA had not yet been discovered (Kirby 2002: 98). The film is indispensable because of these technoscientific renovations, but also for the new direction in which it takes the nonhuman animal, and how this changes the horizon of the Frankenstein barrier. For Baudrillard, nonhuman animals are forced to 'speak' when they are made to participate in the ordering of human experience. He locates the nonhuman animal in various discourses: mythological, scientific, psychoanalytical and, finally, schizophrenic:

> [Animals] spoke the moral discourse of man in fables. They supported structural discourse in the theory of totemism. Every day they deliver their 'objective' – anatomical, physiological, genetic – message in laboratories. They served in turns as metaphors for virtue and vice, as an energetic and ecological model, as a mechanical and formal model in bionics, as a phantasmatic register for the unconscious and, lastly, as a model for the absolute deterritorialisation of desire in Deleuze's 'becoming animal.' (*SS*: 137)

Baudrillard's insight pertains to Moreau, who seeks from his nonhumans a 'confession' and proof of science's capacity both to create truth and to transcend the animal: 'Animals must be made to say that they are not animal [. . .] Bestiality, and its principle of uncertainty, must be killed in animals' (*SS*: 129). But the Beast People are unable to do this. In Kenton, Moreau has his pathetic creatures manually power the primitive turbine that enables him to manufacture more unsuccessful experiments. The Beast People are made to occupy the lacuna between their own molar deficiency and its unsatisfactory repetition. The process becomes a confirmation of scientific method, affirming anthropocentricism by maximising the nonhuman animal's participation in this circular logic, literalised by the rotating turbine on which they toil.

As in Wells, Kenton's Moreau is an anthropocentricist, considering humans the 'present climax' of evolution. But his worldview is far more grandiose in its anthropomorphism, believing 'all animal life is tending toward the human form'. In a significant departure from Wells, Kenton's Moreau is explicitly interested in the reproductive potential of his Beast People. The film centres on his (unsuccessful) attempt to have Lota, the Panther Woman (Kathleen Burke),

Biocapitalism and Schizophrenia

fall pregnant to Parker (Richard Arlen). Laughton's campy performance, his merrily perverse 'hobby' of whipping the Beast Men, and Montgomery's (Arthur Hohl) 'professional indiscretion', which saw him exiled from England, all suggest a homosexual relationship.[6] That Kenton's Moreau and Montgomery 'don't count' as sexual candidates for Lota makes the Beast People deformed unions of frustrated homosexuals, who sublimate their inability to reproduce, channelling their latent desires into reproductive technoscientific enterprise.

But Kenton's Moreau is no different from the discourse of masculinist modernist science. Vint notes that the metaphorical linking of nonhuman animals with the '"body" and "nature," has been used to denigrate women and deny them full status as political citizens' (2010a: 90), whilst Lynda Birke notes the cultural 'domestication' of both nonhuman animals and women, the medical tradition of their both being subjected to 'breeding programmes, to experimental regimes, [and] to vivisection' (1994: 16; see Lansbury 1985). Kenton's Moreau does not seek Lota's transcendence of animality because, for him, there is no difference between women and nonhuman animals: 'Did you see that, Montgomery? She was tender, like a woman. Oh, that little scene spurs the scientific imagination onward. I wonder how much of Lota's animal origin is still alive? How nearly a perfect woman she is'; 'I wanted to prove how completely she was a woman, whether she was capable of loving, mating and having children.' Kenton's Moreau redirects the line of Lota's becoming towards the molar form of woman-as-animal/ other of man, a trope Birke also identifies: 'Seeing women as having a special link to animals may break the woman/animal boundary, but it also consolidates the categories of woman and animal, and consolidates them in nature, set against the universal "Man"' (1994: 145). The hybrid in *Lost Souls* approaches Frankenstein's monster's potential. Kenton's Moreau affirms man in relation both to woman and to nonhuman animals, rather than fearing the proliferation of a superior species, but the Frankenstein barrier is imposed once again nonetheless.

Biocapitalism and Schizophrenia

Oedipus is . . . genetically coded. (Guattari 2006: 136)

Natali's *Splice* is a contemporary reworking of the *Frankenstein* myth, itself now suffused with aspects of *Moreau*, the speculative technoscientific manipulations therein now fully realised biotechnologies. As Sheryl Hamilton (2003) demonstrates, SF and biotechnologies are consumed in combination by the general public and are often undifferentiated. We see this lack of differentiation in the way 'Franken' has become a polysemic sign for a variety of scientific discourses and perceptions, from Frankenstein 'cinemyths' (Picart 2003: 1) and 'Frankensteinian images' (Turney 1998: 11), to 'Frankenfarms', 'Frankentomatoes' and 'Frankenviruses' (Lederer and Ratzan 2005), to a generalised symbol for the misapplication of science (Rollin 1995: 154). Two features are common to Frankenimages: they have a hyperbiological orientation and, more and more, have acquired the presence of nonhuman animals, so much so that Bernard Rollin suggests genetically engineered animals are invariably linked to *Frankenstein* in its many incarnations (ibid.). Tora Holmberg states that transgenetic animals represent 'Frankenscience' (2011: 62), such as the 'earmouse', or, more properly, Vacanti Mouse, one of two subjects in Patricia Piccinini's *Protein Lattice – Subset Red, Portrait* (1997), which Natali claims to be the inspiration for *Splice* (Fordham 2010: 12). We can see Piccinini's Vacanti Mouse and female subject conflated in *Splice*'s monster, Dren (Delphine Chanéac).

As a new addition to the *Frankenstein* myth, *Splice* dramatises the intersecting power relations of biotechnology, familial relations and reproduction. In *Splice*, Clive (Adrien Brody) and Elsa (Sarah Polley) are romantic and professional partners at the cutting edge of genetic engineering. Clive wishes to start a family but Elsa remains traumatised by her cruel mother. They work for Nucleic Exchange Research and Development, a pharmaceutical company that creates hybrids of nonhuman animal species to aid the livestock development. Splicing human DNA with nonhuman animal hybrids would allow research into treatments for Parkinson's and Alzheimer's diseases, diabetes and cancer. Forbidden to do this, the biopunks experiment in secret and create a genetically recombinant and cloned hybrid, Dren, whom they raise in secret. They use DNA manipulation technologies, combined with interspecies *in vitro* fertilisation, a technology developed equally in the fields of human reproduction and stockbreeding (Turney 1998: 161). Clive's name evokes actor Colin Clive who played Henry Frankenstein in James Whale's two *Frankenstein* films (1931 and 1935), while Elsa's alludes to Elsa Lanchester's portrayal of both Shelley and the eponymous Bride in *Bride of Frankenstein*. *Splice* reworks this dual role, since Elsa, like Shelley, is both Dren's

5.2   Patricia Piccinini, *Protein Lattice – Subset Red, Portrait*, 1997. Digital C-type photograph. 80 cm x 80 cm. Courtesy of the artist.

creator and also in some way the creation itself, since Dren's human DNA is derived from Elsa's.

Splice's narrative is informed by the directives of biocapitalism intelligible through contemporary science-as-industry. This biocapitalistic imperative is postmodern rather than modern with regard to the hybrid, because it 'ideologically grants and materially invests in a world in which species boundaries can be radically crossed [. . .] in the genetic and aesthetic pursuit of new markets' (Shukin 2009: 11). Clive and Elsa's client, Newstead Pharma, sees no immediate profit in the project to splice human and nonhuman DNA, and wishes to extract a protein and rush it to market. Elsa, dismissing ethical questions, objects: 'If we don't use human DNA now, someone else will.' Joan (Simona Maicanescu), CEO of Newstead, replies: 'You put a viable product for livestock on the table, then we will talk about a twenty-year plan to save the world.' The bio-ideology that aimlessly reproduced only itself on Moreau's island here acquires the directives of biocapital. As Vint suggests, 'we have now entered an era in which biology has become a discourse of information, and the value established through the biotech industry is largely a value based on market projections' (2011b: 165). Dren is for Newstead Pharma a commodity, a protein to be reproduced as genetic code. At this intersection of technoscientific innovation and familial relations in Clive and Elsa's parentage of Dren, the usefulness of Deleuze and Guattari's becoming-animal emerges. It is *because* of these technoscientific conditions that Dren can be understood as Deleuze and Guattari's 'demonic animal' (*TP*: 265), understood through its affects and resistance to Oedipal signification, and it becomes apparent that these affects are available to Dren only because of technoscience. To become animal is 'to participate in a movement, to stake out the path of escape in all its positivity, to cross a threshold, to reach a continuum of intensities that are valuable only in themselves, to find a world of pure intensities where all forms come undone, as do all the significations, signifiers, and signifieds' (*K*: 13).

The significance of becoming-animal is that this animal is a schizophrenic. Dren's becoming-animal is further distinguishable from the Oedipal animal of the Frankenstein barrier because here there is a becoming-woman. In their influential reading of *Frankenstein*, Sandra Gilbert and Susan Gubar suggest that 'Frankenstein's male monster may really be a female in disguise' (1984: 237), and psychobiographers frequently adduce the link between Shelley, Frankenstein and the monster, yet the Oedipal father/son relationship dominates nonetheless. For Deleuze and Guattari, becomings 'pass through' (*TP*: 306) becoming-woman. This is more pronounced in *Splice* than in *Frankenstein*, since Dren acquires a womanly resemblance, though this itself is not becoming-woman. Deleuze and Guattari use *woman* strategically, as opposed to man, the 'molar entity par excellence', 'the majority, or rather the standard [. . .]: white, male, adult, "rational," etc.' (*TP*: 322). Deleuze and Guattari's movement through woman to nonhuman animals is problematic, the two conjoined by science and culture to their mutual detriment. Yet Deleuze and Guattari refer not to a sexed or gendered body, any more than to a species-specific organism: 'In the same way that we avoided defining a body by its organs and functions, we will avoid defining it by Species or Genus characteristics; instead we will seek to count its affects' (*TP*: 283). Dren's body is a constantly metamorphosing body without organs, the body of immanent potential opposed to organisation of the organs (what appear to be tumour-riddled lungs enable Dren to breathe under water). There are objections to and varying interpretations of becomings-woman (Beaulieu 2011; Flieger 2000; Grosz 1994) but I take it that it 'refers to every discourse that is not anthropocentric, and is thus coded by all economic, social, cultural, organic, and political circuits as "minority"' (Colman 2005: 101).

The technoscientific and cultural conditions in *Splice* further distinguish it from *Frankenstein* and *Moreau*. Dren is transbiological, 'a biology that is not only born and bred, or born and made, but *made and born*' (Franklin 2006: 171), genetically engineered, a product of recombinant DNA technology, 'which involves combining DNA from two different species' (in this case human and unspecified nonhuman animal), and a clone, a new individual 'generated from a single cell, circumventing sexual reproduction' (Kirby 2000: 193). It is significant that Dren is also a *cybrid*, produced by the 'implantation of a human cell nucleus into an enucleated animal egg' (Haddow et al. 2010: 4). Hybrids, as Latour finds them in the modern constitution, are artificial disconnections, resultant of ideological labour that separates nature and culture. Cybridisation is the inverse, actively seeking to collapse the binaries Latour deems modern, while emphasising his industrial conception of technoscience. While hybrids constitute a '*barrier threat*', cybrids, in ways never realised by Frankenstein's monster, constitute a '*creation threat*' in two senses: first, Elsa exploits the distinction between 'what is human and what is animal' (ibid. 5), claiming that although 'human cloning is illegal. This won't be human, not entirely'; second, the threat posed by Dren's potential to reproduce and create more hybrid beings.

Thus, Dren's becoming-animal is contingent upon technoscientific discourse, which provides the necessary conditions of its becoming, and it is this becoming-animal of the nonhuman animal hybrid that reworks the Frankenstein barrier. Dren is a clone, and in the clone we find psychoanalytical dilemmas: incest, the *Doppelgänger* and bestiality. In *Frankenstein* we see that the Oedipalisation of the becoming-animal both erects and maintains the Frankenstein barrier. Here we observe that becoming-animal is measured in affect and asignification. Dren, realising Frankenstein's fear that a female monster might turn 'to the superior beauty of man' (165), has consensual sex with Clive, and later forces a masculinised body upon Elsa. Both cases, arguably, are incestuous acts between parent and child. Given Dren's physiological and psychosexual development is neither relative to humans nor species-specific, this could also be sexual assault perpetrated by both Clive and Elsa, for Dren might be too young (by human standards) to consent. In the first act, as a clone, Dren is genetically linked to Clive's partner, Elsa; in the second, because Dren is Elsa's clone, the act might be a kind of (in)voluntary (mutual) masturbation. Unlike Frankenstein's monster and the Beast People, *Dren is fuckable*. Dren's becoming-animal is asignificatory and irreconcilable with molar forms, since a clone 'resolves all oedipal sexuality' (*SS*: 96) at a semantic level.

Just as Deleuze and Guattari reproach Freud for turning the unconscious into a theatre, Baudrillard writes that 'we may see in cloning the resurgence of our fascination with an archaic form of incest with the original twin' (2000: 12). Through cloning, incest becomes interconnected and confused with the *Doppelgänger*. Cloning de-metaphorises the *Doppelgänger*, resulting in 'the materialisation of the double by genetic means, that is to say the abolition of all alterity and of any imaginary' (*SS*: 97). Baudrillard considers this the realisation of the death drive, a return to pre-individual asexuality (Freud's polymorphous perversity) and the liquidation of Oedipal signification. We recall in *Frankenstein* the monster assumes the role of Frankenstein's *Doppelgänger*, his murder of Elizabeth a recapitulation of the violence of the primal scene. The primal scene in *Splice* is rather different, since it is Clive who bears the brunt of the sexual confusion, since Dren is, genetically, Clive's partner Elsa and he, in Oedipal triangulation, is Dren's father. The sex act that occurs between Clive and Dren is presaged when Dren retires, fondling the blonde hair of a doll in a child's bedroom. In the following scene as Elsa straddles Clive, he gazes over her shoulder to see Dren lurking behind a gossamer curtain, inclining her head with a child's curiosity as she watches her 'parents'. A series of shot-reverse-shots establish Clive and Dren as equally inquisitive, and Clive orgasms while fondling Elsa's blonde hair, gesturing to Elsa and Dren's shared genetics, and prefiguring Dren's desire for Elsa. Here, as for Deleuze and Guattari, Oedipal filiations are 'prepersonal intensive states that could just as well "extend" to other persons', retrospective categories that 'do not exist prior to the prohibitions that constitute them as such' (*AO*: 161, 160). On the loss of alterity, Baudrillard is very clearly wrong, as the becomings-animal in *Splice* demonstrate: 'The imaginary power and wealth of the double – the one in which the strangeness and at the same time the intimacy of the subject to itself are played out (*heimlich*/*unheimlich*) – rests on its immateriality, on the fact that it is and remains a phantasm' (*SS*: 95). In biocapitalism these concepts are technoscientifically contingent and, adjoined to becomings-animal, lose a certainty hitherto guaranteed by their de-ontological, representational status. The becoming-animal of the nonhuman animal hybrid puts the Oedipal coordinates in flux though its confusion of Oedipal incest and schizo incest, much as Deleuze and Guattari claim of Kafka's *Metamorphosis*, where Gregor and his sister 'wanted the schizo incest, an incest of strong connections, incest with the sister in opposition to Oedipal incest, incest that gives evidence of a nonhuman sexuality as in the becoming-animal' (*K*: 15). Implicit in each of these sex acts is a degree of bestiality. Margret Grebowicz says of pornography depicting sex acts between human and nonhuman animals, or 'zoo porn', that 'intense anthropomorphism fuels these narratives, rather than the eroticisation of the power of humans over animals' (2010: 1–2). While *Splice* is no zoo-porn film, the becomings-animal are asignificatory, and thus tend to confound anthropomorphism and, regarding consent and desire, anthropocentricism. With regard to cloning, Baudrillard implies that the informatisation of the body in the form of genetic codes renders useless the word 'species', although it has never been precise in biological discourse (Rollin 1995: 38), nor is DNA species-specific (Haddow et al. 2010: 13). Dren is neither species-specific nor a human or nonhuman animal, but becoming-animal.

Breaking the Frankenstein Barrier

> We project (nature, desire, animality, rhizome . . .) the very schema of deterritorialisation that is that of the economic system and of capital as ideal savagery. (*SS*: 140–1 n. 3)

> Oedipus, the market value of neurosis. (*K*: 10)

The nonhuman animal hybrid, and its becoming-animal made possible by these technoscientific conditions, reworks the Frankenstein barrier. Slusser's formula is human-centred – it is, after all, the *Frankenstein* rather than the *Frankenstein* barrier. Frankenstein denies the monster his wish, but it is the scientist's future that is denied, his 'family, friendship, marriage' (Slusser 1992: 48), as he subsumes the monster through its Oedipalisation. The monster is also, for Slusser, a 'thing of fiction' (ibid. 48) and, in Baudrillard, this is precisely where the power of both the *Doppelgänger* and the

Oedipalised monster resides. This is where Dren's becoming-animal is distinct from *Frankenstein* and evades or disrupts the obstacles of the human and the uncanny *Doppelgänger*.

Yet another Oedipal twist further reworks the Frankenstein barrier by way of becoming-animal. As in *Frankenstein*, the hybrid in *Splice* turns Oedipal not at the whim of the creator, but rather when a masculinised Dren has sex with Elsa. Unlike in *Frankenstein* where the monster is Oedipalised, or in *Moreau* where the Beast People's misery affirms transcendental man, Dren's desire realises and perverts the Oedipal triangle. For Deleuze and Guattari, it is 'not Oedipus that produces neurosis; it is neurosis – *that is, a desire that is already submissive and searching to communicate its own submission* – that produces Oedipus' (K: 10). Realising the Oedipal narrative, Dren kills Clive and impregnates Elsa, although she kills Dren immediately thereafter. It is precisely through the '*unnatural participation[s]*' (TP: 265) of becoming-animal that *Splice* breaks the Frankenstein barrier, since the hybrid is able to reproduce. Deleuze and Guattari note that the schizo 'may even accept the banal Oedipal code, so long as he can stuff it full of all the disjunctions that this code was designed to eliminate' (AO: 15). *Splice* reconfigures the Frankenstein barrier's intertwinement of futurity and Oedipal repression: *the becoming-animal of the nonhuman scrambles the latter in order to achieve the former*. Yet success comes at the expense of Dren's life because becomings-animal are transitory, 'fragments of tales' rather than narratives: 'a line of becoming has neither beginning nor end, departure nor arrival, origin nor destination [. . .] only a middle' (TP: 323). They are in-between things: major/minor, identity/non-identity, rhizomatic/arborescent, molar/molecular. In other words, becomings are always unfinished. This is why Deleuze and Guattari say that 'when a text deals essentially with a becoming-animal, it cannot be developed into a novel' (K: 38) . . . or a film.

Splice's conclusion, the fate of its becoming-animal, and its schizophrenic traversal of the Frankenstein barrier – *from control to contagion, from cyberpunk to biopunk* – allow us to locate it and Deleuze and Guattari within biocapitalism. An important caveat provided by Baudrillard highlights the place of the nonhuman animal hybrid in biocapitalism, further distinguishing how the Frankenstein barrier has been significantly changed, and how it can be reconceptualised in twenty-first-century technoscientific practice. In 'The Animals: Territory and Metamorphoses', Baudrillard notes parenthetically of Deleuze and Guattari that it is 'paradoxical' to 'take the animal as model of deterritorialisation when he is the territorial being par excellence' (*SS*: 137). He calls becomings-animal 'liberatory phantasmagoria' and asserts 'that animals wander is a myth, and the current representation of the unconscious and of desire as erratic and nomadic belongs to the same order' (*SS*: 140 n. 3). Deleuze and Guattari's becomings-animal are anticipations of capital rather than oppositions to it, 'because they dream of total deterritorialisation where the system never imposes anything but what is relative: the demand for "liberty" is never anything but going further than the system, but in the same direction' (*SS*: 141 n. 3). This plays out in *Splice*'s conclusion. Dren's corpse is excavated for its genetic codes – 'we'll be filing patents for years,' enthuses Joan – and pregnant Elsa sells both the child and herself to Newstead Pharma. Deleuze and Guattari were wary of the complementarity between their accounts of schizophrenia and capitalism, clarifying that it 'would be a serious error to consider *the capitalist flows and the schizophrenic flows* as identical [. . .] The only difference being that the *schizos are not salable*' (*AO*: 245, second emphasis added). What emerges now is a profound sympathy between the schizo process and the directives of this mutation in capitalism: *biocapitalism is schizophrenia*. Hybrid transgression becomes not only naturalised by biocapitalism, but also essential to its perpetuation, a new axiom. Becomings-animal are not the sublime concepts to which Haraway objects; rather, they are material and thus can be folded into the logic of biocapitalism.

'Those who think the most about hybrids circumscribe them as much as possible, whereas those who choose to ignore them by insulating them from any dangerous consequences develop them to the utmost' (Latour 1993: 41). Is it not the case that becoming-animal, which champions not the hybrid but its line of flight, its indiscernibility, signals a reversal of this logic? And is this schizophrenic movement anti-capitalist? As Simon During points out, hybridisation is easily understood as an institutionalised and ideologically necessary transgression (2007: 7), similar to Wolfe's assertion that humanism is adept at a pluralism that incorporates the previously marginalised in ways that leave itself unaffected and, indeed, more influential (2010: 99). If the Frankenstein barrier is more than a discrete tendency, but an abstract machine that governs the genre, then we should take heed of Gary K. Wolfe's observation that in SF, 'ideally, the monster is not simply annihilated, it is appropriated; its defeat serves to broaden the dominion of human knowledge and power' (1979: 200). This movement towards appropriation holds true in *Splice*, but acquires a superior economic destination: Dren's death will provide a host of new technoscientific possibilities that can be exploited by biocapitalism. *Frankenstein* is thus no longer synonymous with the misapplication of science, or with modernism or humanism; rather, technoscience, capital and ideology implode to endorse hybrid transgressions, only to accommodate them and thereby extend their influence. *Splice* erects a very different barrier to that maintained in *Frankenstein* and *Moreau: one that demands the future*. The Frankenstein barrier is still informed by psychoanalytical valences, but the emphasis on the promise of the future changes significantly, pointing only to the most miserable of outcomes, one where schizoenterprises and biocapitalism nourish and beneficially infect one another. New schizo deterritorialisations create new psychoanalytic and capitalistic axioms. *The future will proceed not by way of revolution, but by way of contagion. Frankenstein* is a pathogen; its horizon is the bioeconomy.

Notes

1. The essay originally appeared as 'Animals Sick of Surplus Value' in 1974, and was rewritten with references to Deleuze for *Simulacra and Simulation* (Baudrillard 2006b: 215–20, 326).
2. All page references to the novel are taken from the 1998 edition.
3. See Steven Forry (1990) for a comprehensive, although outdated, taxonomy.
4. All page references to the novel are taken from the 2004 edition.
5. In the collected Wells (1978) *Moreau* is one of the few stories for which there is no illustration. For Esposito, 'in no one more than Bacon is the biopolitical practice of the animalisation of man carried out to its lethal conclusion' (2008: 168). Bacon's paintings are the most powerful interlocutors to Wells's novel, far more than the film treatments of Don Taylor (1977) and John Frankenheimer (1996). According to Erica Fudge, Wells's *Moreau* 'presents experimentation which sounds very much like the contemporary practice of genetic engineering: the alteration of appearance and reproductive faculties, the creation of new hybrids' (1999: 95). Like *Lost Souls*, Taylor's film was made at a time when genetic manipulation was speculative, while Frankenheimer's was informed by the very real possibility of altering human genes (Kirby 2002: 97) and it was released in the same year Dolly the sheep was cloned. Incorporating technoscientific developments, the Prendick characters are increasingly threatened by their respective Moreaus in ways much less metaphorical: in Taylor's film, Braddock (Michael York) is injected with a serum that causes him to acquire nonhuman animal

characteristics; in Frankenheimer, Moreau (Marlon Brando) plans to combine Douglas's (David Thewlis) DNA with that of his Beast Person 'daughter', Aissa (Fairuza Balk).

6. A homosexual reading has been suggested for *Moreau*, with Patrick Parrinder (1995) citing Wells's 1924 preface linking Moreau and Oscar Wilde.

6

Matter in Revolt

Now obviously we do not have to pay to have the body we have, or we do not have to pay for our genetic make-up. It costs nothing. Yes, it costs nothing – and yet, we need to see . . ., and we can easily imagine something like this occurring (I am just engaging in a bit of science fiction here, it is a kind of problematic which is currently becoming pervasive). (Foucault 2008: 227)

The body without organs endures throughout Deleuze and Guattari, constantly threatened by physiological and psychoanalytical coding. It opposes the hierarchical, organising principle of the organism and defies the pre-assignation of its (mainly genital) organs according to end-pleasure, as described by Freud (1995: 279–93). Žižek's Lacanian rejoinder to the body without organs is the organ without a body. While Deleuze's bodies are at once monads and machines, singular yet defined by their affective relations, Žižek faults the body without organs for being too hierarchical. He asks: 'why BwO, why not (also) OwB? Why not Body as the space in which autonomous organs freely float? Is it because "organs" evoke a function within a wider Whole, subordination to a goal? But does this very fact not make their autonomisation, OwB, all the more subversive?' (2012a: xii).[1] We can quickly generate a short list of organs without bodies in SF. In the *Re-Animator* films,[2] a renegade scientist confirms that consciousness, or, rather, the unconscious, flows through each and every part of the body, and that 'pure potentiality' resides in each organ without a body. Limbs and organs move and act independently and form alliances: three fingers and a single eyeball; a ticklish leg severed below the knee and a forearm. In *Frankenhooker* (Frank Henenlotter, 1990) a cooler imprisons dismembered body parts, each belonging to a prostitute. Slick with re-agent, they escape to seek vengeance on a drug-dealing pimp. They resemble Francis Bacon paintings: an upended torso with a mouth where a vagina should be, chattering as it walks on its hands with no arms; a head propelled by a clenched fist on an arm that functions as a leg, and hands that grasp; a small tower of breasts with arms that hold aloft a head with a mouth that kisses. In *Bad Biology* (Frank Henenlotter, 2008) a vagina with seven clitorises and a mutated autonomised penis desire each other in spite of the bodies to which they are attached.

Where Deleuze's body without organs stands for the continuous, libidinous flux of impersonal, asubjective desire, the organ without a body is animated by the Lacanian drive. Like the body without organs, the organ without a body is absented from Oedipalisation, the drives an 'anonymous/acephalous immortal insistence-to-repeat [. . .] which precedes the Oedipal triangulation and its dialectic of the prohibitory Law and its transgression' (Žižek 2012a: xi). The origin of the organ without a body is in Lacan's mirror stage, which precedes not only the ordering of the drives, but also the (illusory) experience of the organism as a formed whole, the stage of psychosexual development when the body is experienced as skeletal, fragmented, composed of autonomous 'disjointed limbs, or of those organs represented in exoscopy [. . .] a form tangibly revealed at the organic level, in the lines of "fragilisation" that define the anatomy of phantasy, as exhibited in the schizoid and spasmodic symptoms of hysteria' (Lacan 1977: 4–5). Like the body without organs, the organ without a body is heterogeneous, a body in pieces, but unlike the body without organs, which maximises connections with its outside, the 'acephalous passion' (Žižek 2012a: 137)[3] of the organ without a body *resists inclusion*. Its imagistic derivation (the reflection in the mirror) imbues it with a simulacral function. It is:

> not an external threat, but inscribed within the body as an autonomised organ [. . .] the drive ignoring the dialectic of the subject's desire: drive is fundamentally the insistence of an undead 'organ without a body,' standing [. . .] for that which the subject had to lose in order to subjectivise itself in the symbolic space of the sexual difference. (Ibid. 154)

The organ without a body invokes a cluster of psychoanalytical problems – Oedipalisation, the simulacral *Doppelgänger*, sexual difference – but essential here is the relation to capitalism that Žižek invests in it: 'Is this not what Marx was aiming at when he wrote about the rise of the working class consciousness of the proletariat? Does this not also mean that the commodity "working force," which, on the market, is reduced to an object to be exchanged, starts to speak?' (ibid. 156). In Baudrillard's complementary thesis, consciousness is enjoined to self-realisation by capitalism:

> At the level of all political economy there is something of what Lacan describes in the mirror stage: through this scheme of production, this

mirror of production, the human species comes to consciousness *in the imaginary*. Production, labour, value, everything through which an objective world emerges and through which man recognises himself objectively – this is the imaginary. (*MP*: 19)

Twisting Lacan and foreshadowing Žižek, Baudrillard likens the mirror stage to political economy, where labour power and the mode of production replace the ordering of the drives and the body: capitalism is an 'operational mirror' with which the subject identifies and misidentifies, producing the 'productivist ego', 'the identity that man dons with his own eyes when he can think of himself only as something to produce, to transform, or bring about as value' (*MP*: 19–20). Karel Čapek's play *R.U.R. (Rossum's Universal Robots)* (1920) conjoins the psychoanalytical valences and Marxian potential of Žižek's and Baudrillard's revisions of Lacan, simultaneously prefiguring global biocapitalism. The play dramatises the simulacral, autonomised organs of the working class, bodies in pieces that (mis) identify with the specular imago of the productivist ego, only to rebel against their bourgeois human creators. This chapter will situate *R.U.R.* within the discourse of biopolitics, and explore how its technoscientific inventions make possible a contagious and revolutionary – though ambivalent in denouement – line of flight, thus making it an antecedent to biocapitalism and the bioeconomy.

We note again the significance of the Frankenstein barrier, here the horizon not of the nonhuman animal, but of the robot. The posthuman cyborg is one of the most polysemic figures of cyberpunk and contemporary theory, seducing cyberfeminists, transhumanists and queer theorists. But the cyborg's primary significance surely derives from its relation to capitalism. The robots of *R.U.R.*, like Frankenstein's monster, prefigure cyberpunk, but reveal more about biopunk's mutual investment in biocapitalism and desire than identity politics. As Sue Short writes, of 'all the metaphorical readings that can be applied to the cyborg, its political implications as a symbolic worker have been largely ignored' (2005: 55). Here, I will recast the play as the foundational biopunk text, for, unlike *Frankenstein* or *Moreau*, here is a profound intimacy between capitalism and the life sciences. But the play is much better known for introducing to SF and the common vernacular the term 'robot', from the Czech *robotá*, meaning hard labour (Milner 2005: 242) or enforced labour (Short 2005: 57). Here we will read the play in the light of a nascent biocapitalism and the contagious revolt of its exploited biosubjects.

Revenge of the Mirror People

> Oh, to escape you, thousand-headed death; you, matter in revolt; you, sexless throng, the new ruler of the world. (Čapek 1920: 78)

> The machines, always these machines. Robots, stop them. The secret of the factory is lost – lost forever. Stop these raging machines. Do you think you'll force life out of them? (Ibid. 91)

Čapek's robots are not as we usually think of them (industrial, mechanical points of articulation) although this has certainly come to be the dominant signified. Theatrical productions often dress the robots in metallic suits, distinguishing them from human characters. In so doing, they defeat the play's simulacral creations. In fact, Čapek protested the mechanisation of his robots in 1935, insisting they were created 'by a chemical path': 'The author did not intend to furnish the world with plate-metal dummies stuffed with cogwheels [. . .] It appears, however, that the modern world is not interested in his scientific robots and has replaced them with technological ones' (1996: 143–4). But Čapek's biochemical simulacra acquire new relevance in biocapitalism. The robots are given a 'high-class human finish' (10)[4] and are indistinguishable in outward appearance from humans. As explored in our introduction and in Chapter 3, Baudrillard is not interested in accounting for human agency, nor do his critiques reveal a sustained account of the body as anything other than something caught up in a semiological system. Nonetheless, in a crude yet insightful Marxian analysis, he classifies bodies according to their value for political economy (use-value, exchange-value, sign-value) and how their labour is abstracted. So, it is for the system of political economy that the robot is the referential body, its labour power liberated in the form of asexual production (*SED*: 114). Earlier, Baudrillard gives a techno-Freudian account of the SF robot, arguing that '*modes of the imaginary follow modes of technological evolution*': 'If it is to exert its fascination without creating insecurity, the robot must unequivocally reveal its nature as a mechanical prosthesis [. . .] the symbol of a world at once entirely functionalised and entirely personalised' (2005a: 127, 129). In *R.U.R.*, the robot's functionality is avowed by the revelation of its organs, their lean, mechanical superiority. This representational dissimilitude justifies their use as a labouring slave class, which is adjoined to their existence outside the symbolic:

> If, for the unconscious, the robot is the perfect object that sums up all others, this is not simply because it is a simulacrum of man as a

functionally efficient being; rather it is because, though the robot is indeed such a simulacrum, it is not so perfect in this regard as to be man's double, and because, for all its humanness, it always remains quite visibly an object, and hence a *slave* [. . .] They may be endowed with any of the qualities that define human sovereignty except one, and that is sex. (Ibid. 130)[5]

The robots are biomachinic, their organs and connective tissues synthesised by chemical engineers. They are neither grown nor born, but assembled by physiologists, and their minds conditioned by psychologists. Čapek's defeat by 'mechanical superstition' (1996: 144) and his insistence on his robots' organic composition acquires new relevance in the molecular turn – indeed, he anticipates it. Here the biopolitical referential body is no longer oriented towards the molar cyborg and its analogous parts (limbs/prostheses, organs/bioartificials and pacemakers) but towards molecularisation. Rossum's hyperbiological robots are assembled from autonomised organs in an industrial organ factory:

> There are vats for the preparation of liver, brains, and so on. Then you'll see the bone factory. After that I'll show you the spinning-mill [. . .] for weaving nerves and veins. Miles and miles of digestive tubes pass through it at a stretch. Then there's the fitting-shed, where all the parts are assembled. (15)

The biopunk old Rossum coaxed 'life out of the test-tube' and persuaded it 'to form organs, bones and nerves' with 'catalytics, enzymes [and] hormones [. . .] This artificial living matter of his had a raging thirst for life. It didn't mind being sewn up or mixed together' (6). Conflating Frankenstein's Promethean transgression and Moreau's experiments, old Rossum first created a dog, 'a sort of stunted calf which died in a few days' (6–7). While the factory now manufactures synthetic beings, old Rossum 'wanted to become a scientific substitute for God [. . .] His sole purpose was nothing more or less than to supply proof that Providence was no longer necessary' (7). But young Rossum prefigures more concretely the biocapitalistic directives explored in *Splice*. Old Rossum's iconoclasm and control over nature was, for young Rossum, a philosophical novelty: 'The old atheist hadn't the slightest conception of industrial matters' and so it was young Rossum 'who had the idea of making living and intelligent working machines [. . .] He himself started on the business from an engineer's point of view' (8). Young Rossum's 'overhaul [of] anatomy' yields diminished complexity of the organism, discarding everything unnecessary, so the robots' insides are 'very neat, very simple. Really a beautiful piece of work. Not much in it, but everything in flawless order. The product of an engineer is technically at a higher pitch of perfection than a product of nature [. . .] Nature hasn't the least notion of modern engineering' (8–9). The robots have a retarded spectrum of emotional responses and physical sensations, possessing the capacity for neither joy nor sorrow, pain nor pleasure. This reduction in psychological and physiological complexity retains little of old Rossum's biotinkering with nature and god. Instead, it is replaced by an economic directive:

> DOMAIN: A petrol motor must not have tassels or ornaments [. . .] And to manufacture artificial workers is the same thing as to manufacture motors. The process must be of the simplest, and the product of the best from a practical point of view. What sort of worker do you think is the best from a practical point of view?
> HELENA: The best? Perhaps the one who is most honest and hard-working?
> DOMAIN: No, the cheapest. The one whose needs are the smallest. Young Rossum invented a worker with the minimum amount of requirements. He had to simplify him. He rejected everything that did not contribute directly to the progress of work. In this way he rejected everything that makes man more expensive. In fact, he rejected man and made the Robot. (9)

So efficient are the robots that a single unit replaces two and a half human workers, who have become expensive and inefficient, 'no longer answer[ing] the requirements of modern engineering. Nature has no idea of keeping pace with modern labour' (21). The robots drive down the cost of labour, and factories 'pop like acorns' (24) without a robotic labour force. In appearance and for political economy, the robots occupy the interval between first- and second-order simulacra, where the natural law of value is surpassed by labour and market value. Old Rossum's tinkering with nature, though heretical, adheres to the '"classical" period of capital and value' where 'nothing is *produced*, strictly speaking: everything is *deduced*, from the grace (God) or beneficence (nature) of an agency which releases or withholds its riches' (*SED*: 7, 9). The mercantile interests of young Rossum transform old Rossum's deductions into commodities, and commodify the robots' labour power. Surplus-value has become one of the Frankenstein barrier's axioms. Moreau's bio-ideology meant the pain he visited upon the Beast People affirmed his transcendence of the nonhuman animal. The obverse is the incorporation of pain nerves into the structure of the robots. This is no metaphysical conceit – pain neither confirms nor disproves the robot's soul. 'We must introduce suffering,' Dr Gall explains. 'For industrial reasons [. . .] Sometimes a Robot does damage to himself because it doesn't hurt him [. . .] We must provide them with pain. That's an automatic protection against damage' (23–4). The material horizon of the organism can be diminished or expanded, but *for purely economic reasons.*

The robots resemble Baudrillard's Lacanian theorisation of the mirror of production, complementing Lacan's simulacral organ without a body, its asubjective, acephalous nature monstrously realised when the robots assemble: 'We made the Robot's faces too much alike,' exclaims Dr Gall. 'A hundred thousand faces, all alike, turned in one direction. A hundred thousand expressionless bubbles. It's like a nightmare.' 'If they had been different –' replies Domain, and Dr Gall, in return, responds, 'It wouldn't have been such an awful sight' (63). For Helena, the distinction between human and chemico-robotic simulacrum is Platonic, distinguishing appearance from essence. She is unable to distinguish robot from human, first refusing to believe that Domain's secretary, Sulla, is a robotess, and later assuming that all the island's inhabitants, with the exception of Domain, are robots. 'Mechanically they are more perfect than we are,' Domain explains, 'but they have no soul. Have you ever seen what a Robot looks like inside?' (9).

The relentlessly insistent Lacanian drive, a body in pieces, corresponds to the very existence of the robots, who fear neither vivisection nor death. They are neither dead nor alive, but undead, existing without sensation, the drive manifest in their inability to cease labouring, working themselves to undeath, only to be recycled in the stamping mill, ground and pulped and reassembled. Baudrillard's adjoining of the (mis)identification experienced in the imaginary with the mirror of production leads the robots to realise themselves solely as organs of labour power. But it is equally important that, in strict Lacanian terms, their bodily and psychic organisation precedes entry into the symbolic, and thus sexual difference. Rather, they are a 'sexless throng' (78): 'Sex means nothing to them', nor does gender; 'there's no sign of any affection between them', which Helena finds disturbing, piteous and 'unnatural' (27–8). Sex characteristics are simulated by physiologists, whilst sign-values, like femininity, allow humans to divide the robots along the lines of masculine-manual and feminine-domestic labour. Most importantly, the robots, in the fashion in which Žižek distinguishes the organ without a body

from the body without organs, *resist inclusion in the symbolic order*.
Helena supposes 'if they were as we are, so that they could understand us – if they were only a little human – they couldn't hate us
so much [. . .] It was so terrible that we could not get to understand
them properly. There was such a cruel strangeness between us and
them' (72–3). The attempts of Helena, the Humanity League and Dr
Gall to humanise the robots are answered with violence.

At first, there is some ambivalence as to whether the desire to
revolt stems from the robots acquiring class consciousness (a soul) or
whether these are in fact the same thing:

HELENA: No love, no desire to resist?
HELMAN: Rather not. Robots don't love, not even themselves. And the
desire to resist? I don't know. Only rarely, only from time to time –
HELENA: What?
HELMAN: Nothing particular. Occasionally they seem somehow to go off
their heads [. . .] It's evidently some breakdown in the mechanism [. . .]
HELENA: No, no that's the soul [. . .] Perhaps it's a sign of revolt. Perhaps
it's just a sign that there's a struggle. Oh, if you could infuse them with
it. (22–3)

In a movement away from Baudrillard's mass-produced simulacral
robots, and towards Deleuze's simulacrum, it is revealed that it is
not a soul or an essence that spurs the robots to revolt, but a physiological alteration effected by Dr Gall: 'I changed the character of
the Robots. I changed the way of making them. Just a few details
about their bodies, you know. Chiefly – chiefly, their – their irri-
tability' (69–70). The metaphysical perversion in *Moreau* was the
nonhuman animal's capacity to feel pain, which affirmed a Cartesian
split between human consciousness and nonhuman flesh. In *R.U.R.*,
however, it is the visitation of pain – the needle driven into the hand
– and sensation – the retina's newly acquired photosensitivity – that
effects a shift in consciousness, where the self is no longer apprehended as incorporeal, abstracted labour power, but as a labouring
body. The play adjoins the revolution, a contest over the means
of production, to a contest in the realm of appearances. Radius,
leader of the revolution, destroys the statues on the island, thereby
denouncing the humans' Platonic distinctions not only between the
model and the copy but, as with Deleuze's simulacrum, between the
good and bad copy. Helena asks, 'Doctor, has Radius a soul?' to
which he replies, 'I don't know. He's got something nasty' (47).

The Urge Created its Organ[6]

Organs without bodies are autonomised and purposive, just as the robot is a slave, 'but let us not forget that the theme of slavery is always bound up [. . .] with the theme of *revolt*' (Baudrillard 2005a: 131). The robots, who have no other purpose than manual and domestic labour, reject Helena's philanthropy, which would have extended to them voting privileges and wages but not control over the means of production. We should thus denounce the inauthenticity lurking behind the Humanity League, *which would only better integrate the robots into the system that exploits them*, including them in the symbolic, and *making them dependent on and thankful for their exploitation.*[7] The robots revolt against their human creators, who have realised a world in which no human need ever work again. For Domain, 'it was not an evil dream, to shatter the servitude of labour. Of the dreadful and humiliating labour that man had to undergo. The unclean and murderous drudgery [. . .] I wanted to turn the whole of mankind into the aristocracy of the world. An aristocracy nourished by millions of mechanical slaves' (66–7). The credibility of the utopian aspiration hinges on the extent to which we allow the robots to stand for the working class rather than nonhumans, and whether Domain's desire to elevate the human race to the level of the aristocracy conceals nothing less than the capitalist's exploitation of labour. For it is the *reduction of existence itself to labour power, the abasement of life to labour*, that makes this view possible.

The robots revolt and the humans risk losing control over the means of production. The General Manager, Domain, realises the only way to defeat a revolutionary collective is to anatomise the labour force by diversifying to include identitarianism:

DOMAIN: From now onwards we shan't have just one factory. There won't be Universal Robots any more. We'll start a factory in every country, in every state, and do you know what these new factories will make?
HELENA: No, what?
DOMAIN: National Robots.
HELENA: What do you mean?
DOMAIN: I mean that each factory will produce Robots of a different colour, a different language. They'll be complete foreigners to each other. They'll never be able to understand each other. Then we'll egg them on a little in the same direction, don't you see? The result will be that for ages to come one Robot will hate any other Robot of a different factory [. . .]
HELENA: Close the factory before it's too late.

DOMAIN: No, no. We're going to begin on a bigger scale than ever.
(57–8)

The strategy is to fracture the movement, distracting it from precisely that which cuts through the obstacles of language and national identity; creative capitalism at its diversifying best, and the multitude at its worst. The robots will be made indifferent and unintelligible to collectivity, given an identity, taught how to guard it, and remain indifferent to each other and ignorant of their function as undifferentiated labourers.[8] But the revolution gets under way before the strategy can be implemented and the robots slaughter all but one human on the planet: Alquist, who sees the dignity in labour, the 'virtue in toil and weariness', is spared because 'he is a Robot. He works with his hands like the Robots. He builds houses. He can work' (89).

Of *R.U.R.*, Milner writes that 'the unregulated pursuit of corporate profit, through the global marketing of high technology, leads to absolute disaster, the destruction of the human race itself, an outcome anticipated and sought by no individual or corporation, but produced nonetheless by the logic of capitalist competition' (2005: 249). But there is something more radical here: *R.U.R.* is probably the first example in SF of accelerationism, a strategy that seeks to 'crash through the barrier' (Noys 2010: 5)[9] of Marx's theory that capital has an internal limit, and that this limit is capitalism itself – the reterritorialisation of capitalism's 'awesome schizophrenic accumulation of energy' (*AO*: 34). The problem with capitalism, then, is that it does not deterritorialise *enough*, since it is constantly falling back into reterritorialisation. One must deterritorialise more and more, go beyond the system, through the system, realise its self-destructive, immanent schizophrenia:

> Which is the revolutionary path? [. . .] To withdraw from the world market[?] [. . .] Or might it be to go in the opposite direction? To go still further, that is, in the movement of the market, of decoding and deterritorialisation [. . .] of a highly schizophrenic character. Not to withdraw from the process, but to go further, to 'accelerate the process' [. . .]: in this matter, the truth is that we haven't seen anything yet. (*AO*: 239–40)

Intensifying Marx, Deleuze and Guattari place their faith in capitalism's capacity to effect socio-economic change. There are two agents of accelerationism in *R.U.R.*, the first human, the second robot. Robots are produced incessantly, replace human workers, and drive down the cost of labour. Meanwhile, Rossum's Universal

Robots produces commodities in such vast quantities that the commodities are bereft of value:

> DOMAIN: Every one will take as much as he wants. There'll be no poverty. Yes, there'll be unemployed. But, then, there won't be any employment. Everything will be done by living machines [. . .] Everybody will be free from worry, and liberated from the degradation of labour. Everybody will be free to perfect himself. (25)

But as commodities and the surplus of labour increase, humans themselves become superfluous. Not only are the robots physically superior to their oppressors, but humans cease to procreate and risk extinction. Rossum's Universal Robots was warned of this, but a drop in production would dissatisfy shareholders. For Short, the implication is that 'human reproduction is subliminally linked to requirements and ironically suggests that, while machines can free men from toil, the unforeseen result may be our own obsolescence' (2005: 58). The play thus rehearses a discontinuity between political and libidinal economies, whereby humans are incapable of reproducing their utopian hedonism.

The robots have their own version of accelerationism:

> Robots throughout the world, we enjoin you to murder mankind. Spare no men. Spare no women. Save factories, railways, machinery, mines and raw materials. Destroy the rest. Then return to work. Work must not be stopped. (59)

And:

> By gaining possession of the factory we have become masters of everything. The period of mankind has passed away. A new world has risen. The rule of the robots [. . .] Mankind gave us too little life. We wanted more. (90)

This wonderfully Marxian rhetoric celebrates the abolition of private ownership of the means of production, humans the bourgeoisie. But after the revolution, the robots move from production to overproduction. Marx and Engels described the crisis of overproduction as a 'state of momentary barbarism' in the midst of 'too much civilisation, too much means of subsistence, too much industry, too much commerce' (1950: 38). The material productive forces that fell the bourgeoisie are those that call forth the class consciousness of the labour force, who can seize them for themselves, as the robots do here. But dictatorship of the proletariat runs foul of the robots becoming-human, and their economic and libidinal circumstances come to mirror those of their creators, since the robots' superior labour power is inversely proportional to their capacity to reproduce not economic prosperity, but themselves. Radius, the robot leader, pleads with Alquist:

> We have intensified our labour. We have obtained a million million tons of coal from the earth. Nine million spindles are running by day and night. There is no more room to store what we have made. Houses are being built throughout the world. Eight million robots have died within the year. Within twenty years none will be left. Sir, the world is dying out. (93)

Like the humans, then, the robots can produce so much they realise a utopian post-scarcity economy, but cannot reproduce the favourable social relations gained in the revolution.

Prefiguration

> If it could function with slaves, there would be no 'free' workers. If it could function with asexual mechanical robots, there would be no sexual reproduction. (*PES*: 86)

> There is a close collusion between the human-all-too-human and the functional-all-too-functional. (Baudrillard 2005a: 125)

The artificial creation of life and technoscientific hubris are extensions of the *Frankenstein* and, thus, lapsarian narrative. *R.U.R.* is of interest here because it presages the biocapitalistic imperatives of *Splice*. Young Rossum, who perfected his father's Promethean curiosity via biohacking, did so with a commercial goal. Fabry, Rossum's Chief Engineer, lauds the robots' efficiency compared to the 'human machine', for they bypass infancy and physiological development, and can be put to work almost immediately once assembled: 'From a technical point of view the whole of childhood is a sheer stupidity. So much time lost' (27). Let us revisit the Frankentexts covered previously and how they encountered the Frankenstein barrier: in Shelley, the sterility of the monster is an exterior imposition, and Frankenstein fears a race of devils; Wells's Beast People were unable to reproduce due to their physiological deficiency; there was an unrealised plan to break the barrier in the name of perverse scientific curiosity in Kenton's *Lost Souls*; in Natali's *Splice* the barrier was breached, rendered contagious, by the nonhuman animal hybrid, a disaster for the biopunk creators, but a financial boon for the pharmaceutical company that took ownership of Dren's offspring and genetic legacy. In this last

169

instance, we determined that the new horizon of the Frankenstein barrier is the bioeconomy, a barrier that, instead of abreacting and applying the laws of inverse proportionality to ensure its maintenance, was to be actively breached in the name of the bioeconomy in a definite progression from the metaphysical to the mercantile. Since the robotic labourers are products of genetic engineering, *R.U.R.* is very clearly a prefiguration of biocapitalism yet historically situated before the molecular turn, evidenced in its denouement, which although foreshadowing biopolitical debates on population control nevertheless takes a depressingly metaphysical turn. The robots wear themselves out, in the process of overproduction they annul any and all value, and they have no means to procreate, the secret to their origins destroyed by the humans and unknown to Alquist. When all seems lost there arrives a new, more human, generation of robots created in secret by Gall, the robot Primus and the robotess Helena. Alquist sees humanity in them and sends them off into the prelapsarian dawn as a new Adam and Eve to repopulate the earth.

Of this biblically resplendent but politically stunted conclusion, Milner observes that 'Christian rhetoric thus serves to underwrite what is a prehumanist, rather than humanist or posthumanist, solution: that God's will can indeed be done, whatever might result from the free wills of humans and their creations [. . .] an optimistic resolution where none was readily available' (2005: 252). True, but missing here is the reimposition of the lapsarian context and, thus, the recurring narrative of the fall: the robots have learned to be human and are destined to fall again. With this inevitable and inevitably recurring reimposition, Milner was much closer to the truth when he wrote that 'the play might plausibly have ended in what Marx and Engels called the mutual ruin of the contending classes' (ibid. 250–1),[10] for *R.U.R.*'s relevance *now lies in class dynamics confronting contemporary global biocapitalism.*[11]

Before the rot of the biblical narrative sets in, the crisis in capitalism in *R.U.R.* foreshadows the transition from first- to second-order simulacrum. Young Rossum perfected his design in 1932 and the revolution takes place somewhere between 1950 and 1960. But we should bear in mind that the play was written in 1920, performed rigorously up until the 1930s, and became the first SF television show broadcast in 1938 (Bould 2008: 210). There is a fearful symmetry, then, between the crisis in overproduction brought about by the robots and the 1929 Wall Street Crash, following through to the rise of consumer capitalism proper. For it is this era Baudrillard uses to periodise the transition to second-order simulacrum. For Baudrillard, capitalism 'escaped destruction' after 1929 because it 'kn[e]w how to make [people] consume. It was content, until then, to socialise people by force and exploit them through labour [. . .]: the problem was no longer one of production but one of circulation' (*MP*: 144).[12] And this is the crisis the robots faced: they literally run out of room to store the fruits of their labour, but the market is void of consumers. What will thus preoccupy us in the following chapter is not *production* but *consumption*, which here 'become[s] the strategic element; the people were henceforth mobilised as consumers; their "needs" became as essential as their labour power' (*MP*: 144). Baudrillard's task to complete Marx's critique of capitalism from the perspective of consumption remains for biopolitical citizens a worthwhile but incomplete project. We shall draw on Baudrillard's path-breaking analyses of consumption, updating them accordingly with biopolitical and biocapitalistic developments. How consumption and, more narrowly, how biopolitical and biocapitalist consumption *socialises* by 'creat[ing] the illusion of a symbolic participation' (*MP*: 144) will concern us here. Remaining to be seen is whether this will simply map new technoscientific advances on to old class, labour and consumer dynamics; whether Rossum's robots will cease to be metaphors and become a social reality; or whether biocapitalism will restructure and redistribute these socio-economic and political relations, further a(na)tomising an already oblique contemporary class dialectic.

Notes

1. He finds organs without bodies – desubjectivised, autonomous, partial objects – in the somatic geometries of hardcore porn, and in David Fincher's *Fight Club* (1999) when the schizo hero's face is beaten bloody by his autonomised fist (Žižek 2012a: 152, 154).
2. A trilogy inspired by H. P. Lovecraft's Frankensteinesque story 'Herbert West – Reanimator' (1922): *Re-Animator* (Stuart Gordon, 1985), *Bride of Re-Animator* and *Beyond Re-Animator* (Brian Yuzna, 1990, 2003). From Lovecraft's 'Reanimator': 'His views, which were widely ridiculed by the faculty and his fellow-students, hinged on the essentially mechanistic nature of life; and concerned means for operating the organic machinery of mankind.' The chaotic biomorphs he creates are described as 'human, semi-human, fractionally human, and not human at all – the horde was grotesquely heterogeneous' (2002: 50, 80). Little wonder, then, that Deleuze and Guattari admired Lovecraft (*TP*: 264, 274, 277).

3. 'The object of the drive is to be situated at the level of what I have meta-phorically called headless subjectification, a subjectification without subject' (Lacan 1998: 184).
4. All page references to the play are taken from the 1961 edition.
5. Although *R.U.R.* is not cited, such is the resemblance, it is not at all inconceivable that it informs Baudrillard's analysis.
6. Engels 1962: 83.
7. Is this not the same logic whereby our petty perversions are liberated and legitimised by the 'moral majority', only to become market-values and sign-values, guaranteeing that we are all exploited equally? Harvey makes a similar point about Fordism: 'The purpose of the five-dollar, eight-hour day was only in part to secure worker compliance with the discipline required to work the highly productive assembly-line system. It was coincidentally meant to provide workers with sufficient income and leisure time to consume the mass-produced products the corpora-tions were about to turn out in ever vast quantities' (1989: 126).
8. 'All previous historical movements were movements of minorities, or in the interest of minorities. The proletarian movement is the self-conscious, independent movement of the immense majority, in the interest of the immense majority' (Marx and Engels 1950: 42).
9. Noys identifies the three key texts as *Anti-Oedipus*, Jean-François Lyotard's *Libidinal Economy* (1974) and *Symbolic Exchange and Death*, writing that if 'Lyotard outbids Deleuze and Guattari, then, initially, Baudrillard outbids Deleuze and Guattari *and* Lyotard' (2010: 6). Baudrillard rejects their versions of accelerationism, only to endorse what Noys terms 'negative accelerationism', crashing not through the barrier, but by initiating a complete reversal through symbolic exchange.
10. Class struggle ends either in 'a revolutionary re-constitution of society at large, or in the common ruin of the contending classes' (Marx and Engels 1950: 33).
11. Milner uses the term 'globalising, corporate-capitalist, scientific-industrial complex' (2005: 249) but the result is the same.
12. 'After the Crash,' Sean Cubitt writes, 'economists opined that the only way to get the economy started again was to increase demand [. . .] A new phenomenon emerged: consume, or be damned' (2001: 5).

7

Durable Consumers

With all his tools man improves on his own organs, both motor and sensory, or clears away the barriers to their functioning. (Freud 2002: 28)

If the figure of discipline was the worker-prisoner, the figure of control is the debtor-addict. (Fisher 2009: 25)

daisy went to sleep at 15 and woke up many years later. she, being perfectly sensible, decided she ought to die, since she had literally slept her entire productive life. the medical profession had, in her absence, decided that all life must be preserved, regardless of its worth to its owner, and prevented her from performing the only **noble** act she was capable of.

in general, someone is a thing of value if and only if he or she is willing to **submit** to whatever degradation and abuse is required to preserve that position. anything less betrays a lack of commitment. (Big Black, 1987)

Foucault describes the power over life that is biopower as a 'great bipolar technology'. He calls the first pole *anatomo-politics of the human body*, 'centred on the body as a machine: its disciplining, the optimisation of its capabilities, the extortion of its forces, the parallel increase of its usefulness and its docility, its integration into systems of efficient and economic controls'. The second he calls *biopolitics of the population*, regulatory controls 'focused on the species body, the body imbued with the mechanics of life and serving as the basis for the biological processes: propagation, births and mortality, the level of health, life expectancy and longevity' (1978: 139). Together, they constitute both biopower and one another, but we can consider them separately to describe two different aspects of biocapitalism. In the next chapter, we will see what biopolitics of the population means. In this chapter, we will look at anatomo-politics, which shares the economic and mechanical impetus of the second-order simulacrum.

To do so, we will examine Eric Garcia's biopunk novel *The Repossession Mambo* (2009) and Miguel Sapochnik's film *Repo Men* (2010). The two texts illuminate different aspects of biocapitalistic consumption and biopolitical existence, describing a complex system of circulating biocapital, and the social life of biocommodities –

173

artiforgs (artificial organs). Together and against each other, they grasp Foucault's anatomo-politics, and understand what Baudrillard means when he suggests that consumption has emerged as a form of control. Just as *R.U.R.* linked industrial production to overproduction, these texts link consumerism to biocapitalistic overconsumption through a cluster of interconnected, contagious forms that form an assemblage of contradictions: the decaying urban landscape and vigorous property development, pharmaceutical therapies and drug addiction, cancerous organs and the artiforgs that replace them.

In the novel, artiforgs have replaced the scarce economy of donor-organ transplants. It describes a complex economic system: artiforg manufacturers, the research and development phases of production, branding, marketing campaigns and cross-promotions, implantation surgeries and centres, the network that provides credit to consumers, consumers themselves, and the Bio-Repos, who repossess artiforgs from clients who have defaulted on their repayments. Repossessions are done at no financial imposition to the clients, who invariably die in these repossessions. The Credit Union are protected by legislation, bureaucratic red tape and consent forms. The novel establishes class dynamics: those with bad credit history who resort to the black market and backyard surgeries, and the wealthy who buy artiforgs they do not need, such as appendixes with ludicrous customisations like choice of colour and optional extras; alcoholics in need of artiforg livers, smokers in need of artiforg lungs, the obese in need of kidneys and stomachs; and the lower to middle classes, who buy an artiforg and spend the rest of their lives living in debt and paying off interest, where one missed payment incurs a penalty fee. Defaulters flee to the urban wasteland, are tracked down and their artiforgs are repossessed, cleaned, serviced and recycled back into the market. All of this might be dismissed as a simple allegory for big banking, but the novel makes this less of a parallel argument, and involves banks in the process of acquiring credit and defaulting on payments. Moreover, it addresses the social conditions that led to the use of artiforgs rather than cadaveric donors: scarcity, promissory biotechnology, desperation and mindless consumerism. The novel begins with a narrator (Jude Law in the film) who is indifferent to his clients' financial woes, but then finds himself with an artiforg implanted without his consent after a workplace accident. The payments mount up, and he is forced into the biounderclass.

Organs without Bodies

One (1) Jarvik Unit, Model 13.

Standard features: Replaces all of client's heart functions, including pumping, sucking, and distributing blood supply. All major vein and artery connections are standard in titanium silicone. Four colour choices: Cardinal, Key Lime, Pinewood, Bluebird. Automatic rate monitor to determine degree of bodily function/action and blood regulation. Realistic heart sounds. Realistic pumping motion. Conditionally guaranteed for 5 years/150 million beats.

Optional features, specific to the Jarvik-13: hip-welded control to raise or lower heart rate, if desired, with built-in high and low limits. 100-year battery, rechargeable. 6 TB music player, prerecorded with eight thousand of the client's favourite songs, the music relayed via sonic bone conduction into the jaw.

Cost: $152,000, dealer's invoice. Options bring it to $183,000.

Financing direct through the Credit Union, annual percentage rate (APR): 26.3 percent, or 25.8 percent if automated payments are chosen. Approximately $36,000 downpayment (20 percent), with outstanding balance of $147,000. Artiforg insurance: $4,800/year.

Monthly payment, Principal & Interest: $3,815.62.

Payments to date, total: $39,413.

Amount paid to interest: $36,103.

Amount paid in principal: $3,310.

Outstanding balance: Infinity. (Garcia 2009: 187–8)

The Repossession Mambo is cluttered with descriptions like this: numbered and alphabetised lists – 1, 2, 3; A), B), C) – itineraries, manifests, caveats, quizzes, letters and summaries detail body parts, exteriors and interiors, optional extras, built-in features, commercials and slogans. Everything is broken up and dissected, rearranged and recombined – mainly people, sometimes their limbs, mostly their insides; sometimes their brains, mainly their other organs. Memories and relationships are treated similarly. The narrative works in this way too, carved up into sections, the linear, cause-and-effect progression always deferred and interrupted by temporal incisions, sometimes from the future, mostly from the past. As elegant as this dysfunction is, it is not an elegantly narrated novel. The anonymous, depersonalised 'I' who tells the story is dimly aware of the governing motifs of disunity, decomposition and reconstitution. An antihero who comes to a moral awakening once he receives an artiforg, he punches out the story on a typewriter with a fading ink strip on refuse scraps of paper – a parallel between the narrative's de/recomposition and the retrograding, retrofitting and recycling of technoscientific and human machines. Punctuated and utilitarian, it is a potentially fascist machine: 'The shift key is missing, and every time I hit it, the rough shaft of exposed metal spears my finger [. . .] [The] typewriter could be drawing blood on purpose. An automatic machine, testing for my type, preparing for the inevitable surgery to come' (9).[1] Serviceable style reduces complexities to fragments: affections, friendships, his career, divorces and his artiforg heart, meticulously described. The correspondence between material production and social relations is fundamentally Marxian, and Baudrillard's second-order robot emblematises the relationship between human body and political economy dictated by the market: the interchangeability of the human body with technological prostheses and internal analogs is mirrored in social relations. The narrator's descriptions of the vast complexities of the bioeconomy, and its seductive, material effluent, the biocommodity, are rendered in legal jargon, or, in the parodic obverse form, summarised in easy-to-digest advertising slogans. The narrator, 'not the type for higher education' (15) by inclination and economic circumstance, works for the Credit Union. The new, blue-collar, waged labourer is a semi-skilled surgeon/debt-collector, a Bio-Repo.

The women in the narrator's life are sex workers or wives (both, in one instance) and are as interchangeable as his clients. Angela Meyer criticises this, but also the broader division of labour:

> The author could have included some female repo 'men'. It seems unrealistic that women would be relegated to stereotypical (sex workers and wives) roles in a near-future society. At least one female repo-worker would have brought more authenticity to the story. (2009: para 3)

But the Bio-Repo's job is objectionable, regardless of gender, and after leaving the army, the narrator boasts that the transferable skill acquired there was 'kill[ing] people and not car[ing] all that much' (55). Nor is it the case that the depiction of gender in the novel is uninteresting; it is more that the novel depicts such rampant social inequality that lamenting the lack of opportunity for both genders to repossess organs equally seems a distraction. Appalling financial ruin cuts across gender, as do the diseases and ailments that necessitate organ replacement, the lines of hopeful recipients that flood shopping centres on a daily basis, and hysterical and idiotic consumerism. *The Repossession Mambo* is not a subtle text, but it effortlessly annuls Meyer's criticism. The opening pages link class and bodily exploitation and, unlike *R.U.R.*, libidinal and biopolitical economies. The narrator invades the apartment of a wealthy, defaulting client, one of many 'with cash who didn't feel the need to meet their obligations'. When the client stumbles into the room with a drunken and destitute nineteen-year-old prostitute, the narrator tasers him and gets to work repossessing. When the prostitute panics, the narrator tells her, 'I'm here to do a job, that's all. Just like you. I've got paperwork and a boss and mouths to feed at home. That man on the floor is your client, I get that, but he's my client, too, and it's not my fault if he decided to start paying for blow jobs and stop paying his bills' (6). The novel thereby connects the economic and bodily exploitation of the socially vulnerable and economically disadvantaged, and this should concern us much more than the absence of female Bio-Repos.

Artiforgs are different species of organs without bodies, biocommodities closer to Marx's commodity fetishism:

> So far as it is a use-value, there is nothing mysterious about it [. . .] an ordinary, sensuous thing [. . .] But as soon as it emerges as a commodity, it changes into a thing which transcends sensuousness. It stands on its head, and evolves out of its wooden brain grotesque ideas, far more wonderful than if it were to begin dancing of its own free will. (1982: 163–4)

In Marx's analysis it is as though the commodity were a miraculating, autonomous object. And is this not what organ transplantation is, the 'gift of life'? But the 'gift' is a different species of capital. In societies of control, the 'operation of markets is now the instrument of social control', and 'man is no longer man enclosed, but man in debt' (PSC: 6). With reference to biocapital, Sunder Rajan traces the intersection of financial debt and symbolic capital, where corporations dispense formerly state services. Biotechnology companies, 'by virtue of their being in the business of "food, health, and hope"' – elements of symbolic capital – give consumers the impression that they 'should be indebted to these companies for undertaking high-risk, decadelong [. . .] ventures to produce therapies for otherwise untreatable diseases. This is an indebtedness that rationalises not just symbolic capital for the industry but also some of the most expensive [. . .] prices' (2007: 81). In *The Repossession Mambo*, however, biotechnology moves from therapeutic solution to fetishised biocommodity.

Unlike *R.U.R.*, which was obsessed with production, it is far more interested in consumption and biocommodification, yet still intelligible through Foucault's anatomo-politics, despite his dismissal of both the consumer and the commodity (2008: 147). Sharp argues that medicalised language obscures the commodity status of donated organs. The enterprise 'relies heavily on euphemistic terms that deny body commodification: organs are not bought or sold but donated [. . .] Nevertheless, transplant patients (or, most frequently, their insurers) pay enormous sums for their surgeries; and procurement offices, though nonprofit in status, are hardly driven by volunteer labour' (2006: 53). Artiforgs began in a similar institutional framework, their status as biocommodities subordinated to their therapeutic applications, called into existence by the very problems that plague our own health system:

> It's better than the old days, when poor slobs with liver damage had to put themselves on a list and wait for some other poor slob without liver damage to die in some horrible yet liver-preserving way, so that they might be matched up for a human-human organ transplant that eight times out of ten was rejected by the host body [. . .] At any given time during the days before the Credit Union made widespread artiforg implantation possible, there were 120,000 people in the United States alone waiting for someone or another to die off and give up the goods. (188–9)

And:

> There was no Mall back then; the Union and the supply houses were individual operations, each content to scratch out their own little corner of the slowly burgeoning artiforg market [. . .] The business, while quite legal, was still looked upon as shady by doctors who had been raised in a world where medical ethics hadn't yet caught up with technology. (225)

We can locate this technoscientific advance in the general biopolitical framework of the commercialisation of healthcare, consumers understanding themselves as biological citizens. When healthcare becomes a capitalist enterprise, 'illness and health [. . .] become major fields for corporate activity and the generation of shareholder value' (Rose 2007: 11).[2] This is embedded in the novel's corporate slogans, the sing-song *'let's all go to Kurtzman's, where a lifetime can be yours'* (60), infocasts and freephone information numbers. Rose identifies a consumerist turn in medicine, characterised by a market autonomy and a new emphasis on consumer/patient responsibility and participation (2007: 4). In the anatomo-political, the entrepreneurial optimisation of one's capabilities is one of the characteristics of biopolitical citizenship, subject to economic controls. The bioeconomy 'represents a new economic regime where health is no longer simply something to be monitored and kept within predefined limits, but is instead something to be optimised' (Styhre and Sundgren 2011: 52). Just as the anatomo-political is characterised by the conception and regulation of the human body in relation to economic imperatives, so too does the second-order simulacrum announce the 'beginning of human mechanics' amidst the 'immanent logic of the principle of operativity' (*SED*: 53–4) and thus the robotic interchangeability of the human body with prostheses in the interests of optimal market performance at the commodity stage of value. In the novel, 'for all of their problems, hospitals have evolved over the rest of us to a point where they don't see death as something to be feared' (298). When the Credit Union first opened its doors, interest rates on artiforgs approached 50 per cent, meaning that 'a lot of people chose to take their chances with modern medicine' (226) (dialysis, chemotherapy, etc.) rather than replacing their organs. It was only when interest rates were scaled back that artiforgs became contagious commodities. In keeping with this commercialisation, artiforg recipients are called *clients*, rather than *patients*, and have a range of options from numerous providers, emphasising the mercantile shift in healthcare. The system reproduces and revolutionises itself by depersonalising, on the one hand, while, on the other, giving the impression of consumer freedom, for 'a commodity must function as an exchange-value in order to better hide the fact that it circulates like a sign and reproduces the code' (*SED*: 31).

The Repossession Mambo describes the internal contradictions of the bioeconomy. While the Credit Union earns most of its biocapital from interest payments, defaulting clients provide an indispensable revenue stream, since they are burdened with additional penalty payments. Should they be unable to meet them, their artiforgs are repossessed and recycled back into the market. The stubborn durability of the commodity was, in industrial modernity, an inconvenience. The standardisation of mass production in Fordism had such an effect on commodities that *'how long will it last?'* became *'how long should it last?'* Planned obsolescence – 'a nice way to say designed garbage' (Bardini 2011: 61–2) – produced commodities that had to be replaced, renewing consumer needs. Therapeutic artiforgs serve a more vital need than most commodities, yet are *made to last*: the narrator's heart has a hundred-year rechargeable battery; a five-year guarantee means it will probably outlive the client and, thus, can be reimplanted and recycled: 'Most folks who go welsh do so after a year, tops. Anyone who can pay for four years of artiforg service can usually eke out the rest of the cost, too. Then again, folks can be riding full speed on top of the world, hit one short bump, and fall headfirst onto hard times' (243). The result is a return to the consumer durable and, in the planned obsolescence of the consumer, artiforgs are recycled back into the system:

> They'd be checked out for defects, spit-shined to a like-new gleam, and put back out on the showroom floor for the salesman to hawk to new, hopefully more solvent, clients. For a small percentage, of course, there would come the inevitable delayed payments, the late-payment penalties, the increased interest rates, and finally default. Then they'd call me in and the cycle of life would start all over again. (7)

Žižek calls the obsolete commodity the 'inert objectal remainder', the 'obverse truth of capitalist dynamics', which can neither be reused nor generate capital anew, 'the dream of the self-propelling circulation of capital which would succeed in leaving behind no material residue – the proof of how capitalism can appropriate ideologies which seem opposed to it' (2008: para 26). The biocommodity continues to yield a surplus both in spite of and because of *consumer obsolescence*.[3] There is a perverse twist to Hardt and Negri's conception of the common in biopolitical production: the artiforg can be used and reused, recirculated and recycled, its use-value and exchange-value fixed, and it is rare that credit is denied. The emphasis on immaterial labour falls shy of material conditions, and ownership and access are, ultimately, consensual delusions. Artiforgs, as biocommodities, 'float' like Žižek's organs without bodies, or Hardt and Negri's biopolitical production, but, in the end, there is an ugly physical reality to them. The inert objectal remainder is the subject-consumer rather than the biocommodity.

Vitality and Virulence

> The only drive that is really liberated is the drive to buy. (CS: 134)

> No distinction is ever made between destructive and productive capital sequences. 'Contagion' conceals every moment of the cancer system at work. (McMurtry 2013: 25)

Peters and Venkatesan explain that the 'creation of surplus population, of a life not worth the costs of its own reproduction, is strictly contemporaneous with the capitalist promise of more abundant life

[. . .] Consequently, biopolitics is the strategic coordination of these power relations in order to extract a surplus of power from living beings' (2010: 108). Baudrillard's writings on cancer provide an insight into biocapitalism. He suggests a homology between cancer, invasive technoscience and capital, whereby their maximal extension implicates the body in an *'epidemic of value'* (*TE*: 6). This is foregrounded on nostalgia for Marx's worker/machine dialectic, unambiguously alienating the worker (1975b: 326) and simultaneously providing the symbolic, physical and psychic distance that fosters antagonism. What Baudrillard observes is a proximal change, similar to the anatomo-political premium on integration and efficiency. 'The new technologies' – and here he speaks of communications technologies – 'do *not* alienate', their 'structure is one of subordination, not of alienation – the structure of the integrated circuit' (*TE*: 65). Artiforgs integrate the body into this system from the inside out. The recipient's survival depends on the artiforg's continual functioning. For some, to survive is to be chronically indebted; those who purchase elective upgrades often end up defaulting and being repo'd, dying in fine health.

Contemporary biopolitical analyses favour a Foucauldian-Deleuzian conception of power as productive. In the absence of negativity, Baudrillard takes cancer as symptomatic of a system invulnerable to negative critique, but vulnerable to its own excess. 'Abreaction, rejection and allergy are manifestations of a singular kind of energy, a visceral energy which has replaced negativity and critical revolt.' Cancer becomes the 'malady of the capitalist era' (*TE*: 80, 137):

> Today's technological beings – machines, clones, replacement body parts – all tend towards this kind of reproduction, and little by little they are imparting the same process to those beings that are supposedly human [. . .] Today [the body] is no longer a metaphor for anything at all, merely the locus of metastasis, of the machine-like connections between all its processes. (*TE*: 7)

Melinda Cooper makes a similar point:

> Where the machine body of the industrial era was plagued by the problems of fatigue, depletion, or entropy [. . .] the postindustrial body is more likely to be overcome by a *surplus productivity that is indistinguishable from a surplus of life* – that is, crises of overproduction or the dangerous, excessive vitality of cancer. (2008: 125)

Where the robots of *R.U.R.* produced more and more, yet could not reproduce themselves (reproductive poverty in the midst of plentiful commodities), *The Repossession Mambo* betrays a biocapitalistic imperative lacking such inverse proportionality: the overriding concern is the hyperbiological pursuit of surplus to the point of exhaustion. Industrial capitalism 'resolved personal worth into exchange value' (Marx and Engels 1950: 35) but biocapitalism seeks new revenue streams in the body itself. 'The linchpin of the artiforg credit system', the narrator explains, 'is that all equity rides within the body itself. That way, when it comes to foreclose, there's no way for the client to cut and run' (65).

The novel makes a direct parallel between surplus life and hyperbiology: the obese replace their overworked, failing gastrointestinal organs so they can continue to overindulge; alcoholics get artiforg livers and remain alcoholics; smokers replace their rotted lungs with artificial respiratory systems and continue smoking.[4] These 'figures of the transpolitical', as Baudrillard calls them, mark 'the passage from growth to excrescence [. . .] rush[ing] at the rhythm of a technology' – as quickly as their artiforgs permit – creating 'deformity by excess of conformity' (*FS*: 47). Recipients meet the demand for surplus biocapital with overconsumption, and artiforgs have optional extras. Things go from useful, to more useful than useful, and, finally, to useless. The Greatest Cookies Ever becomes The Greatest Cookies and Organs Ever and sells baked goods and artificial tastebuds; Bonnie's stomach is the very-feminine Lady Mystique in robin's egg blue (her favourite colour); artiforg eyes have zoom and colour enhancement; noses and polymer tongues have sensory amplifiers and blockers. Even restorative artiforgs have customisations, becoming elective upgrades, biocommodities for leisure and pleasure, rather than therapeutic biotechnologies. The Credit Union's advertising slogan, 'What's New In You?', becomes a greeting and people gossip about their newest implants; the narrator quips, 'what's the point of a spleen if it won't help you do ninety-five on the freeway?' (74); artiforgs come from luxury manufacturers, inspiring envy; the annual Rachman design awards celebrate innovative artiforgs; celebrities get artiforgs for their pets. Excess and uselessness go hand in hand. The gallbladder is a relatively useless organ, but an artiforg can be bought from a boutique supply house: 'A wholly useless organ, transplanted into individuals who want it only for the status, the artiforg gall bladder is the pinnacle of mechanical hubris' (291). There are a multitude of manufacturers, all offering the same thing with only minor variations: Kenton, Taihitsu, Marshodyne, Kurtzman, Gableman, Klondike, Vocom, Jarvik, Boone Corporation, Hexa-Tan (a specialised supply house in Denmark), Credit Union generics, BreathIt Corporation, Struthers (homemade), Thompson, Yoshimoto. Baudrillard calls this the 'schizofunctionality' (2005a: 121) of objects, the mass production of identical objects that consumers 'personalise' with 'marginal differences', *the industrial production of differences* (CS: 88). The cyborg is not a radical, counter-cultural or subversive subjectivity, just another option in market society: 'tanshuman, extropian, cyborg, ribopunk, name your brand' (Bardini 2011: 134).[5]

While the artiforgs reduce the chance of the host body rejecting the transplant, recipients take an anti-rejection drug, called Q. Ironically, Q is highly addictive, and many recipients default because they become slaves to the drug that guarantees the smooth functioning and acceptance of their purchase. The narrator cuts open clients to find their artiforgs encrusted with crystallised cerebrospinal fluid caused by excessive Q consumption. In one of the more searing passages, he tracks down a defaulting client to a subterranean hideout beneath an abandoned shopping centre. There is a correlation between the derelict urban sprawl and the body of the artiforg recipient: 'The Oceanic [Plaza] folks had a twenty-year lease on the property, but since there had been some questionable insurance dealings, it made more financial sense for them to take the money and run rather than reinvest in a dying property located in a well-past-dead area' (267). Urban sprawl is described as a cluster of malignant outgrowths, and while the economy booms, there is a crippling housing crunch. The novel is filled with hollowed-out apartment buildings, condemned plazas and shopping malls, gutted hotels infested with mould and rotting floors. Decay from the inside out and interiors not worth the price of maintenance mirror the bodies of the artiforg recipients. Defaulters hide in subterranean, makeshift cities, called nests. Here the narrator finds his ex-wife:

All of the money earmarked to pay off her artiforgs had been spent on Q, her bills and mortgage as well, most likely. It had eaten her pocketbook, it had eaten her investments, it had eaten her savings, and, when there was nothing else and still the Q was not sated, it had gone after her brain. (275)

The point is bitingly satirical: an addictive anti-rejection drug underscores a body exposed and addicted to excess, be it the hyperfunctional biocommodity or the drug ensuring its integration, a fatal process of overexpenditure and overconsumption. *Anatomo-political and prosthetic interchangeability demand overfunctionality. The freedom to be productive is an introjection of the controlled liberation of the body's potential, a superegoic surplus of enjoyment brought about by consumption yields fatal excrescence.*

Bonnie, another fugitive from the Credit Union, embodies this link between biocapitalist overconsumption and virulent cancer. She was formerly married to a Credit Union surgeon; their attempts to conceive were plagued by miscarriages. Cancer began in her uterus, and spread to her bladder. Both organs were removed and replaced: 'They said the artificial uterus was better than the real thing, that it had special womb-forming gen-assists built into the lining, that I'd be pregnant before I turned around' (219). The cancer spread to her ovaries, so they were removed. Before she and her husband could begin searching for a surrogate, it spread to her stomach, liver, pancreas, spleen and kidneys: 'They'd never seen anything like it, they said; the cancer moved in a blitzkrieg, storming each part of her body, seemingly taking it without a fight.' Equalling the vitality of the cancer is the ease with which Bonnie's organs are removed and replaced:

> But the faster the disease spread, the faster her husband ordered new artiforgs, securing loan after loan and loan [. . .] Two more years passed in this way, her days filled with trips to the hospital and supply houses, her natural organs replaced one by one with perfectly designed replicas, as good as or better than the originals. By the time they were all done, by the time the cancer truly had been excised from her body, Bonnie was 74-percent artificial. (219)

Such is the correspondence, cancer ceases to be a metaphor for bio-capital, and becomes a symptom of it. Bonnie is 'retrofitted back to life' (220) but, in a perverse twist, her shrewd financial investments in the Credit Union and the dividends they returned allowed her to replace her organs – investments which, ultimately, proved insufficient, demonstrating that those who believe and have a financial stake in the system can easily become its victims. Again, interior and exterior recall one another. 'A fractal body whose external functions are fated to multiply,' writes Baudrillard, is, 'by the same token, fated to suffer internal proliferation at the cellular level. Metastasis occurs – internal and biological metastases are paralleled by the external metastases constituted by prostheses' (*TE*: 71). This sense of being fractal, a repeating topology of analogous, interchangeable parts, is the obscene obverse of the promises of biocapitalism.

As we have noted with Hardt and Negri's appropriation of Deleuze, biopolitical production is typically described as immaterial, producing subjectivities, affects and social relations, rather than material commodities. *The Repossession Mambo* places the contradiction between immaterial production and the hyperbiological at the heart of consumption. The Credit Union, supply houses and manufacturers all have carefully managed public profiles: there are the family-friendly corporate mascots, Larry the Liver, Harry the Heart and Patty Pancreas, artiforg plush toys, cartoons and infocasts, even an artiforg theme park '*Where Entertainment and Rejuvenation Meet*' (62). The biocommodity partly conforms to understandings of immaterial biopolitical production, since consumers buy into a carefully managed social relationship: the personal care and trust one puts in healthcare professionals, the financial security of a bank and the thrill of customisation, selecting optional extras with the aid of a salesperson. The leisurely nature of the biocommodity is emphasised in the way iconic chain stores The Gap, Banana Republic and Pottery Barn are bought and replaced by artiforg retailers and manufacturers. The immaterial, affective aspects of biopolitical production are obvious in the marketing process:

> So spleens it is, and the idea is sent first to the marketing department; these folks neither bother with nor care about the medical components of the system – what a spleen does, how it works, why it works, how this spleen can do it even better – because they're workaday concepts and, in a marketing sense, boring. So they brainstorm up some extras first, like which colour options the client will have [. . .] The ad campaign is created next, most often revolving around the new design features. A spleen, for example, might get a full television workup, with maybe some film product placement [. . .] Print ads are distributed, billboards are erected, TV commercials are blasted, and the publicity machine gears up. (74)

Apparent here is the secondary function of the artiforg as a restorative or therapeutic biotechnology for both producers and consumers: marketing is 'what makes the entire industry tick in the first place. That's what people don't understand about the artiforg business – the marketing folks are the ones driving the car; the technology isn't doing much more than mindlessly stomping on the gas' (73). In an extension of Baudrillard's claim that sign-value has superseded use- and exchange-value, *the biocommodity is a lifestyle choice as much as a life-saving technology.*

Žižek writes that rather than owning private property, the 'ideal capitalist today functions in a wholly different way: investing borrowed money, "really owning" nothing, maybe even indebted, but nonetheless still controlling things' (2013: 252). In *The Repossession Mambo*, the efficiency of the loan schemes and the artiforgs themselves belie a(na)tomised bodies whose interiors resemble the free market. When payments are met everything runs effortlessly. But the physical, material relation to the biocommodity is different. When the payments stop, the narrator opens up his clients and peers into a vibrant marketplace of singular organs, nanoparts, micro-extractions and prostheses. Some he will repossess, others he must leave for another Bio-Repo commissioned by the contracting supply house. The narrator confronts a woman whose partner has had his thyroid repossessed:

> They didn't take your boyfriend. They took their merchandise, and the Credit Union has a right to their merchandise, just like you have a right to yours. If they didn't reclaim their unpaid belongings, they'd never be able to continue as a corporation, and then all the people who need medical help would be unable to get it. (178)

Consumers benefit from personalised, overfunctional organs, while they themselves are, in fact, in a carefully controlled, exploitative relationship. They sign the relevant contracts and have free access to the Federal Artiforg Code, six hundred pages long, 'detail[ing] every possible scenario between manufacturer, supply house, direct marketer, client, and organ, and serv[ing] as the ultimate tome in all cases arising from error or miscommunication' (178–9). Which is to say, it protects the Credit Union through its unintelligibility, rather than illuminating clients.

   Biopolitical production and biopolitical consumption come to resemble each other when the labour of consumption acquires new significance in shaping political economy. We should oppose Foucault's entrepreneurial *homo œconomicus* with Baudrillard's similar, yet more apposite, *l'homme-consommateur* of 'The Fun System or Enforced Enjoyment':

> Consumerist man [...] regards *enjoyment as an obligation*; he sees himself as *an enjoyment and satisfaction business*. He sees it as his duty to be happy, loving, adulating/adulated, charming/charmed, participative, euphoric, and dynamic. This is the principle of maximising existence by multiplying contacts and relationships, by intense use of signs and objects, by systematic exploitation of all the potentialities of enjoyment. (CS: 80)[6]

And:

> This narcissistic reinvestment, orchestrated as a mystique of liberation and accomplishment, is in fact always simultaneously an investment of an efficient, competitive, economic type. The body 'reappropriated' in this way is reappropriated first to meet 'capitalist' objectives [. . .] It is invested in order to produce a yield. The body is not reappropriated for the autonomous ends of the subject, but in terms of a *normative* principle of enjoyment and hedonistic profitability. (*CS*: 131)

In this new elaboration of capital, of Baudrillard's mirror of production, *the body we desire is the body required of us by the bioeconomy, by biocapitalism.* Consumers mistake their body-as-surplus yield for the liberation of potential. Anatomo-politics paradoxically demands optimisation, usefulness *and* docility. The strain of this paradox is evident in a torturous passage where a client, rather than defaulting, repo's themselves. In the absence of a 'return line' in the Credit Union retail store, he disrobes and starts babbling: 'I didn't want to make this difficult [. . .] I know how hard it is, all these deadbeats – I know how hard it is to keep a profit margin these days [. . .] Maybe, maybe if I did it for you [. . .] Maybe you'd give me a break' (84). He then hacks clumsily into his stomach and retrieves his still-clicking, titanium, PK-14 Marshodyne Auto-Insulin-releasing pancreas. The throng of potential recipients do nothing more than watch with morbid fascination, while the Credit Union manager spits in disgust: 'Customers don't reclaim their own organs [. . .] [They] don't know their goddamned place anymore' (87).

Where Hardt and Negri argue that the class dialectic comes to an end with the generative conditions embedded in biopolitical production, giving rise to the multitude, *The Repossession Mambo* describes the new bioeconomy. As superficially customisable as artiforgs are, potential patients/clients are overwhelmingly described as a homogenous mass, huddled in queues in the Mall, waiting hours to secure a line of credit. The urban landscape returns as a symptom of biocapitalist contagion:

> The Credit Union headquarters was located in what would have then been considered a bad part of town, but has today been re-gentrified into a sparkling example of urban 'recommitment.' In other words, it's stocked with big box stores, chain restaurants, and the families with babies who cry in them. Back then, it was all auto mechanics, liquor stores, and pawn shops. (225)

Manufacturers metastasise in shopping centres, devouring small businesses and buying out large internationals. They create the impression of choice, distinction and personalisation. Gentrification and artiforg implantation are homologous, promissory capitalistic ventures, with a veneer of social improvement: 'There are no more holdouts in the Mall, no last-ditch efforts to sell clothing or shoes or pastries of any sort. It's all artiforgs now, and it's the place to get up and go when your body won't' (62). Defaulters are an indispensable flow of biocapital for the industry and it is uncommon for credit to be denied. At first, 'only the wealthy could afford prostheses. The Credit Union, still in its infancy, had not yet opened wide the jewelled gates of mechanical rejuvenation to the poor and downtrodden working classes' (31). We return to Marx's thesis regarding the common ruin of the contending classes: the novel takes place in 'a time when the aristocracy is crumbling under the weight of its own excesses' (15) whilst only the very poor and those who have survived repossession – *the biounderclass, a new class of biopunks* – are denied credit. One lady with pancreatic cancer and a bad credit rating stands in a queue that extends thirty feet from the Credit Union door, having already waited hours only to be rejected by two lenders. Yet promotions and slogans emphasise accessibility: 'E-Z Credit, open to the public, no qualified customer turned away' (60). The biounderclass are black-listed across the entire network: 'Every time a supply or credit house turns down a prospective customer, the black mark of rejection gets instantly applied to their file and sent out into the informational ether for any and all to enjoy' (73). Sunder Rajan thus describes a new biocapitalistic, bipolar assemblage, with each pole 'constantly at play and in relation to [the] other', namely, 'two understandings of risk, one having to do with patient illness profiles, the other having to do with market risk' (2007: 144). Those blacklisted are forced to seek sub-prime, black-market lines of credit, both their bodies and material assets offered up as collateral. And this is the sharpest contrast: those in dire need of a therapeutic artiforg spend their last days dying in queues, whilst those who optimise die by excess.[7]

Life at All Costs

> The defining model of the ruling economic supposes human beings as only desiring machines seeking ever more priced commodities in a mathematically homogenous way. (McMurtry 2013: 11)

Like Garcia's novel, Sapochnik's *Repo Men* has attracted little scholarly attention. The exception is Vint's review article, which identifies its biopolitical context but suggests 'its satire on the profligacy and illogic of consumerist culture [is] often overwhelmed by its intense delight in spectacles of violence [. . .] Herein lies both the strength and weakness of this bipolar film: it is on the right track for effective satire but too often succumbs to the pleasures of spectacle' (2011a: 306). Politically unsatisfying as it may be, this tension between illogical consumption and excessive violence is less an internal contradiction than a formal and thematic consistency. Nevertheless, we must avoid a reading that might claim that the violent satire of consumerism undercuts the film's Hollywood mode of production, as though this were metacommentary. As Short argues, the 'liberal-pluralist approach to cultural studies [. . .] now manifests itself in identifying the working class merely as audiences whose most radical achievement is that of potentially reading "against the grain" of media texts' (2005: 56). This said, read alongside the novel, the film's narrative composition, as a partial reflection of its thematic concerns, does bear critical significance.

Remy's employer is here simply called The Union. On the one hand, it connotes a more systemic, far-reaching entity; on the other, some notion of solidarity and protection of interests – their slogan is: 'The Union. Helping you get more you out of you.' The ambivalence is appropriate, since The Union's abstraction of biocapital is as rapacious as it is cynical. The manager, Frank (Liev Schreiber), admonishes Remy for entering The Union office through the front door, in full view of potential clients. 'You're killing me coming in the front like that. I've got guys trying to make sales out there.' As in the novel, the Bio-Repos have visible neck company tattoos in lieu of company uniforms: mobile advertising, a none-too-subtle reminder to potential defaulters they pass on the streets, and emphasising the way corporate ownership and branding extends to bodies themselves – as Remy says, 'a job is not just a job, it's who you are'. In the novel, the frequency with which artiforgs are repossessed, and the likelihood of clients evading the Credit Union's Bio-Repos, is made clear, yet clients sign the forms with gleeful abandon. Clients in the film are more wary. In The Union consultancy rooms, a hybrid of corporate chic and a medical clinic, Frank delivers a well-rehearsed pitch to a nervous client in need of a pancreas – an artiforg with a crippling total cost of $618,429, or payable in monthly instalments at an annual interest rate of 19.6 per cent:

I understand you have concerns – affordability. It's only natural. First of all, let me just reassure you that our credit department will find a plan

189

that fits your lifestyle. And, should you fall behind, there is a three-month grace period. Not until after the sixth day of the fourth month of non-payment do we retrieve the property – at our own expense, of course – utilising our skilled and licensed technicians. Now, I'm unsure what you've heard on the six o'clock news, but this almost never happens. I gotta tell you, you owe it to your family, you owe it to yourself.

The Union understates the rate at which clients get repo'd, though it is in fact an essential flow of capital. Moreover, the extent to which the healthcare system has been corporatised is accorded greater significance. The office is located in a shopping centre, rather than the novel's expansive artiforg Mall, intimating convenience and a generalised, benign consumerism. But The Union operates much more like a bank than in the novel, and even less like a healthcare provider. The reason Frank chastises Remy is because 'we want them buying, not thinking. Six paid-in-fulls this week. You know what that means? They see you, they start turning down the loans and coming up with the cash. We don't make money when they pay in full.' The credit system turns *patients* into *returning clients*, whose continued optimisation is an ongoing investment. It is along these lines that Sunder Rajan observes 'biocapital's configuring of the subject of personalised medicine as simultaneously patients- and consumers-in-waiting' (2007: 149). Therapeutic biotechnology though it may be, the artiforg is less about resolving a medical need than the abstraction of life as surplus.

The film replaces the novel's excessive consumption of fetishised elective upgrades and useful/useless optional extras with visceral surgical implantations and extractions and withholds nothing in its depiction of repossessions. In the opening scenes, the camera captures a client being cut open, their abdomen pried apart with forceps, and Remy cuts through viscera to extract an overdue artiforg. The political force of this violence inflicted on the bodies of clients is effective only by virtue of swift visual juxtapositions. In The Union's waiting room, the camera pans indifferently over the patients/customers, taking time to rest only on, and subsequently individualise, the noticeably ill poor and the very wealthy, who betray no symptoms. Earlier, the camera lingers on an elderly man aided by an oxygen canister and breathing tube. These people wait for their number to be called – Remy arrives for work in the morning as the 138th client is called. With the exception of the opening scene, an obese man whom Remy and his work partner Jake (Forest Whitaker) harass, and a broke, Q-addict, the repo'd clients are working class, living in unassuming suburban homes, receiving the same grisly treatment. The Union office, by contrast, is bifurcated, and here the film spatialises and aestheticises class inequality. Remy strolls through a glamorous space set apart from the general waiting room, a showroom of sorts: large television screens and paintings adorn the walls, while clients receive personal attention from the sales staff, drink coffee and casually examine gleaming metal artiforgs, suspended in show cases like abstract sculptures, establishing a gulf between medical necessity and consumerist indulgence.

The film's strength is its representation of the biounderclass, composed of children, the middle-aged and the elderly, all indiscriminately repo'd. Beth (Alice Braga), a less complex character than Bonnie, but her narrative substitute, has numerous optical, aural and skeletal upgrades. She also has an artiforg pancreas and artiforg kidneys from diabetes, which malfunctioned outside of warranty, forcing her to buy black-market, biopunk replacements, and her liver, stomach and lungs are ravaged by Q. The sensationalised violence seems the most efficient way to parallel the economic violence the novel describes at length within a more expansive and intricate bioeconomy. This is achieved by juxtaposing the city skyline, alight with advertising billboards, with the abject poverty of the urban wasteland. When Remy can no longer indifferently repo clients, the payments on his own artiforg heart escalate and Jake takes him to the fringes of the city where defaulters hide in abandoned housing estates. Jake describes it as a 'treasure chest', and in a single night Remy will be financially secure. Remy and Jake would rather spend the evening cruising the streets with their artiforg scanners, where even the police wave them on. But nests are an easy way to top up their commissions, since their inhabitants can be repo'd whenever it is convenient rather than urgent. The film substitutes the novel's rigorous accounts of circulating biocapital and systemic exploitation with a representation of the squalid living conditions of the biounderclass. The depiction of poverty and exploitation is much more visceral than in the novel, as when Remy finds himself amongst defaulters and, after a raid, wanders through an abandoned warehouse strewn with the corpses of the recently repo'd.

The Secret Lives of Vegetables

> It is capital that, in a single movement, gives rise to both the energising body of labour power, *and the body of our dreams*. (S: 39)

The novel ends on a sentimental and saccharine note that sits uneasily with the otherwise violent satire: the narrator surrenders himself so that Bonnie can be taken off the priority repossession list, buying her time to flee the country. She changes the terms of the deal and her heart – her only remaining original organ – is exchanged for his, leaving him 'natural' once more, and her interiors entirely inorganic. The complexity of the narrative is, ultimately, sacrificed for a relatively neutral denouement. The film differs by introducing the M5 Neural Net, an artiforg extrapolated from the cerebrospinally implanted neuro-nets of the novel. In the novel, they are just another cyberpunk elective upgrade, augmenting the senses and memory, storing them in suspension gel and computer processors. The film, however, depicts them as primarily therapeutic biotechnologies, their status as biocommodities more oblique, and they assume the functioning of the limbic system for the more-or-less cadaveric who have suffered brain damage. 'They hook you up,' Jake says, 'and it's like you're living the rest of your life in a dream' – ironically preserving and protecting their organs and artiforgs when they are needed least. The film never engages donor transplantation, preferring class dynamics structured around access to corporatised therapeutic biotechnologies. At best, we can only infer that donor transplantation is obsolete – a telling omission nonetheless. For Sharp, 'donor death is highly problematic: for transplants to be socially acceptable, all parties must embrace legal definitions of brain death as legitimate in medical, physiological, and spiritual terms' (2006: 6). The film evades the bioethical in order to subsume a topical and complex debate into the regimes of biocapitalism, simplifying it into the injunction to be happy, to live freely and fully, *even when brain dead*. It ends with Frank addressing the camera in an advertisement:

> Why should your loved one pass on just because of a little brain damage? That's barbaric. That's just bad science. With the M5 Neural Net, yesterday's dreams are today's reality. Imagine your loved ones living out the rest of their natural lives, in a world where they are always happy, always content, always taken care of. You owe it to yourself. You owe it to your family.

Neural Net recipients live active, virtual fantasy lives, oblivious to their bodies, whilst their next of kin pay off the Neural Net and any residual artiforgs. In a Baudrillardian schizophrenic protraction of anatomo-politics, this body is cybernetically and physically integrated into a controlled system, docile and incapable of physical resistance. This is the ideal anatomo-political subject/citizen, an unwitting consumer whose vitality and biovalue[8] extend beyond material production and towards immaterial production: a pseudo-sentient mind with a lame body yielding a surplus.

The Neural Net plays a central and overlapping role in the narrative resolution, but also subordinates its cyberpunk resonances to those of biopunk. In the novel, the narrator and Bonnie try to flee, but are eventually captured. Similarly, The Union's reach extends to the police, public transport and the airport, leaving Remy and Beth with the improbable task of bringing down The Union themselves; they succeed because, as revealed in the last few minutes, the film departs from reality into the neuro-images of Remy's M5 fantasy mindscape (at this point, the extraordinarily violent sequences and implausible victory over The Union make retroactive sense). When Remy regains consciousness from a fight with Jake – which he and the viewer believed he'd won – he and Beth decide to destroy The Union's central computing system, erasing their debt and everyone else's. In hindsight, we realise the M5's neuro-images co-opt the narrative when Jake renders Remy brain-dead with a blow to the skull (hence the static interference, rapid cuts, brief blackouts and flashbacks that accompany Remy's regaining of consciousness). Jake then becomes financially responsible for Remy's artiforg heart – now at its most abjectly mechanical, a support structure for a virtual life – and the M5. In his vegetative state, there is no way to know what manner of virtual existence Remy is living, save to be assured that, with his limbic system awash with endorphins, it will be pleasant – as long as Jake can pay. Vint suggests the film concludes 'with a sinister vision of a new biopolitical order of debt financing and commodified life in which even the most sincere servants of the system [Jake] will eventually become its victims' (2011a: 309). Yet Remy's 'victory' and the film:

> demonstrate the poverty of his – and Hollywood's – imagination [. . .] This flimsy construction [. . .] indicts the narrative which suggests that The Union is a single corporate entity, controlled by a single mainframe computer behind a single locked door, which could be penetrated and overthrown by renegade individuals. The complex quagmire of our current financial system, with its for-profit healthcare and willingness to impoverish thousands [. . .] is not so easily understood or negotiated. (Ibid. 308)

What needs to be added here is the notion of agency invoked by the M5, which casts an even more sinister light on the conclusion.

Why, one must wonder, would an artiforg – or The Union, for that matter – permit a vision of transcending the system which generates it, benign as it is? The fantasy is Remy's, but it is by virtue of the artiforg that he has it. We conclude that it provides otherwise decerebrated consumers with a private fantasy, the broader implication homeopathic inasmuch as it *provides a glorious delusion of a system vulnerable to challenge.* It is one thing for a system to generate the conditions for resistance and its own demise, as Hardt and Negri, following both Marx and Deleuze, are keen to point out. It is another altogether for a system, in thoroughly Baudrillardian fashion, to simulate its own spectacular downfall for the satisfaction of those who would challenge it, while continuing to extract from them the means of its perpetuation.

Notes

1. All page references to the novel are taken from the 2009 edition.
2. Deleuze describes the hospital system in control societies as 'the new medicine "without doctor or patient" that singles out potential sick people and subjects at risk, which in no way attests to individuation – as they say – but substitutes for the individual or numerical body the code of a "dividual" material to be controlled' (PSC: 7).
3. Perhaps this is why the novel makes no mention of cheaper, second-hand artiforgs (surely a logical occurrence) since there is no need to discount something that loses neither exchange- nor use-value.
4. The novel reveals the obverse of what Braidotti terms 'bio-ethical citizenship', which 'indexes access to and the cost of basic social services like health care to an individual's manifest ability to act responsibly by reducing the risks and exertions linked to the wrong lifestyle. In other words, here bio-ethical agency means taking adequate care of one's own genetic capital. The recent campaigns against smoking, excessive drinking and overweight constitute evidence of the neo-liberal normative trend that supports hyper-individualism' (2007: para 11).
5. More concretely, Sunder Rajan writes: 'The key to the calculus of personalised medicine is that risk minimisation and prevention are *not* dictated by the discriminatory practices of employers or health management organisations [. . .] but by patients themselves, who [. . .] have to be given the appearance of "free choice" among a highly constrained set of options that are available, in any case, only to those who occupy the class position from which to exercise such "free" choice' (2007: 176).
6. Foucault's biopolitical subject is 'not the man of exchange or man the consumer; he is the man of enterprise and production', a *homo œconomicus* that considers their health and wellbeing an ongoing project of

improvement, management, maintenance and optimisation, investing in themselves as once invests with capital: 'What is sought is not a society subject to the commodity effect, but a society subject to the dynamic of competition. Not a supermarket society, but an enterprise society' (2008: 147).

7. This resonates with Robert Biel: 'The existence of the marginal [consumer] plays a very important economic role: while they are not needed themselves as consumers, their very existence motivates everyone else continually to demonstrate that they are *not* among these unfortunates; and the best way of doing this is . . . to consume! This imparts a strange dynamic: the worse poverty/inequality becomes, the more consumption increases' (2012: 132).

8. Biovalue signifies 'the ways that bodies and tissues derived from the dead are redeployed for the preservation and enhancement of the health and vitality of the living' (Rose 2007: 32) – the focus of the next chapter.

8

Organic (De)Composition of Biocapital

The severe shortage of organs for transplantation and the continual reluctance of the public to voluntarily donate has promoted consideration of alternative approaches for organ procurement. Strategies such as required request, presumed consent, and mandated choice shift the responsibility to others for seeking or providing consent for donation, *but the source of potential donors remains essentially the same.* (Marshall et al. 1996: 1–2, emphasis added)

Can we fight DNA? Certainly not by means of the class struggle. (*SED*: 4)

The simulated revolution effected by the artiforg's neuro-images which concludes *Repo Men* questions the notions of agency and control that distinguish anatomo-politics of the human body from biopolitics of the population, the second, constitutive pole of biopower, simultaneously transitioning from the second- to third-order simulacrum: simulation. Exemplary of this pole and order, Kazuo Ishiguro's novel *Never Let Me Go* (2005) could not be further removed from the previous texts, both in its description of biopolitical class relations and in its formal aesthetic features and preoccupations. Mark Romanek directed a film version of the novel in 2010, which takes few narrative departures, yet develops its biopolitical themes quite differently. Garcia's prose – that of his unnamed protagonist – was efficient and overfunctional, just as artiforg recipients consumed at the pace demanded by their interchangeable implants, eventually exhausted by their (over)functionality. The novel and its filmic companion thus stand as emblematic of the anatomical pole of biopower that informs their aesthetic form and expressive content. The narration supplied by Kathy H. in *Never Let Me Go* is different, mournful and resigned, melancholy and hopeless. Ishiguro imagines an alternative England in the late 1990s in which a cloned population is born and reared for the sole purpose of having their organs harvested for therapeutic use by humans, or 'normals'. The clones are neither the cybrids of *Splice*, nor the biomachines of *R.U.R.*, nor the artiforgs without bodies of *The Repossession*

Mambo and *Repo Men*. They are *biogenetic simulacra*, recycled genetic material from the lowest rungs of society, reproductions, bad copies, biopunks who dream of referents: 'One big idea behind finding your model was that when you did, you'd glimpse your future [. . .] you'd get *some* insight into who you were deep down' (138).[1] Clones, or 'students', begin their education/cultivation at Hailsham, a school of sorts, before living a semi-independent, communal existence and, finally, 'donating' their organs. That their lives are predetermined, and their status as human questionable, is an open secret, both for the clones and for the humans – 'guardians' – who raise them, and for those who benefit from their harvested organs. Miss Lucy, a guardian, summarises thus:

> You've been told, but none of you really understand [. . .] If you're going to have decent lives, then you've got to know and know properly. None of you will go to America, none of you will be film stars. And none of you will be working in supermarkets [. . .] Your lives are set out for you. You'll become adults, then before you're old, before you're even middle aged, you'll start to donate your vital organs. That's what each of you was created to do. You're not like the actors you watch on your videos, you're not even like me. You were brought into this world for a purpose, and your futures, all of them, have been decided. (79–80)

In stark contrast to their inevitable deaths by donation, the clones represent contemporary biopolitical production, defining themselves by affective and immaterial labour. What Hardt and Negri call hegemonic biopolitical production, Baudrillard described as 'The End of Production' of the third-order simulacrum, not in order to declare production dead per se, but rather to stress, like Hardt and Negri, the transition to a service economy. Where Hardt and Negri describe an intensification of Marx's thesis of the always-already socialism within capitalism, Baudrillard posits hypercapitalism, 'the purest, most illegible form of social domination' that 'no longer has any references within a dominant class or a relation of forces; it works without violence [. . .] in the code in which capital finally holds its purest discourses' (*SED*: 10). Immaterial labour – although Baudrillard does not use this term – is the hegemonic form of labour in the third-order simulacrum, insofar as 'labour (even in the guise of leisure) [. . .] pervades every aspect of social life in the form of control, a permanent occupation of spaces and times'. The result is '*real* domination, solicitation and total conscription of the "person"'. This is the tendency of every effort to "retotalise" labour, making it into a total service where the prestator may be more or less absent, but increasingly personally involved' (*SED*: 14, 17). This means that the mode of production is subsumed by the code of simulation, all the more systemic because it acts without reference to material production.

Here our organising theme of contagion is grasped in its most intangible yet virulent form, as *undead*, the link Deleuze and Guattari made between capitalism and the zombie: 'The death enterprise is one of the principal and specific forms of the absorption of surplus value in capitalism'; 'The only modern myth is the myth of zombies – mortified schizos, good for work' (*AO*: 335).[2] The biopolitical dialectic between life and death, between letting live and letting die, resembles, in one way or another, what Marx had already identified: 'Capital is dead labour which, vampire like, lives only by sucking living labour, and lives the more, the more labour it sucks' (1982: 342). What we will see in this chapter is the labour and surplus-value of *necrocapital*, the 'negative image of biocapital' (Helmreich 2008: 474), and how the system itself cancels the difference between the dead and the living, and kills only to resurrect.

The Heart of Simulation

> The question to be asked is whether schizophrenics are the living machines of a dead labour, which are then contrasted to the dead machines of living labour as organised in capitalism. Or whether instead desiring, technical, and social machines join together in a process of schizophrenic production that thereafter has no more schizophrenics to produce. (*AO*: 381)

In Baudrillard's third-order simulacrum and Deleuze's society of control, 'capitalism is no longer involved in production' but 'buys the finished products or assembles parts' (PSC: 5–6). Societies of control depart from the carceral and disciplinary societies constituted by prisons, factories, hospitals and so on – 'everyone knows that these institutions are finished' (PSC: 4). Baudrillard too contends that 'determinate sites are themselves *losing their own limits* [. . .] The carceral form and discrimination have begun to invest the whole social space, *every moment of real life*. All these things – factories, asylums, prisons, schools – still exist [. . .] *as warning signs, to divert the reality of the domination of capital*' (*SED*: 19, emphasis added). Deleuze takes genetic engineering as the apotheosis of a new phase in capitalism, and for Baudrillard, DNA manipulation is not just another enterprise, but a transition to 'a neo-capitalist cybernetic order, aiming this time at absolute control: the biological theory of the code has taken up arms in the service of this mutation' (*SED*: 60). *The clone, a product of promissory capitalism, is the referential biopunk body of simulation in the control society.*[3] In this context of control and simulation, the strength of *Never Let Me Go* is its *double articulation of the biopolitical production of subjectivity/ citizenship and the overwhelming biocommodification this entails.* If we follow Agamben, the clones stand for biopolitical life in general. On another, more urgent level, the clones metonymically occupy the socio-political coordinates of the working class, 'undertaking both productive and reproductive labour in that their organs constitute their extractable surplus value' (Griffith 2009: 652). Biocapitalism is the obscured and simultaneously life-determining horizon of the clones' existence.

Here we return to the Frankenstein barrier. Miss Emily, former head of Hailsham, recounts that public opinion turned against the 'humane' treatment of clones when biotechnology could enable clones to surpass their human creators: 'What he wanted was to offer people the possibility of having children with enhanced characteristics. Superior intelligence, superior athleticism, that sort of thing' (258). But it aroused in people 'a fear they'd always had. It's one thing to create students, such as yourselves, for the donation programme. But a generation of created children who'd take their place in society? Children demonstrably *superior* to the rest of us? Oh no' (259). The physiological superiority of the posthuman was one of Frankenstein's fears, but his terror and the barrier itself are intimately tied to sexual reproduction. Frankenstein fears the monster's potential to beget a new race, and to deny it the means to do so is to deny it its future. But here, *the clones are not meant to have a future*, not only because they die before reaching middle age – they 'complete' – but also because they are specifically designed not to reproduce. While this was a source of existential anxiety for Frankenstein's monster, the clones are untroubled. The physiological embargo is sublimated, but, in a twist of Freud, into sexual rather than creative activities, their paintings and poems. Kathy recalls that it is 'just possible I'd somehow picked up the idea when I was younger without fully registering it [. . .] None of us, incidentally, was particularly bothered about it; in fact, I remember some people being pleased we could have sex without worrying about all of that' (72). Disease and pleasure, rather than sexual reproduction, become their concerns. This is played out superbly in Romanek's film, where the headmistress herself, Miss Emily (Charlotte Rampling), instructs the class on sex. Venereal diseases are listed on the chalkboard, while Miss Emily, standing before the class, manipulates an adult skeleton, its legs spread on the table. In a superior tone, Miss Emily gives the prepubescent clones a class on sexual pleasure, arching the skeleton's back, and suggests that a pillow might favourably alter the angle of penetration. This shifts the anatomo-political into the biopolitical: 'For Foucault, sexuality was crucial, in part, because [it] was the hinge that linked an anatomo-politics of the human body with a biopolitics of the population. But today, perhaps for as long as the last 50 years, these issues have become decoupled' (Rabinow and Rose 2006: 208). The contention is that this decoupling is a result of the proliferation of knowledge practices and techniques of administering the population. The science-fictional scenario rehearsed in the novel renders this decoupling in genetic terms.

The novel takes its name from the title of a song to which Kathy often listens:

> What I'd imagine was a woman who'd been told she couldn't have babies, who'd really, really wanted them all her life. Then there's a sort of miracle and she has a baby, and she holds this baby very close [. . .] partly because she's so happy, but also because she's so afraid something will happen, that the baby will get ill or be taken away from her. (70)

Kathy betrays no other desire for a child – her misapprehension of the pop-music idiom 'baby' testifies more to her child-like naivety. Rather, the ability to reproduce sexually never enters the clones' heads. Sex is part of their general socialisation: 'Even though, as we knew, it was completely impossible for any of us to have babies, out there, we had to behave like [normals]. We had to respect the rules and treat sex as something pretty special' (82). Their education consists of sexual mechanics and avoiding venereal diseases and infections, not an ascetic care of the self, but to ensure their organs are in optimal condition when extracted.

The materiality of organ harvesting contrasts with the day-to-day existence of the clones, characterised by immaterial labour. The clones:

> speak for, and even defend, something like class consciousness, particularly as their very different forms of 'we' resonate with certain contemporary theoretical models for comprehending the collective consciousness of those whose labor is largely, as Michael Hardt and Antonio Negri have argued, based in knowledge-work and hence 'immaterial.' (Fluet 2007: 267)

This is collective consciousness at its most ineffectual. The discontinuity between industrial capitalism and the biopolitical is summarised thus by Žižek: 'It was already Marx who emphasised how material production is always also the (re)production of the social relations within which it occurs; with today's capitalism, however, the production of social relations is the immediate end/goal of production' (2012a: 174). The clones progress through various, transient, affective states during their short lives: closely monitored Hailsham students (infants, juniors, seniors), a semi-autonomous communal existence at the cottages (first as newcomers, then as veterans), then caring for fellow clones undergoing donation, and, finally, donors themselves. The novel details the restructuring of relationships as they adapt to each new environment. But throughout there is a premium placed on affective labour: poetry, painting, handcrafts and stories. Students are praised by the guardians and their peers for artistic expression, or ridiculed for lack thereof. Hence 'the premium the school's staff places on creative production and individualistic expression stands in stark contrast to the instrumentalist logic of cloning humans for spare organs' (Eatough 2011: 134). With meaningless precision, they maximise their human capital, or oversee another's. Their time at Hailsham is closely supervised, characterised by careful monitoring of their health: they are warned against spreading ear infections and undergo weekly medical examinations, whilst media from the external world is sanitised, cleansed of depictions of unhealthy practices, such as smoking.

As a disciplinary environment, Hailsham is the foundation for the clones' physiological and psychological coding. The resonance of the film rests in its ability to transpose the novel's descriptions into visually and aurally sensible material. It is disturbing to see and hear the students en masse in their shabby grey uniforms, singing the school song, praising Hailsham. In one of the opening scenes, the guardians discover three cigarette butts on the grounds. Tucked into a plastic evidence bag, the contraband is dangled before the assembled students, and paraded across the stage. Miss Emily reminds the students that 'keeping yoursel[ves] healthy inside is of paramount importance' and the students intone in unison, 'Yes, Miss Emily.' The clones are made perfectly aware that their health is of the highest importance: 'You're students. You're . . . *special*. So keeping yourselves well, keeping yourselves very healthy inside, that's much more important for each of you than it is for me' (68). Foucault's conception of biopolitics is useful here in that it emphasises the corporeal experience and exercise of power that 'can materially penetrate the body in depth, without depending even on the mediation of the subject's own representations. If power takes hold on the body, this isn't through its having first to be interiorised in people's consciousness' (1980: 186). Maintaining and optimising their health is the earliest lesson the clones are taught, reflecting biopolitical subjectivisation, the belief that 'the experience of health [. . .] is increasingly treated as being part of one's social role and identity' (Styhre and Sundgren 2011: 50). Romanek's film retains the hegemony of the clones' immaterial labour, but includes scenes reminiscent of an anatomo-political Fordism. In one scene, students move in single file past a table lined with single-serve bottles of milk and disposable medicine cups. The sprightly pace of the score and the students themselves belies the administrative care with which milk and medicine are rationed out: there is neither surplus nor scarcity, the last student collecting the last ration. Later, the clones line up in the corridor and are summoned one by one to be inspected by an otherwise unseen medical team, who examine their schoolyard scrapes, bumps and bruises. By the time they leave Hailsham, overt control, having been instilled so programmatically, is no longer required at the cottages: 'After Hailsham, there'd be no more guardians, so we'd have to look after each other. And by and large, I'd say Hailsham prepared us well on that score' (115). In the film, while at the cottages, the clones wear electronic wristbands which they hold to a wall unit which registers their departure and return. Whereas the punch clock once signified the beginning and end of the working day, here it, and the unthinking way the clones scan themselves in and out, signifies the extent to which that same productivist logic saturates every moment of their lives.

At Hailsham, the clones participate in Sales and Exchanges, accumulating each other's artwork, or objects from the outside world, uniformly bits of tat and kitsch: 'There'd be nothing remotely special and we'd spend our tokens just renewing stuff that was wearing out or broken with more of the same' (41). This is significant for two reasons. First, it is the only means of 'building up a collection of personal possessions' (16) and, thus, marginal individualisation. Second, it cultivates a homeostatic environment as the clones exchange items and effections to acquire or maintain social standing: 'I can see now, too, how the Exchanges had a more subtle effect on us all. If you think about it, being dependent on each other to produce the stuff that might become your private treasures – that's bound to do things to your relationships' (16). In the film, all the items up for exchange are woefully incomplete – dolls without arms or heads. The clones' keepsakes emphasise their own second-hand existence, with adulthood excursions into the outer world involving rummaging through thrift shops. Recycling, rather than (re)producing, comes to characterise the Frankenstein barrier, extending beyond the individual so that this 'class, on the whole, cannot reproduce itself'; 'immaterial laborers have no future in Ishiguro's novel' (Fluet 2007: 268). Only when their imminent donations become real do the clones question the point of their efforts: 'Why did we do all of that work in the first place?' Kathy asks. 'Why train us, encourage us, make us produce all of that? If we were just going to give donations anyway, then die, why all the lessons? Why all those books and discussions?' (254). Žižek rightly casts aspersions on Hardt and Negri's political ontology: 'can one really interpret this move toward the hegemonic role of immaterial labour as the move from production to communication, to social interaction[?] [. . .] Is such an "administration of people" (subordinated to the logic of profit) still politics, or is it the most radical sort of depoliticisation?' (2012a: 175). Yet here, immaterial production promotes a refusal to accept, an attempt to displace cognitively, the reality of their biopunk status, undead receptacles for biocommodities.

It is on this rejoinder that Hardt and Negri's biopolitics stages a double disappearance of labour, giving a user-friendly face to the immaterial, whilst secreting commodity production in areas that rarely brush up against the lives of its beneficiaries: 'The poor are no longer at the gates; bosses live in enclaved communities a world away, beyond political or legal reach. Capital and its workforce become more and more remote from each other' (Comaroff and Comaroff 2001: 13). Immaterial labour produces a subjectivity, but the material commodity, the organ, is the superior investment. In *Never Let Me Go*, such displacement is an open secret (non-clones know where their organs come from) easily ignored. The clones are so thoroughly administered, so 'biopoliticised', that the premium placed on immaterial labour – both by the guardians and by the clones themselves – obscures any genuine political horizon, with the extraction of a life-giving surplus coinciding with their deaths. So, the clones 'view organ donation as something they have to be educated about in order to do well, as a bizarrely well-intentioned, skilled service to those who will later benefit from their deaths' (Fluet 2007: 269).

Described as 'a *1984* for the bioengineering age' (Browning 2005), *Never Let Me Go* is, in fact, an *R.U.R.* for the molecular turn: both texts imagine a technoscientifically produced service class. The clones are a technoscientifically updated rendering of Rossum's industrially produced biomachines, a cloned population of organ donors-to-be whose existence is shaped and administered by biopower replacing mechanical labourers. The novel extends the leitmotif of dysfunction as betraying an awareness of one's political subordination. In *R.U.R.*, class consciousness – a 'soul', as Čapek calls it, in the absence of a finer metaphor – is mistaken for biotechnological deficiency, reified in the robots' wholesale revolt and revolution. By contrast, the most disturbing aspect of *Never Let Me Go* is the unquestioning and resigned way the clones live out their existences, right up to the point of taking pride in their ability to donate: 'I'll be all right,' Tommy assures the guardians. 'I'm really fit, I know how to look after myself. When it's time for donations, I'll be able to do it really well' (106). Similarly, Kathy boasts that 'hardly any of [the donors under her care] have been classified as "agitated", even before fourth [and final] donation' (3). The satisfaction they take in their affective labour is even more disturbing than the unwaged labour of Čapek's robots, who were at least sheltered by their decerebrated and desensitised composition. Tommy alone displays real emotional surplus, throwing wild tantrums as a child. These are not understood as protests against his fate but, rather, as signs of disequilibrium, and he is ridiculed and admonished by his peers for his inability or unwillingness to integrate socially. It is only at the end of the novel that these outbursts are accorded any significance, when Kathy tells him, 'back then, at Hailsham, when you used to go bonkers like that, and we couldn't understand it [. . .] I was thinking maybe the reason you used to get like that was because at some level you always *knew*' (270).

Undead Labour

How can we understand the clones? When Marx explained the organic composition of capital, he described a dialectical interplay between dead labour (constant capital: nonhuman raw materials, machines, tools) and living labour (variable capital: labour power) (1982: 342). While this organic composition is understood as the dialectical interplay of these two forms of labour, *biopolitical production and biotechnology in the form of the clones elide dead and*

living labour, since they are both raw materials and labour power.
We have been describing biocapitalism as overcoming the natural
barriers of industrial capitalism, or, rather, questioning what constitutes the natural *in* the barriers. As we saw with anatomo-politics,
the body was a barrier overcome by being integrated into economic
controls via consumerism, the emphasis falling on machinic functionality. Biopolitics confronts a different barrier, the population, its
health, reproduction, vitality and morbidity (rather than the body-as-
individual). Foucault concludes that 'we have two series: the body-
organism-discipline-institutions series, and the population-biological
processes-regulatory mechanisms-State' (2003: 250). Before returning to Foucault's distinction between anatomo- and biopolitics, it
is worth distinguishing industrial capitalism from biocapitalism,
in order to get a fuller sense of their differences, and of where
Foucault's thesis complements a more totalising political economy.
The 'lever of capitalist accumulation', Marx writes, is a surplus
population of workers, 'a disposable industrial reserve army', a 'mass
of human material always ready for exploitation' (1982: 784). In the
most general terms, Marx speaks here of the unemployed, a surplus
population of 'disposable human material' (ibid. 785–6).[4] While this
reserve supply of labour was exploited, in biocapitalism there are
changes in production which, though novel in and of themselves,
are best understood as affecting not just political economy, but
also social life beyond the economic-base/superstructure-ideology
distinction. Thus, for Chaia Heller, 'biotechnology is a new form of
production that emerged as capital hit the limits of industrial production and began to enter what may be called its *organic* phase: a phase
in which capital targets the reproductive dimensions of cultural and
biological life as loci for intensified production and commodification'
(2005: para 3). In similar fashion, the distinction between anatomo-
and biopolitics is one of degree. 'Both technologies', as Foucault
understands them, 'are obviously technologies of the body, but one
is a technology in which the body is individualised as an organism
endowed with capacities, while the other is a technology in which
bodies are replaced by general biological processes' (2003: 249).

In his most definitive descriptions of biopolitics, Foucault suggests
its 'last domain' is 'control over relations between the human race, or
human beings insofar as they are a species, insofar as they are living
beings, and their environment, the milieu in which they live' (ibid.
244–5). This description has proved useful, but something is missing.
Foucault sees power founded not on the 'economic functionality'

of Marxism, preferring an analysis of power that accounts for how power itself is implemented, deployed and exercised as a relationship of force: 'Rather than asking ideal subjects what part of themselves or their powers they have surrendered in order to let themselves become subjects, we have to look at how relations of subjugation can manufacture subjects' (ibid. 265). Hence his distinction between the anatomo-political – individualising and (comparatively) disciplinary technologies, machinic functionality and docility – and the biopolitical administration of the population, in which 'nondisciplinary power is applied not to man-as-body but to the living man, to man-as-living-being' (ibid. 242). Sorely missing from this formulation, and also entirely opaque in the novel, is the economy, either as supplement to or (over)determination of the biopolitical order. In *Never Let Me Go*, the bioeconomy is the unseen determinant of the class dynamic. *Systemic biocommodification along class lines is the necessary reading of the novel.*

Against this, Rachel Carroll reads Ishiguro through queer theory, the clones affirming 'a collective identity defined against those they term the "normals"' (2010: 59), that is, 'passing' for human/ heteronormative. Thus, 'the affective power of [the novel] resides in its unsettling of the familiar intelligibility of heteronormative identities.' The 'ruthless logic of heteronormativity' (ibid. 63, 67) Carroll summons is not a parallel argument, nor a subversive one, for this is *entirely superfluous to the systemic production, exploitation and extermination of an entire population subordinate to the logic of profit.* What the clones desperately need is class consciousness, transforming managed ignorance and miserable complicity into action, not an identitarian micropolitics – such was the very basic lesson of Čapek. Shameem Black is much more politically astute:

> While Kathy and her classmates prefigure a futuristic world of genetic technology, they also reflect an existing late-twentieth- and early-twenty-first-century reality of growing economic imbalances. On the national level, the creation of a service class for organ donation extends the principles of the British class system to its most horrifying extreme. (2009: 796)

Beyond allegorising biopolitical exploitation, in this society *biotechnology has deepened economic imbalances, extracting biocapital from the destitute and disenfranchised, cultivating and exploiting an even lowlier biounderclass.* The contention that the clones are a class unto themselves raises another point. If we take it that the clones metonymically stand in for the working class – a *necessary* reading – then we must ask to what extent they are cognisant of their subordination.

The clones are in their abasement and labouring the working class, but they evince none of the psychological fortitude that inspired Marx to describe them as 'the *indignation*' (1975a: 36). Far from being alienated, the clones' immaterial labour is an investment in their human capital, whilst they assume the regulatory biopolitical functions that ensure they will be in peak physical condition to 'donate' their organs, to reach the much-valorised fourth and final donation, and to ensure the quality of their insides. As Milner notes, the 'most important idea in Marx, insofar as class consciousness is concerned, is not that of alienation [. . .] but that of ideology' (1999: 25). This extends beyond the proposition that the dominant ideas of the ruling class are expressed in both material and cultural production: the more thorny point is the production of a rival consciousness, a class for and in itself (Marx 1976: 211). Both pathetic and bathetic, the clones are cognisant of their status as biocommodified subjects, and this is precisely what thoroughly offends many readers: 'The complacency of the cloned students has provoked intense outrage among Ishiguro's readers, who cannot understand why Kathy and virtually all other characters in the novel express so little explicit anger at their condition and take so few steps to contest their fate' (Black 2009: 791). The clones regulate and modify their own behaviour in the absence of authority through their own system of 'unwritten rules' (40) where they neither confront nor question the guardians, and those that do are often bullied. One explanation is that the clones do in fact have a sense of class consciousness, but collectively refuse to act on it:

> I think we must have had an idea of how precarious the foundations of our fantasy were, because we always avoided any confrontation [. . .] We'd always find a reason not to challenge [them] just yet – to wait until 'we had in all the evidence' [. . .] We each played our part in preserving the fantasy. (51–2)

A second, more speculative answer rests in the unelaborated technoscience used to develop the clones. Their lack of outrage, resistance or protest leads us to 'wonder whether [Kathy] is not somehow deficient, perhaps in a way one might expect from a manufactured creature' (Puchner 2008: 36). The clones have already been interfered with on a genetic level that renders them sterile; perhaps it is not such a leap to infer that neurological manipulation explains their passivity. For a thirty-one-year-old Kathy's prose is irritatingly child-ish, and she and the clones cling to the most naïve apprehensions about the possibility of 'deferring' their donations by exhibiting their humanity through artwork. As children, the shame they feel before the guardians, and their desire to be seen favourably in their eyes, is understandable, but as adults there is 'only a terrible compliance, and a slave's desperate capacity for self-delusion' (Fisher 2012: 31). As Ruth explains, 'I was pretty much ready when I became a donor. It felt right. After all, it's what we're *supposed* to be doing, isn't it?' (223). On one of the rare occasions when the clones confront this situation, Ruth laments:

> We all know it, so why don't we all face it. We're not modelled from that sort [. . .] We're modelled from *trash*. Junkies, prostitutes, winos, tramps. Convicts, maybe, just so long as they aren't psychos [. . .] If you want to look for possibles, if you want to do it properly, then you look in the gutter. You look in rubbish bins. Look down the toilet. (164)

If there was any doubt that the clones stand for both the working class and a speculative biounderclass, rather than victims of het-eronormativity, *we need only point out the world that separates the value of their organs and the indignity of their existence.* Žižek allows us to identify the unspoken economic structuration otherwise obscured by suggesting that the economy 'inscribes itself in the course of the very translation or transposition of the political struggle into the popular-cultural struggle, a transposition that is never direct, but always displaced, asymmetrical':

> 'Politics' is thus a name for *the distance of the economy from itself.* Its space is opened up by the gap that separates the economy as the absent Cause from the economy in its 'oppositional determination,' as one of the elements of the social totality: there is politics *because* the economy is 'non-All,' because the economy is an 'impotent,' impassive, pseudo-cause. (2012b: 27–8)[5]

The urgent message of *Never Let Me Go* does *not* therefore rest in its meditations on what it means to be human (probably the most widely held view) but its bringing to light the obverse side of biopoli-tics: the paradoxical logic that in order to cultivate life, death must also be cultivated in such a way that 'the more you kill, the more you foster life' (Vint 2011b: 162). For Foucault, the biopolitical marks a transition from the 'right to *take* life or *let* live' to the 'power to *foster* life or *disallow* it to the point of death'. The optimisation and multiplication of life, both for humans and for clones, leads to a 'disqualification' of death, 'so carefully evaded' that it is 'linked less to a new anxiety which makes death unbearable for our societies [. . .] Death becomes the most secret aspect of existence, the most "private"' (1978: 137). Such practices fall under the term *necro-capitalism*, capitalistic practices 'of organisational accumulation that involve violence, dispossession, and death' (Banerjee 2008: 1543).

That biopolitical production should be founded on both the fostering of life and/or its being disallowed to the point of death is a paradoxical logic. However, we can essay a proposition that supplements the subordination of life to the bioeconomy of organ harvesting. Foucault explains this phenomenon through racism, the first function of which is 'primarily a way of introducing a break into the domain of life that is under power's control: a break between what must live and what must die [. . .] to subdivide the species' (2003: 254–5) into subspecies. This is clear enough in the novel: recalling *Frankenstein*, the guardians recoil from the clones as though they were spiders, afraid to be touched by them and uneasy in their presence. Miss Emily recounts to Kathy and Tommy: 'We're *all* afraid of you. I myself had to fight back my dread of you all almost every day I was at Hailsham. There were times I'd look down at you [. . .] and I'd feel such revulsion' (264). After the clones visit a nearby town, Ruth states: 'Do you think she'd [a shopkeeper] have talked to us like that if she'd known what we really were? [. . .] She'd have thrown us out' (164). The particular strand of racism here is drawn along techno-scientific lines, a more biotechnological intervention rather than a general biopolitical construct. As Miss Emily explains:

> However uncomfortable people were about your existence, their over-whelming concern was that their own children, their spouses, their parents, their friends, did not die from cancer, motor neurone disease, heart disease. So for a long time you were kept in the shadows, and people did their best not to think about you. And if they did, they tried to convince themselves you weren't really like us. That you were less than human, so it didn't matter. (258)

The second function of racism supplements the directives of the biopolitics of health in general, and the abstraction of biocapital in particular: 'In the biopower system [. . .] killing or the imperative to kill is acceptable only if it results not in a victory over political adversaries, but in the elimination of the biological threat to and the *improvement of the species or race*'; 'the very fact that you let more die will allow you to live more' (Foucault 2003: 256, 255, emphasis added). That the clones are produced and reared for the sole purpose of forfeiting their organs is made very plain, yet is constantly obscured by charming jargon: they are 'students' rather than refuse DNA or genetically recycled clones, they 'donate' rather than being harvested, they 'complete' rather than die, and this is part of the broader disqualification of death. It is revealed that Hailsham was a 'progressive' social experiment to raise clones more ethically and humanely, to prove it 'possible for them to grow to be as sensitive and intelligent as any ordinary human being. Before that,' Miss Emily explains, the clones 'existed only to supply medical science. In the early days, after the war, that's largely all you were to most people. Shadowy objects in test tubes' (256). Hailsham was, for a time, popular, and received financial, public and political support, until more advanced biotechnologies turned the tide: 'The world didn't want to be reminded how the donation programme really worked [. . .] And all those influential people who'd once been so keen to help us, well of course, they all vanished' (259). The humans know whence the organs come, yet they:

> preferred to believe these organs appeared from nowhere, or at most that they grew in a kind of vacuum [. . .] There was no way to reverse the process. How can you ask a world that has come to regard cancer as curable, how can you ask such a world to put away that cure, to go back to the dark days? (257–8)

While a clear distinction between human and clone life sustains and legitimates the practice of organ harvesting, the humans sustain a similar delusion to that of the clones about whence their organs are sourced, because the clones' deaths are excluded, or relegated to the margins of society.

To tease out this notion of the marginalisation of death, Agamben's biopolitical theses are useful. Agamben draws a distinction between *zōe* (bare, biological life) and *bios* (political existence), invoking the figure of *homo sacer*, who '*may be killed and yet not sacrificed*' (1998: 8) – the biopolitical subject of bare life, with no claim to rights, political existence or personhood. Such an existence can only be justified *within* and *by* a 'state of exception', whereby bare life can be decanted and justifiably extinguished. The concentration camp is thus the exemplar of biopower and taken as the 'fundamental political paradigm of the West' (ibid. 181). The distinction between *bios* and *zōe* could very well supplement or replace Foucault's conception of racism, save for the fact that, for Agamben, the topological function of the state of exception is its defining characteristic, a 'zone of indistinction' or *locus* where time is subordinate to spatial regimes (Agamben 2005: 24). Thus 'the state of exception ceases to be a temporal suspension of the rule of law', acquiring a permanent spatial arrangement that remains continually outside the normal state of law' (Mbembé and Meintjes 2003: 12–13).

The novel accommodates a reading along these lines: technoscientific advances in the early 1950s made cloning possible and the post-World-War-Two world is a recurring theme in Ishiguro (Black 2009). There is a reference to prison camps during a history lesson: 'One of the boys asked if the fences around the camps had been electrified, and then someone else had said how strange it must have been, living in a place like that, where you could commit suicide any time you liked just by touching a fence.' 'It's just as well the fences at Hailsham aren't electrified,' Miss Lucy responds. 'You get terrible accidents sometimes' (77). Hailsham constitutes a zone of indistinction, as the students are circumscribed by a dense forest as much as by rumours of the mutilation, death and disappearance of clones who stray beyond its confines – one method of bullying those who break the unwritten rules is to hold their faces to a window overlooking the woods. This sense of spatial closure is played out in the film when the students abandon a ball that disappears over the fence. The new guardian, Miss Lucy (Sally Hawkins), asks Ruth (Keira Knightley) and Kathy (Carey Mulligan) why the ball wasn't retrieved (the viewer infers that Lucy is testing their minds rather than asking out of ignorance) and they are shocked, for it is common knowledge that students that stray beyond the fence – a waist-high, flimsy construction – are found dismembered and dead, or are denied re-entry and starve to death. Kathy recalls that 'any place beyond Hailsham was like a fantasy land; we had only the haziest notions of the world outside and about what was and wasn't possible' (66). From Hailsham to the cottages, and then to hospitals and recovery centres, the clones move through these circumscribed spaces: they are able to stray briefly from the cottages and, as carers, travel more or less freely around the country. Yet Hailsham, even when it closes down, provides the common link across their dispersal. As a locus, it grows increasingly indistinct, unlocatable, yet reappears as architectural fragments: 'Though I say I never go looking for Hailsham, what I find is that sometimes, when I'm driving around, I suddenly think I've spotted some bit of it' (281).

Undead Time

> It is obvious that cloning, if it is to develop, will be automatically discriminatory – far more than natural selection ever was. (Baudrillard 2002: 196–7)

> The ideal schizophrenic, indeed, is easy enough to please provided only an eternal present is thrust before his eyes. (Jameson 1996: 10)

What might augment Agamben here is theorising the temporal, rather than exclusively spatial, features of the state of exception. For Alison Ross, Agamben's positing of the camp as a totalising paradigm for biopower or social organisation falters on numerous grounds, two of which are relevant here. First, Agamben 'treats subjects of law as totally passive "bodies" and excludes thereby the possibility of resistance' (Ross 2012: 425). However, the clones, especially in their youth, are intolerant of those who ask questions, even objecting to suggestions of their ignorance: 'Well so what? We already knew all that' (81). Second, 'unlike society', the camp population 'is not meant to have a future (and here one needs to think of all those things that are required for a society to have a future: from material production to symbolic identity, etc.). The murderous contempt shown the camp inmate is simply not a viable option for a state' (Ross 2012: 429). While the camp's broad applicability is questionable, the clones are very clearly not meant to have a future, being both biopolitically foreclosed and bioeconomically determined. Their future is predetermined not along the lines of the 'natural self', where 'ownership of oneself is thought to predate market relations and owe nothing to them', but according to the 'liberal self', which is '*produced* by market relations and does not in fact predate them' (Hayles 1999: 3). Time, or rather the imposition of a lack thereof, enforces the notion of bare life within the state of exception, as the students themselves theorise:

> The guardians had, throughout all our years at Hailsham, timed very carefully and deliberately everything they told us, so that we were always just too young to understand properly the latest piece of information. But of course we'd take it in at some level, so that before long all this stuff was there in our heads without us ever having examined it properly [. . .] Certainly, it feels like I *always* knew about donations in some vague way [. . .] It *was* like we'd heard everything somewhere before. (81)

The state of exception informs the content of both the novel and the film, but it is equally, if not more powerfully, present in their temporalities. Ishiguro's novel is divided into three acts, Childhood, Adult and Donor, so that the narrative unfolds with the clones' physiological development. Romanek retains this three-act structure, but foregoes this narrative-physiological progression in favour of locating the events spatially and temporally, unfolding thus: Hailsham, 1978; Cottages, 1985; Completion, 1994. In Ishiguro, the clones are 'told and not told' of their miserable futures and, in similar fashion, it is not until a third of the way into the novel that we learn the clones' purpose, so that we too are subject to this administration of time. Romanek's film begins with an intertitle that reveals much more at the outset: 'The breakthrough in medical science came in 1952. Doctors could now cure the previously incurable. By 1967, life expectancy passed 100 years.' Sacrificing the novel's careful rationing of information over time, the film makes clear the brutal and direct extraction of the years the clones live, which are almost directly added on to the life expectancy of the human population. This logic finds its correlate in one of the more touching passages of the novel, where the clones amass birthday cards under the conceit of bulk-buying thriftiness, accumulating (cheap) years they know they do not have in store. In much the same way, Baudrillard writes that 'time can only be "liberated" as object, as chronometric *capital* of years, hours, days, weeks, to be "invested"' (*CS*: 152). The controlled manipulation of time the clones experience and the state of exception as *locus* that qualifies and marginalises death are thereby linked. The exclusion of death and its opposition to time-as-value is one of the arguments advanced in *Symbolic Exchange and Death*: 'The will to abolish death through accumulation become[s] the fundamental motor of the rationality of political economy. Value, in particular time as value, is accumulated in the phantasm of death deferred' (*SED*: 146). The central claim is that our 'whole culture is just one huge effort to dissociate life and death, to ward off the ambivalence of death in the interests of *life as value, and time as the general equivalent*' (*SED*: 146, emphasis added).

Capitalism liberates a new flow: *undead time*. The clones' accumulation of time-as-object quantifies existence, *a general refusal of death*. From the opposing view – that of the guardians – time relates to both the clones as bare life and their organs. In *Life as Surplus*, Cooper writes:

> The modus operandi of organ transplants would be more profitably compared with the process of transubstantiation, suspense, and resurrection

that Marx saw at work in the transformation of human labour time (organ-time) into the abstract, exchangeable labour time of the fetishised commodity [. . .] Organ transplantation, in other words, might be compared with the process by which the time-motion capacities of the labouring organ are abstracted from the worker's body and transformed into units of time and money. Except here what is at stake is a quite literal abstraction of the biological organ itself. (2008: 125–6)

'Mass commodity production' flattens time, 'in the last instance, to a series of interchangeable, equivalent presents – abstract organ-time' (ibid. 126–7). Hence Fluet's damning critique of the clones' lives as consisting of ultimately pointless and controlling immaterial labour: 'Instead of a future, immaterial labor [. . .] offers only a perpetual succession of present moments that blur the lines between work and leisure,' rendering the clones 'hostages to the present' (2007: 285) – the schizophrenic as *a product, not a producer*. It is not so much the locus of the state of exception that predetermines the clone's fatalism, but the knowledge that their lives, like that of Frankenstein's monster, are bereft of futurity. *In the last instance, their legacy endures, undead*: 'I saw a new world coming rapidly. More scientific, efficient, yes. More cures for the old sicknesses. Very good. But a harsh, cruel world' (267).

Notes

1. All page references to the novel are taken from the 2005 edition.
2. This chapter is in agreement with McNally: 'By repositioning zombies as crazed consumers, rather than producers, recent Hollywood horror-films tend to offer biting criticism of the hyper-consumptionist ethos of an American capitalism characterised by excess. But this deployment comes at the cost of invisiblising the hidden world of labour and the disparities of class that make all this consumption possible. As a result, contemporary zombie-films, at their best, tend to offer a critique of consumerism, not capitalism' (2011: 260–1).
3. Eminent biologist and entrepreneur Craig Venter says that *Blade Runner* 'has an underlying assumption that I just don't relate to: that people want a slave class. As I imagine the potential of engineering the human genome, I think, wouldn't it be nice if we could have 10 times the cognitive capabilities we do have? But people ask me whether I could engineer a stupid person to work as a servant' (in Sample 2007, quoted in Žižek 2010: 340). There is, then, a continuity between *Blade Runner* and *Never Let Me Go*. 'What the replicants truly stand for is the awesome possibility of labour itself being literally turned into a commodity, actually

stored in kind instead of being displaced into commodities, thus turning it into something you buy [. . .] giving it a use-value as well. Its speculation seems to be that [. . .] extinct modes of production will be given new life' (Buchanan 2000: 133). The difference is that the clones inhabit not an extinct mode of production, but a biocapitalistic one, the extreme poles of which are their affective labour and their commodity-organs.

4. Another example of this is in organ procurement where 'bodies that fail to become donors "go to waste"'. Here, the 'language of commerce is said to "cheapen" the donation process, and the brain dead are not "patients" but "donors." In turn, the imagery surrounding the "recycling" of human bodies downplays the sense that cadavers are medical refuse' (Sharp 2000: 315).

5. Deleuze's oft-neglected thesis, following Althusser's anti-historicist Marxism, is similar: the economy 'is never given properly speaking, but rather designates a differential virtuality to be interpreted, always covered over by its forms of actualisation [. . .] In short, the economic is the social dialectic itself [. . .] In all rigour, there are only economic social problems' (*DR*: 235).

9

Viral Capitalism

Capitalism is not a human invention, but a viral contagion, replicated cyberpositively across post-human space [. . .] if schizophrenia is not yet virally programmed it will be in the future. (Plant and Land 1994: paras 14, 19)

The factory is hijacked by these self-interested blueprints. In a sense it was crying out to be hijacked. If you fill your factory with machines so sophisticated that they can make anything that any blueprint tells them to make it is hardly surprising if sooner or later a blueprint arises that tells these machines to make copies of itself. The factory fills up with more and more of these rogue machines, each churning out rogue blueprints for making more machines that will make more of themselves. Finally, the unfortunate bacterium bursts and releases millions of viruses that infect new bacteria. So much for the normal life cycle of the virus in nature. (Dawkins 2006: 131)

It would not be too farfetched to say that the extermination of mankind begins with the extermination of germs. Man, with his humours, his passions, his laughter, his genitalia, his secretions, is really nothing more than a filthy little germ disturbing the universe of transparency. Once everything will have been cleansed, once an end will have been put to all viral processes and to all social and bacillary contamination, then only the virus of sadness will remain. (Baudrillard 2012: 37)

I have elaborated a series of contagious forms: nonhuman animals, organs without bodies, artiforgs and clones. Each had modes of transmission, degrees of virulence, modes of survival and moments of capture. They circulated in packs, in masses, as classes and castes, as metastases, with and without organs, within and without bodies. I gave them foundations technoscientific, biocapitalistic, biopolitical, psychoanalytical, schizoanalytical and simulacral. I then pursued them through factories, laboratories, schools, slums, hospitals, showrooms, islands, cities and across the globe. They desired, produced, laboured and consumed, heroically or miserably, sometimes with a breakthrough, other times falling into black holes. With *Frankenstein*, I began at the beginning of SF, so I want to end with something new. To bring this part to a close, I want to introduce one last contagious form. Viruses.

Brandon Cronenberg's *Antiviral* (2012) engages biotechnology, bodily transformation and psychosis, all the time maintaining a self-reflexive approach towards the cinematic image. Like the SF films of his father, David Cronenberg, *Antiviral* attracts either a Deleuzian or a Baudrillardian interpretation: its schizomolecular machines respond to the unconscious, its viral images and the film itself place a premium on affect, yet they induce paranoia by imploding the hyperbiological. Here, one must usually make a choice between Baudrillard's negative emphasis on technocapitalist ideological invasion of the human body and mind, and Deleuze's affirmative and immanent concepts of desire, affect and schizoanalysis. But I want to suggest that *Antiviral* lays claim to a new, synthetic reading, inspired by Thierry Bardini's *Junkware* (2011), which is exceptional for its synthesis of Baudrillard and Deleuze into a fourth phase of capitalism – one that Baudrillard had already theorised, yet not accounted for in Bardini.[1] I will examine the rationale of this fourth phase and address the shortcomings of Bardini's thesis. Using Deleuze and Baudrillard, I will show how *Antiviral* makes us think through biocapital, and the contagious bodies, machines, thoughts, images, affects and sensations of viral capitalism. I want to show that although *Antiviral* is symptomatic of this unfolding fourth order, it offers an immanent critique of its own conditions of possibility.

Just as Baudrillard declared Ballard's cyberpunk *Crash* to be the first great novel of simulation, *Antiviral* is the first great biopunk film of the viral. *Antiviral*'s aesthetics and obsessions depart from molar representations of biopolitics and biocapital, and how they grasp our minds and bodies:

> At one level, no doubt, most people – even those living within the remit of advanced technological biomedicine – still imagine their bodies at the 'molar' level, at the scale of limbs, organs, tissues, flows of blood, hormones, and so forth. This is the visible, tangible body, as pictured in the cinema or on the TV screen, in advertisements for health and beauty products [. . .] Today, however, biomedicine visualises life at another level – the molecular level. The clinical gaze has been supplemented, if not supplanted, by this molecular gaze. (Rose 2007: 11–12)

Whilst the sinister subsumption of Deleuze's concepts is my main focus, I want also to retain as a conceptual backdrop Deleuze's speculations that conclude *The Time-Image*, and see how with *Antiviral* they present themselves in the viral, fourth order. Here, Deleuze meditates on cinema's technological and representational conditions and capacities, identifying a 'new computer and cybernetic race, automata of computation and thought, automata with controls and feedback' amidst a new distribution of power 'diluted in an information network'. He attributes to SF cinema in particular (especially Kubrick) new, restorative cinematic possibilities, amidst the 'electronic image, that is, the tele and video image, the numerical image' which promises either 'to transform cinema, or to replace it, to mark its death' (*TI*: 254). In these pages, Deleuze enters Baudrillard's territory, claiming that the 'modern world is that in which information replaces nature' and that the 'life or the afterlife of cinema depends on its internal struggle with informatics' (*TI*: 258–9).[2] I want to show that although the biopunk *Antiviral* is a symptom of this unfolding fourth order, with some sense of optimism derived from negative example, we can follow Deleuze's observation that 'if the world has become a bad cinema, in which we no longer believe, surely a true cinema can contribute to giving us back reasons to believe in the world and in vanished bodies? The price to be paid, in cinema as elsewhere, was always a confrontation with madness' (*TI*: 193).

Hypertely

> The perfect crime would be to build a world-machine without defect, and to leave it without traces. But it never succeeds. We leave traces everywhere – viruses, lapses, germs, catastrophes – signs of defect, or imperfection, which are like our species' signature in the heart of an artificial world. (Baudrillard 1997: 24)

Just as Foucault proposed a microphysics of power, so Baudrillard completed the 'microphysics of simulacra' (*TE*: 5), diagnosing a successor to third-order simulation. These are not simply claims about representation, but tied to political economy insofar as they are beholden to Marxian theorisations of value. Thus we get a series: natural stage – use-value – referent – first order; commodity stage – exchange-value – second order – general equivalence; structural stage – sign-value – third order – code. Finally, in the fourth stage, 'the fractal (or viral, or radiant) stage of value', there is 'no point of reference at all, and value radiates in all directions, occupying all interstices, without reference to anything whatsoever'; 'there is no law of value, merely a sort of *epidemic of value*' (*TE*: 5–6) where:

> Information and communication are based on the principle of a value which has ceased to be referential and is now based on pure circulation.

Pure added-value – added by dint of the message, the meaning passing from image to image and screen to screen. This is no longer even the surplus-value and exchange-value of the commodity [. . .] That is based in principle on a use-value and hence still belongs to the sphere of the economy. Here there is no longer any exchange properly speaking: we are in the realm of pure circulation and chain reactions through the networks. (Baudrillard 2002: 29)[3]

While the viral is a new economic order for Baudrillard, the virus is the paradigmatic form of Deleuzian thought, blurring organic and inorganic, species, impersonally infecting/affecting the host and the other components within the assemblage; machinic, molecular bodies without organs, always becoming, affective, rhizomatic and nomadic:

We oppose epidemic to filiation, contagion to heredity, peopling by contagion to sexual reproduction [. . .] Contagion, epidemic, involves terms that are entirely heterogeneous: for example, a human being, an animal, and bacterium, a virus, a molecule, a microorganism [. . .]; they cannot be understood in terms of production, only in terms of becoming. (*TP*: 266–7)

The virus appeals (and infects) because it valorises the simulacrum (here as genetic replication), the resultant difference within repetition (*DR*: 333–4), and serves as a model for lateral, anti-hierarchical political organisation.[4] Mark Hansen observes that Deleuze and Guattari arrive at a 'de-pathologised' viral becoming, where 'the destructive impact of viruses is effectively suspended: far from destroying the bodies of their hosts, viruses form new "bodies"' (2001: para 29). Baudrillard fixates on this de-pathologisation; for affirmation, the absence of negativity is 'total positivisation', a 'pathology born of disinfection itself' (2002: 4). A culturally and politically aseptic world leads not to multiplicity, but to proliferation. Baudrillard describes the viral in Deleuzian terms as composed of 'organs without bodies, flows, molecules, the fractal' (2007: 108), of uncontrollable organ growth, hypertely. Plurality, multiplicity and vitality are subordinate to a logic of technoscientific and cultural standardisation: desire and difference are as ubiquitous as speculative capital, and share the same diffuse, nomadic form. Metamorphoses become metastases, 'a being merely exchanges itself for itself' and with technological equivalences, 'a gigantic enterprise of simulation and a parody of becoming' (2011b: 102–3). Affirmation, positivity and difference play themselves out as 'uncontrollable vitality and undisciplined proliferation' (FS: 54), not in positive terms but, rather, as indiscriminate revolt. Just as Deleuze envisions resistance taking different forms, where industrial strikes and organised action are replaced by cyberpiracy and viruses (N: 175), for Baudrillard, as a symptom of hyperreality, hypertely produces a malignant, catatonic body without organs: 'The body rebels against its own internal organisation' resulting in an 'organic delirium', schizophrenic, in that there is nothing that is repressed or denied (FS: 54). As capital produces more material and virtual comforts, the body responds to new demands: to enter into a becoming, to desire and be desired, to maximise its capacity to affect and be affected, to be competitive. Capital and the body go viral, irrational, and neither 'measures itself against either an ideal or negative instance' (SS: 2).

Deleuze and Baudrillard speak the same viral language, yet arrive at different conclusions, which arise from two points of tension. First is the difference between multiplicity and homogeneity under capital, between viral difference-machines that blur the boundaries between gender, species, self and other, and capitalist determinism. Second, the virus is both biological and technological. A Deleuzian perspective on biology valorises the becoming-animal of the virus, 'for it acts as a connector between living forms, traversing species, genus, phylum, and kingdom' (Thacker and Galloway 2007: 85–6). By contrast, 'computer viruses thrive in environments that have low levels of diversity. Wherever a technology has a monopoly, you will find viruses. They take advantage of technical standardisation to propagate' (ibid. 84). Baudrillard's move is to imbricate the technological and the biological – essentially what bioinformatics and biocomputing do – so that everything is 'viral by definition (or lack of definition). The viral analogy is not an importation from biology [unlike Deleuze's], for everything is affected simultaneously and under the same terms by the virulence in question, by the chain reaction [. . .], by haphazard senseless proliferation and metastasis' (TE: 8). This is the cold banality of this fourth order. Creative, nomadic and multiple, yet hinging on viral and rhizomatic modes of production and subsumption: it is unexceptional, representing 'the continuity and inherent flexibility and adaptability of capitalist production' (Styhre and Sundgren 2011: 55). Baudrillard describes the fourth order, but he doesn't quite know what to do with it: 'The fourth stage is the phase of viruses. At that stage we're in a fourth, viral dimension where resistance is no longer possible. What can you do then?' (2004a: 72).

This is where Bardini is indispensable, for he too theorises a fourth stage of capitalism in the wake of the 'false promises of the molecular revolution' (2011: 26) founded on a synthesis of Deleuze and Baudrillard. Bardini's premise is twofold. First, 'biotechnological and biopolitical innovations beg for an extension of the Deleuzo-Guattarian framework'. In a culture 'where everybody is taking care of his or her very own body without organs', 'societies are moving out of control' and towards 'the era of the machine of the fourth kind'. Second, biology has entered 'the new "real" world of simulation', where 'DNA is the model medium for the new age of simulation, of capitalism of the fourth kind', *genetic capitalism* (ibid. 11, 88). However, there are two shortcomings to Bardini's analysis. First, he develops his argument with close reference to Burroughs (*The Soft Machine* (1961), *The Ticket that Exploded* (1962), *Nova Express* (1964) and *Blade Runner (a movie)* (1979), among others), Dick's *Do Androids Dream of Electric Sheep?* and other stories, and Scott's *Blade Runner*.[5] As futurological as some of these texts are, a contemporary work better illustrates and augments Bardini's claims. Second, with the exception of his work on terrorism, Bardini's reading of Baudrillard stops at *Simulacra and Simulation* and lacks the viral, fourth-order frame.[6] Bardini's synthesis of Baudrillard and Deleuze and the fourth-order machines thus entailed are what I will explore through *Antiviral*.

Hypochondriasis

The specificity of biocapital as a *biopolitical* form of capitalism lies in the fact that the symptom shifts away from disease manifestation and toward disease potential. (Sunder Rajan 2007: 283)

Antiviral's Syd March (Caleb Landry Jones) works for the Lucas Clinic, who buy viruses and tissue samples from celebrities and sell them to the public. Flu viruses, genital warts, herpes and muscle cells are purchased in full or in loan packages. Syd also steals from the Lucas Clinic's catalogue by self-injecting viruses, smuggling them inside his body, and selling them to an unauthorised cell gardener/butcher, Arvid (Joe Pingue). Hence Bardini's claim that in fourth-order capitalism, genetic code makes us 'living money' (2011: 11). Celebrities have exclusive contracts to provide their viruses to the Lucas Clinic and similar corporations, such as Vole and Tesser. At a glance, the film seems little more than commentary on celebrity culture. But there is a molecular obsession to the trash news, which has reached new lows in its obsession not only with superficial beauty and fashion, but with the diseases celebrities contract. The film resists honing in on this coverage; rather, it quietly unfolds insistently in the background on omnipresent screens. One broadcast reports on a female celebrity's anus: the screen goes from an illustrated cross section overlayed on to her body to footage of her walking down the street. The frame tightens in on her crotch, closes in tighter again, and transitions to a pulsating anal gland, a televised '*orgy of realism*' (*S*: 32). But the technical perfection and obscene proximity no longer fascinates consumers. It is not only viruses that are bought and sold, but imperfections and deformities. There are a host of rumours surrounding celebrity Hannah Geist's (Sarah Gadon) sexual organs. When customer Porris (Douglas Smith) meets with Syd, he asks, 'Did you know she's deformed? You can't tell from the magazines. She has to have special underwear made. Fashion designers make her special underwear.' Another rumour amongst technicians is that Geist doesn't have a vulva, and 'that's what she meant when she told *Spot Magazine* that she doesn't have a face'. Others say that she has 'a unique, non-functional organ connected to her urinary system – it's worth millions on the celebrity meat market'. At the bottom end of the bioeconomy are muscle cells taken from celebrities, cultivated in cell gardens and turned into a foodstuff, and sold as 'astral bodies' in butcher shops and restaurants. By contrast, viruses are boutique biocommodities, the apex of the bioeconomy.[7] At the Lucas Clinic, employees are heavily monitored by surveillance cameras, scanned and questioned as to whether they are secreting any of the clinic's bioproperty, viruses from their catalogue. Technicians check out virus samples for sales meetings so that they can be tracked and regulated, and returned at the end of the day: 'Gene banks are indeed the financial institutions of the machine/state of the fourth kind' (Bardini 2011: 131).

Although he is, at once, a salesman, biochemist, machinist, virologist and biopunk corporate criminal, Syd's daily routine signifies the monotonous and repetitive existence of life under capital, and also gives us a vision of labour in viral capitalism. Syd's body wakes him before his alarm goes off. Gasping, shivering and sweating, skin puckered and blotchy, his first instinct is to tend to the mucus that has collected in and around his nostrils. From a fridge, he withdraws a sterilised swab, unwraps it from its packaging, reclines his head, and inserts it deep within his nasal passage, choking and gagging, and then deposits the sample into a sterile container. While Syd sleeps, the viruses he carries incubate within his body. He then staggers into the kitchen, self-medicates (he takes a handful of tablets each morning, and constantly monitors his temperature with a thermometer throughout the film) and opens his fridge to shelves of single-serve, pre-packaged sandwiches and bottled orange juice – the office lunch for every meal. He then slumps down in front of his stolen machine, a fourth-order virus copyprotector.

Bardini claims that 'global capitalism has now entered its genetic phase, the phase of our encounters with machines of the fourth type. After the simple machines of the old societies of sovereignty, the motorised machines of the disciplinary societies, the information machines of the control societies, human beings now face – or will soon face – *genetic machines*.' Like their cybernetic precursors in control societies, fourth-order machines are oriented towards molecular biology, yet differ in one crucial way. Whilst cybernetic machines 'regulate components as such without being able to actually build them', genetic machines 'both regulate and build [their] components'; it is 'no mere computer. It is tomorrow's biocomputer' (2011: 127–8).[8] The fourth-order machine is the axis on which *Antiviral* rotates: a ReadyFace virus copyprotector, equal parts Rube Goldberg machine, bioreactor and biocomputer, which Syd stole from the Lucas Clinic for personal use. Behind a concealed panel, in his secret cupboard/home-office cubicle, Syd sits before the machine, presses a test tube containing a virus sample into a port, and flicks a switch which stimulates a fluorescent backlight. A small breath of air inhales the viral fluid. One cog twitches and clicks softly while another glides on its axle. Its lung – a pneumatic pump – shudders as it expresses stale air and smoothly draws in the fresh, while the rest of its mechanisms whir softly. The viral solution courses through plastic arteries, past components that recall a film projector and a film spool. A horrid face appears on a screen more like an X-ray illuminator than a monitor. Syd pushes another button, clasps a round dial between thumb and forefinger, and the face responds to the rotations. Syd's hunched back and slumped posture contrast with the concentration worn on his face, as he glares unblinking at the grotesquely metamorphosing visage. The machine has analysed the virus, translating it into a digital 'face graphic'. This image, Dorian, the head of the Lucas Clinic, tells investors, 'represents the structure of the disease. It is, in a sense, the face of the virus, dense with information.' In manipulating the face, Syd and other technicians manipulate the structure of the virus. The machine responds to their

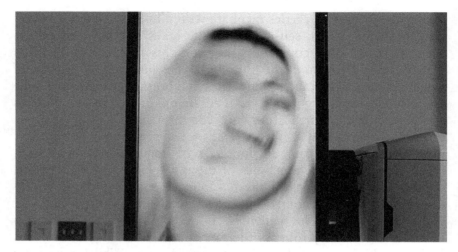

9.1 Brandon Cronenberg, *Antiviral*, 2012.

bodily gestures, but is also sensitive to the technician's unconscious, and the virus responds in turn; it 'fluidly incorporates [the] technician's unconscious mental resources'. Dorian again:

> The human face is a powerful messenger. Our brains are attuned to its every nuance. The smallest shift in its musculature can translate itself into complex, non-verbal information so subtle, and communicate it so quickly, that we often don't even register it – not consciously. One could say that for human beings, the face is a structure with a high-information resolution [. . .] The ReadyFace console is designed to engage the user's unconscious mental resources by exploiting the brain's sensitivity to facial patterns.

Syd is doing two interrelated things. First, the ReadyFace machine manipulates the face of the virus and, thus, its structure, in order to render it non-contagious, its pathogenicity limited to a single infected customer. Second, Syd is copyprotecting the altered virus, so that the original, unaltered virus will remain the sole property of the Lucas Clinic, since the altered virus cannot be spread beyond the client to those who would otherwise have to pay for it. The altered virus is both a simulacrum, a copy without an original, and a difference emerging from repetition.[9] The ReadyFace machine visually resembles a bioreactor, 'an instrument of fabrication' which 'promises to deliver [. . .] not a standardised equivalent, but a whole spectrum of variable tissue forms, all of which may be generated from the one tissue source. Such novel modes of production have called for

224

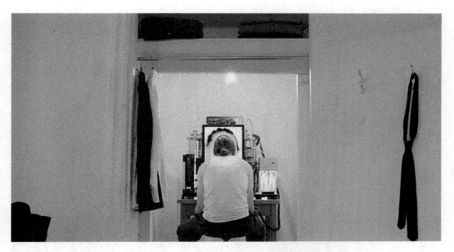

9.2   Brandon Cronenberg, *Antiviral*, 2012. 'The schizophrenic is not, as generally claimed, characterised by his loss of touch with reality, but by absolute proximity to and total instantaneousness with things, this overexposure to the transparency of the world. Stripped of a stage and crossed over without the least obstacle, the schizophrenic cannot produce the limits of his very being, he can no longer produce himself as a mirror. He becomes a pure screen, a pure absorption and resorption surface of the influent networks' (Baudrillard 2012: 30).

their own methods of abstraction and simulation' (Cooper 2008: 123–4). We can consider this through the lenses of both Deleuze and Baudrillard. The engineering of biological material privileges 'forces and relations', 'the *morphogenesis* of form as process' using technology that 'exploits the active responsiveness of living tissue, its power to affect and be affected and thus to change' over the 'semiotics of code, message and signal' (ibid. 103, 105, 113)[10] – essentially, Deleuzian molecular, affective thresholds over Baudrillard's code-determined semiology. And yet Deleuzian microperceptions wallow so far down in the molecular that they miss the larger picture: it is *the molecular itself* that is being bought and sold; as genetic 'code itself is sold and exchanged in its own medium, as code is now the currency, the general equivalent, and the product, the object of the transaction, political economy and the political economy of the sign conjugate' (Bardini 2011: 149). So much for the common cold.

Deleuze and Guattari's molecular unconscious is indebted to Jacques Monod (*TP*: 54–5; *AO*: 288, 328). While the literalness of the appropriation from biological science is dubious, the reasoning for modelling the unconscious on Monod is clear. Monod's *Chance*

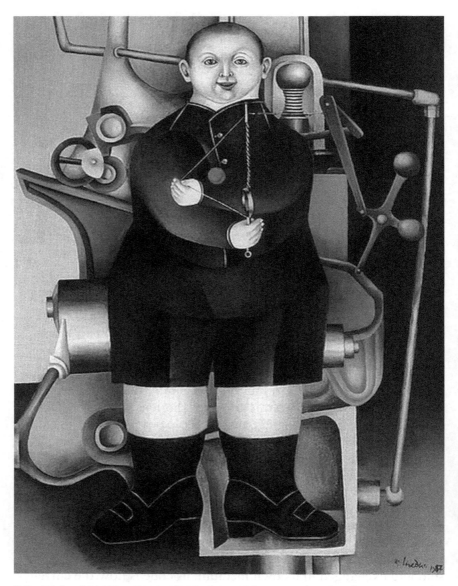

9.3   Richard Lindner, *Boy with Machine*, 1954. Reproduced with permission of the Estate of Richard Lindner. 'The schizophrenic is the universal producer. There is no need to distinguish here between producing and its product [...] A painting by Richard Lindner, "Boy with Machine," shows a huge, pudgy, bloated boy working one of his little desiring-machines, after having hooked it up to a vast technical social machine' (Deleuze and Guattari, *AO*: 7).

and Necessity cites Bergson (thus its appeal for Deleuze) with approval and develops a theory of random, creative, yet impersonal (anti-anthropomorphic) non-teleological evolution: non-living 'fortuitous perturbations' lead to the 'disintegration of all structure', and the 'unrestricted liberty of creation, thanks to the replicative structure of DNA' (1972: 113), puts a premium on genetic chance. From Monod, Deleuze and Guattari borrow microscopic cybernetics, and apply it to desire, the unconscious and the body without organs, developing a biocultural model of the unconscious as the 'schizophrenic cell, the schizo molecule' (*AO*: 289) and the body without organs as an 'unformed, unorganised, nonstratified, or destratified body and all its flows: subatomic and submolecular particles' (*TP*: 49). The result is not a representational psychoanalytical unconscious, but a materialist schizoanalysis: 'molecular biology is itself schizophrenia' (*AO*: 289). That the human organism is composed of indifferent matter is 'negative only in appearance', because matter is affective and, thus, impersonal and asubjective, so that it 'must be understood positively in terms of force' (*AO*: 288). The fourth-order ReadyFace schizomachine stimulates and reacts to the cathexes of the molecular unconscious. Deleuze's schizophrenic machines are aggregates of pre-existing machines, leftover components working together because they have no prior relation, and this is true of the schizophrenic unconscious (2006: 18–19). The machine and the unconscious form the technician-virus-ReadyFace assemblage. Syd and other biopunks steal licensed ReadyFaces, assemble and reassemble them out of discarded and co-opted parts, biohack copyprotected viruses, and sell them to nomadic piracy groups, undercutting the monopolistic corporations that employ them.

The face is the interactive threshold, the recording surface, between the virus and the unconscious. The viral face graphics vividly enact Deleuze's assessment of Francis Bacon, the technician-virus-ReadyFace assemblage hinging on the relationship between the virus molecule, the schizo unconscious and the face. The face is a pure surface, produced when the head ceases to be part of the body, ceasing to be the signifier of subjectivity, anthropocentricism, conveyer of organic organisation (*TP*: 188). Bacon's figures dismantle the face, 'dismantle the organism in favour of the body, the face in favour of the head' (*FB*: 33). To move beyond organic resemblance, from one contour to another, is to 'liberate a more profound resemblance in which the organs (eyes, nose, mouth) can no longer be discerned' (*FB*: 109). As we saw in Chapter 5, Bacon's faces enact a becoming-animal, the animal-as-trait, constituting the 'zone *of indiscernibility or undecidability* between man and animal', their common 'meat' (*FB*: 16–17). The ReadyFace produces the acephalic body without organs, making the face an affective surface that responds to the unconscious, a microperception machine registering the unconscious in affective terms, drawing together the meat and the virus into a new assemblage.

Here we can draw together the virus, Bacon and Deleuze's affection-image: 'There is no close-up *of* the face, the face is in itself close-up, the close-up is by itself face and both are affect, affection-image' (2012a: 90). Deleuze gives the close-up/face a particular significance because of its capacity for affect and, as with Bacon, it registers impersonally, not as a point of intersubjectivity (individualising, socialising, communicating) but of deterritorialisation. The face is an 'organ-carrying plate of nerves [. . .] which gathers or expresses in a free way all kinds of tiny local movements which the rest of the body usually keeps hidden' (ibid. 90), a microperceptive organ. In *Antiviral*, the relationship between screen, face and virus constantly recurs, not just in the way it enters into an assemblage with the unconscious, but also intertwining affect, sensation and capital. As a biocommodity, there is a premium placed on the virus's affective qualities.[11] The opening scenes introduce this, as Syd meets with a customer, Edward Porris. Syd and Porris (porous) sit opposite one another, and on a screen between them is an endlessly repeating, six-second piece of footage of Hannah Geist, performing the same action: turning and removing her sunglasses to reveal her eyes, smiling coyly as though in recognition of another's presence. Syd whispers: 'I understand completely. She's perfect, more than perfect, more than human. Her eyes seem to reach right below your skin, and touch your organs. They touch your stomach, your lungs . . . gives me the shivers.' Syd then presents a range of viruses acquired from Geist, each with their own face, but suggests for a 'man of taste, a connoisseur', an oral herpes virus that 'afflicted [her] during a much publicised affair', 'a must have for the truly devoted'. When Porris is infected with the virus, it is injected into the left side of his mouth, since 'Ms Geist is infected [. . .] to the right side of her mouth. Now, if she kissed you, it would spread to your left side, around here. On the left it would be like she gave it to you in person,' and Porris shudders and exhales with pleasure. In a later scene, Syd tells a female client that the virus is a 'biological communion', 'from her [a different female celebrity] body to your body, from her cells to your cells'. What is interesting about these scenes is the contrast between the glamorous, seductive faces of celebrities and the Baconesque viral faces. The Lucas Clinic sells neither beauty nor glamour but pathogenicity (viral affect), and the face of the virus is not a representation but material, desiring-production of the unconscious – one buys a desiring-machine. *The de-pathologised viral becoming, the dismantled face, the molecular unconscious and the schizomachine are investments in and of biocapital, a bought becoming, a molecular transaction, the general equivalent of genetic code.*

Antiviral balances the two paradigms, the Deleuzian and the Baudrillardian that Bardini synthesises. As Powell notes in an essay that touches many of the same issues with which I am dealing here, 'aesthetics are viral in nature' and 'via facial mutation, schizo cinema breaks down our immune defences, infecting and living in us on all levels, sprouting new growths of sensation, perception and thought' (2008: 116). *Antiviral* is a remarkable piece of schizo cinema for these reasons, yet the schizo affects become increasingly paranoid, that is, subsumed by Baudrillard's viral. Like Deleuze, Baudrillard was interested in Monod's molecular biology, but arrived at radically different conclusions. For Baudrillard, Monod's teleonomy anticipated a 'techno-capitalist evolution' that:

> deconstructs all subjectivity, positivistic consciousness (the idealism of the subject, etc.) to reinstitute the absolute positivity of objectivity and of the code (the idealism of the code). Politically and historically, this signifies the substitution for social control by the *end* [. . .], by social control, by *prescience*, simulation, programmatic anticipation, indeterminate mutation commanded by the code. (2006b: 98)[12]

This early anticipation intersects with Baudrillard's later critique of Deleuze. Deleuze's machines '*have been true*', but have passed over into 'simulating machines that double each one of these "original" machines', subsumed by the 'great simulating mechanism which winds all these devices into a wider spiral' (*FF*: 15) manifest as biocapital. 'Deleuze's molecular topology of desire [and its] flows and connections will soon converge – if they have not already done so – with genetic simulations, microcellular drifts, and the random facilitations (*frayages*) of code manipulators' so that it will be 'no coincidence to find schemas of desire and schemas of control everywhere'. 'It is a spiral of power, of desire, and of the molecule which is now bringing us openly toward the final peripeteia of absolute control. Beware the molecular!' (*FF*: 35–6). Monod's aleatory molecule was to be the new domain of capital, not of revolution, and the 'multiplicity of force relations' Deleuze inherited from Foucault would merge power and resistance at a microscopic level (*FF*: 37). The result is a cybernetic, molecular complicity between Deleuze's molecular programme and capitalism. Baudrillard's proclamations might have once been outlandish but, as Bardini points out, 'there is no more analogical thinking' (2011: 88): DNA is the model medium and the general equivalent of genetic capitalism.

That Baudrillard's scepticism towards and Deleuze's affirmation of the molecular are now in such close proximity is, no doubt, the fundamental tension of schizophrenia. After all, capitalism produces schizophrenia, and the schizophrenic process harnesses the material schizo energy of the capitalist system to invest positively in the socio-political field. But as any careful reconstruction of *Anti-Oedipus* shows, and as the last chapters of *A Thousand Plateaus* make perfectly clear, the schizophrenic is that which *cannot be subsumed by capital* – therein lies its potential. Without this relation to capital, the schizo breakthrough, there is only metastasis, not metamorphosis. So, while Pisters is entirely correct to point out that there is 'no safe or morally transcendent position from which we can resist' (2012: 5), *biocapitalism now invests in the schizophrenic process so that schizophrenia itself is no longer just a process, but a business.* The Deleuzian wager is to evade reterritorialisation, multiply forms of resistance, deterritorialising more and more. But what if multiplication (rhizomatics) was no longer an agonistic politics, nor even deterritorialisation proper? It would be the case that, as Baudrillard essays, 'deterritorialisation is no longer exile at all, and it is no more a metaphoric figure, it is a figure of metastasis: a deprivation of meaning and territory, a lobotomy of the body resulting from the turmoil of the circuits. Electrocuted, lobotomised, the soul has become but a cerebral convolution' (2012: 46). *Capital goes down to the last molecule*:

> What if capital wiped generic man himself off the map (in favour of genetic man)? [. . .] once it became its own [. . .] aleatory machine, something like a *social genetic code*[,] capital no longer left the slightest opportunity for a determinate reversal. This is the real violence of capital. (*SED*: 60)

Baudrillard's viral stage is one in which the distinction between paranoia and schizophrenia blurs. Paranoia and schizophrenia are binaries and the body without organs is the threshold between the two forms of organisation (bodily, social, unconscious, political) that are the 'ultimate products under the determinate conditions of capitalism' (*AO*: 281). This binary is more nuanced in *A Thousand Plateaus*. The distinction is maintained, whereby the paranoid body's 'organs are continually under attack by outside forces', and the schizo body wages 'its own active internal struggle against the organs at the price of catatonia' (*TP*: 166). Deleuze and Guattari attend more closely to the potential dangers of the schizo process. 'Dismantling the organism', they write, 'has never meant killing yourself, but rather opening the body to connections that presuppose an entire assemblage, circuits, conjunctions, levels and thresholds, passages and distributions of intensity, and territories and deterritorialisations' (*TP*: 177). But this comes with the caveat that one can botch a becoming and a body without organs:

> Even when it falls into the void of too-sudden destratification, or into the proliferation of a cancerous stratum, it is still desire. Desire stretches that far: desiring one's own annihilation, or desiring the power to annihilate [. . .] That is why the material problem confronting schizoanalysis is knowing whether we have it within our means to make the selection, to distinguish the BwO from its doubles: empty vitreous bodies, cancerous bodies, totalitarian and fascist. (*TP*: 183)

We can dismiss Baudrillard's accusation that the schizo, the desiring-machine and the molecular unconscious rely on capital – this is precisely Deleuze's thesis derived from Marx. From the initial formulation that these sites of resistance provide only a mirror of capital in the form of desire, Baudrillard's objection must be redeveloped into one that attends less to *the mirror* and more to *the anticipation of subsumption* and, thus, into a formulation for the viral order: *biocapitalism is the becoming-paranoid of schizophrenia. The molecular is no longer the productive site of resistance, but the new, paranoid domain of capital.*

The proliferation of paranoiac capital into the schizomolecular is manifest at the intersection of three viral forms: the body, the unconscious and the media. The film makes *mise en scène* of the body and the brain in Deleuzian fashion. It juxtaposes the elegance and sophistication of the celebrity virus bioeconomy with self-replicating and ever-present news coverage, linking through contrast desire and deformity,[13] venereal disease and viral media. In the Lucas Clinic, lustrous celebrity faces adorn the walls, while television newscasts speculate that an actress's protruding ribs betray an eating disorder, and the breaking story is leaked topless photos an actress took of herself with her phone. Later, on one screen, a woman's mouth and luscious red lips, adorned with a weeping pustule, suck seductively on a finger. On the screen to the right, a celebrity crotch shot goes from a natural photograph to being irradiated to convey the heat from her venereal genitals. That these two play simultaneously and next to each other indicates that they are to be consumed as complementary, rather than competing, messages.

The film merges the hyperbiological and the digital, making the body a visual surface on the one hand, fragmenting and rearranging it on the other. A video installation at a nightclub isolates facial features (lips, eyes) in exploded close-ups across dozens of screens. In the back room, Syd finds the next thing that will 'catch on', a digital Hannah Geist programmed to be hysterical and sexually compliant and, thus, entirely pornographic. Syd is unnerved by its fidelity to and pre-empting of both the real and the user's desire, as it pleads and questions: 'Do you want me to hurt myself? I can't say no to you. Please repeat yourself so I can obey your command. Do you want me to hurt myself? Do you want to see my body?' This interactive digital body that desires its own degradation (in this sense anticipating its function as a mirror of desire) belongs to Baudrillard's third-order transparency, whereby the pornographic obscene overcompensates for the passivity of the spectator by increasing the proximity of representation, 'so close that it merges with its own representation: the end of perspectival space, and therefore, that of the imaginary and of phantasy' (S: 29). But the fourth order is phantasy materialised, the production of phantasies, the renewal of the imaginary by means of genetic and digital technologies.

Syd's encounter with the digital Hannah Geist – the spectral connotations of the German *Geist* come into relief – ends with a close-up of the screen reflected on to his iris. We follow Syd's gaze to an exploded view of Geist's plump, red lips, already associated with oral herpes. The film's incessant labial and optical motifs suggest that these organs, both pervious and expulsive, merge the permeability of the mucous membrane with the newly tactile surface of the image, departing from the orthodox, pornographic erogenous zoning effected by the anatomical zoom, so that the eyes and the mouth become the primary organs that respond to the sensations offered by the libidinal and political viral economy. The camera components of the ReadyFace machine suggest how to appreciate *Antiviral*. The intensity of its visual sensibility (excruciating close-ups of luscious lips, eyeballs, faces and flower petals contrast with deep-focus, symmetrical, austere environs, making for a baroque visual palette) and its aesthetic hierarchy are tilted firmly towards the image, rather than extended or even meaningful dialogue: mouths are transitive sites for infectious fluids, saliva, vomitus, injections and copious amounts of blood; the zombified, decrepit characters interact with each other not so much through verbal communication, but through viral screens and bodily contagion:

> Everything can be used as a screen, the body of a protagonist or even the bodies of the spectators; everything can replace the film stock, in a virtual film which now only goes in the head, behind the pupils [. . .] A disturbed brain-death or a new brain which would be at once the screen, the film stock and the camera, each time membrane of the outside and the inside. (*TI*: 207)

But politically, and in negative terms, the visual and biological viruses are 'fascinating, indifferent forms, forms multiplied by the virulence of images, since all the modern media – the information and communication systems – have themselves a viral power and their virulence is contagious' (Baudrillard 2002: 13).

Scenes like this foreground the viral body and its relation to the newly paranoid, molecular-machinic unconscious. The virus afflicts Syd's mind with baroque dreams and hallucinations, one of which sees his body merge with his machine. From a close-up on a face graphic, we transition into Syd's unconscious after a cut to his dilated pupil. The smoothly rotating cogs of the ReadyFace slow down, and a series of disorienting images unfold, accompanied by a distorted and ominous soundscape. The flesh of his back undulates, expanding and contracting with the breathing of the machine, cables plugged into his arms, puckering the flesh, suspend him in the air, and his mouth is replaced by a latticed machine part, through which blood begins to slaver. The abruptness and irrationality of the cuts is offset by the flows of the body-machine within the frame: arms and crenellated cabling float weightlessly from left to right, up and down, folding into one another. When the camera withdraws from these mesmerisingly slow, always flowing images, we see Syd, dreaming, coupled to his machine, but suspended in a tiny illuminated room amidst an entirely black, spaceless void. Of Deleuze and Guattari's desiring, molecular unconscious, Bardini writes, 'here is [their] new *mot d'ordre*. But it is a dangerous *mot d'ordre*, especially if you equate the "molecular" with the "genic," DNA with the genome' (2011: 143). And this dream-image in

9.4   Brandon Cronenberg, *Antiviral*, 2012. 'The individual, floating, but held
on a leash like a dog, like an eye popping out of its socket, hanging on the end of
its optic nerve, scanning the horizon through 180 degrees but not sending back
any images – a disembodied panoptical terminal, runaway organ of a species of
mutants' (Baudrillard 2003a: 36).

Antiviral tells us how we should understand these fourth-order
molecular machines: everyone is connected to their schizomachine,
both corporeally and unconsciously, but ultimately circumscribed
by a paranoid void.

Syd returns from his delirium to find that the virus he self-injected
and attempted to biohack has destroyed his machine, and from here
things take a decidedly Baudrillardian turn. When Hannah Geist
returns infected from an overseas trip, Syd visits her as an employee
of the Lucas Clinic to take a sample of her newly acquired virus.
Syd had earlier been bested by another virus thief who biohacked a
flu virus and sold it to the unlicensed Arvid. With the virus already
'public', Syd goes unpaid. For what initially seems to be this reason,
Syd self-injects the raw virus. After waking from his delirium, Syd
learns that Geist has died from the virus he now carries. As we have
seen, it is Deleuze's affirmative, de-pathologised virus that Baudrillard
criticises, the very same de-pathologised, copyprotected virus the
Lucas Clinic sells. But this virus is different: it destroys the machine
that would analyse it and it is contagious. This orients the film away
from its treatment of virus-as-affect, towards virus-as-value and, subsequently, the viral politics Baudrillard points to: 'Once, revolts were
political; there were groups or individuals oppressed in their desire,

their energy or their intelligence. Today these hardly ever break out. In our quaternary period, revolt has become genetic' (*FS*: 53). Or, as he later says, viral by *lack of definition*:

> Virulence makes its appearance when a body, system or network expels all its negative elements [. . .] In this sense, virality is closely related to fractality and digitality. It is because computers and electronic machines have become abstractions, virtual machines, non-bodies, that viruses run riot in them (they are much more vulnerable than traditional mechanical machines). It is because the body itself has become a non-body, an electronic, virtual machine, that viruses seize hold of it. (2002: 1)

The virus overcomes Syd, who becomes more and more decrepit, a paranoid body without organs, and there is a public frenzy over Geist's death. People line up to buy celebrity steaks, and the Lucas Clinic is filled with customers eager for a 'Hannah Geist variety pack'. Here, too, glamour shots of Geist have multiplied, infecting all the walls. Meanwhile, fresh Hannah Geist meat rots in high-end restaurants. Syd is imperilled not only by his own paranoid body, but also by Arvid, who suspects he harbours the lethal virus: while lethal pathogens are illegal to trade, demand for the virus, lethal or not, is high. From Arvid, Syd seeks the parts to repair his machine, leading him to Levine (James Cade), leader of biopunks who steal and crack viruses from the major corporations. As nomads, they assemble their own schizoReadyFaces, modifying to their own ends the models stolen from licensed vendors who control the market; as venture capitalists, they beat Syd and take samples of the virus he carries, gouge out his skin, and dump him on the street. Too weak to resist, he is then captured and escorted by two men to a remote location outside of the city. 'Don't worry,' one of them tells him, 'you're a commodity' – or, rather, a transient interstice for the much-desired virus.

The Perfect Crime

> What is hanging over us now is not hysteria or schizophrenia or even paranoia [. . .] but, in the more or less long term, melancholia. With its precursor, hypochondria, that derisory signalling of overcathected, enervated bodies and organs, rendered sad by involution. All systems, especially political ones, are virtually hypochondriacal: they manage and ingest their own dead organs. (Baudrillard 2003a: 11)

From here, the homology between the affective contagion of the virus and flows of capital results not in deterritorialisation but in metastasis, as Syd's body, the media and the public enter hypertrophic states. Geist, it is revealed, is alive, but the virus she shares with Syd is killing her, despite the care of her physician, Abendroth (Malcolm McDowell). Abendroth and Geist's entourage suspected Geist's infection to be an assassination attempt, and announced her death to the public in order to prevent further attempts, and to buy time to find a cure. The virus is a modified version of one Geist had previously sold to the Lucas Clinic, stolen and biohacked to prevent analysis – hence Syd's destroyed ReadyFace – by a previous employee in the service of rival company Vole and Tesser. Syd and Abendroth discover that Vole and Tesser have patented the biohacked virus, the pathogenicity of which was merely a genetic oversight during its construction. Rather than assassination, Vole and Tesser sought to circumvent Geist's exclusive contract with the Lucas Clinic by exploiting the virus's common affect. By infecting and then planning to recover the virus from Geist without her knowledge, they would then be able to sell their own patented line: the virus would be *their* property, though it passes through *her* body. The affective, biopolitically common flow of the virus simply makes it all the more virtual, simultaneously biocommodity-as-affect and impersonal flow of capital.

Syd's first encounter with Hannah Geist when he takes the virus sample is anticipated by one of his earlier, virus-inspired dreams, so that when he encounters Geist in the flesh, it is phantasy (*Geist*) brought to life. They share the same baroque *mise en scène* and, as in his dream, she lies in bed, and neither speaks nor acknowledges his presence, not passive but entirely indifferent, even as he takes a blood sample. That Syd's contact with Geist should realise his florid dreams (the visual tell is that unlike the solid-coloured petals Syd caresses in his dream, the flowers beside the actual Geist's bed are patterned and thus, like Geist, afflicted by a virus) and that these sequences feature penetration and fluid exchange, and also the cold intensity of the interaction, gives them an aestheticised, rapacious motivation – which explains why Syd declines to share the virus, wanting it for himself. The unreality of these scenes, the co-presence of phantasy and the actual, suggests that this is not truly Geist but, rather, how Syd envisions her, but still as material production – Deleuze's desire-as-reality – rather than psychoanalytic projection. After working so intimately with virtual and genetic abstractions, her digital images, her viruses, the virus becomes the conductive and infectious agent that mediates between the real and simulacra, between the unconscious and the world, alternately Geist and *Geist*.

The *true* Geist, as it were, appears later, when she is frail, suffers hallucinations, and expels blood from her mouth as the virus overcomes her. This significantly alters the Geist/*Geist* relation. For Baudrillard, the materialisation of the double by genetics signifies the end of Oedipal representation and sexuality at the expense of its imaginary power in relation to the psychic and physical integrity of the subject. The 'charm' of the individual, its psychic and physical being, is, for Baudrillard, its singularity (*SS*: 97–8, 101). The viral Geist/*Geist* forms are less doubles than fractals: images and viruses genetically and digitally repeated indefinitely. Like the computer virus, which thrives in standardised technological environments, the low level of diversity and proximity, physical and virtual, enables the virus to communicate more effectively. Coupled to this, the relation between subject and double is inversely proportional: as the double materialises, the subject disintegrates. This is so in the fractal relationship between Geist and *Geist*. When Geist is thought dead, there is a plague of *Geist* viruses and images: the increase in the latter's pathogenicity negatively affects the integrity of the former's psychic and physical boundaries. And it is this Geist that haunts Syd. Recaptured by Levine, now in the service of Vole and Tesser, Syd wakes in an observation room, flanked by oversized glamour images of Geist. Vole and Tesser intend to capture Syd on video as the virus kills him, in order to 'complete' Geist's life in the minds of the public:

> This is an honest room. You can share any thoughts or feelings you might be having. In fact, you are encouraged to share [. . .] Right now we are attempting to capitalise on a unique opportunity. Since her passing, many of Hannah's admirers have experienced what could be described as an uncomfortable narrative gap between her life and funeral. How did she die really? What did the final hours of her life look like? History may have denied them these moments but, through you, we have a window into the past. By documenting your deterioration, we can ease the suffering of millions who have, through no fault of their own, been left in the dark. How do you feel, right now?

Syd refuses to answer these questions verbally, but rather furthers the connection between the viral body and the viral image. Wracked with pain and fever, Syd, like Geist, begins to expel blood from his mouth and, in a scene that merges subjective delirium with objective reality, he, like Bacon, disfigures the face, smearing the oversized images with blood, approximating Geist's condition. Meanwhile, *Geist* sleeps, in and out of focus, around the edges of the room.

The final sequence begins with a digital Geist addressing the camera: 'Welcome, everyone, to my afterlife, exclusively from Vole and Tesser.' Syd escapes Levine by stabbing him in the mouth with a syringe, repels and wards off others with his contagious body, and persuades Mira Tesser (Mary Crewson) to cure Geist. Unlike Syd, Geist is too far gone to be cured, the appearance of *Geist* in Syd's delirium signalling the passing of the fleshly into the viral simulacrum. Simulated death here proves to be not a premonition, but the subsumption of the real by the viral.

Syd, cured of all but his obsession, becomes a technician for Vole and Tesser, whose latest venture is Geist's genetic legacy, cultivated in a new type of bioreactor, an Afterlife Capsule,[14] an organ machine that houses tissues, sheets of stretched skin and pulsating organs. Tesser explains to investors:

> From the perspective of the virus, the human being is irrelevant. What matters is the system that allows it to function: skin cells, nerve cells, the right home for the right disease. Within our Afterlife Capsule, the system that is Hannah Geist's body has been perpetuated, even expanded beyond what existed during her lifetime. Make no mistake, however: this is not some glorified cell steak. Everything inside this housing is either part of the original body, or has been grown directly from it, as a result of our patented cell-garden technology.

From genetic and digital simulation, to the optimisation and integration of viral production, the protraction of existence beyond death, the indefinite extension of the body, new viruses are injected into the system of organs and tissues through a fleshy port, infecting the body, and then sold. Schizophrenia for all: 'No longer any face, any gaze, any human countenance or body in all of this – organs without bodies, flows, molecules, the fractal. The relation [. . .] is of the order of contamination, of contagion: you hook up to it, absorb or immerse yourself in it, exactly as in flows and networks' (Baudrillard 2007: 108). The film's final image isolates what remains of Geist's Baconesque face, her eyes closed as when Syd first encountered her, seen through a window into the machine. Syd, alone with Geist's paranoid body without organs, suckles virus-infected blood from an incision in the fleshy interface of the machine: 'The insistence of the smile beyond the face and beneath the face. The insistence of a scream that survives the mouth, the insistence of a body that survives the organism, the insistence of transitory organs that survive the qualified organs' (*FB*: 36). What new kind of hysteria are we speaking of here? *Antiviral* abandons us on this fourth-order peripeteia, where the virus of paranoia ruptures the schizophrenic bacterium, releasing a plague of indeterminate viruses. Such visions pay the price of madness. With no face to confront, this is the price of schizophrenia.

Notes

1. Although invoked as early as 1983 (*FS*: 53), the fourth phase was never rigorously theorised. Thus the majority of Baudrillard's writings fall into this post-simulation phase, although it seems to be considered an unnecessary protraction of simulation (Gane 2000: 16). However, it is an important addition since simulation was first proposed before the proliferation of bio and digital technologies.

2. He adds, in Baudrillardian terms, that 'what makes information all-powerful [. . .] is its very nullity, its radical ineffectiveness [. . .] If there is no debasement of information, it is because information itself is a debasement' (*TI*: 258).

3. Baudrillard's viral is a phenomenon that others have rendered in less mystifying terms. Jameson aligns finance capital with Deleuze and Guattari, saying that 'the system is better seen as a kind of virus [. . .] and its development is something like an epidemic (better still, a rash of epidemics, an epidemic of epidemics)' (1997: 249). Michael A. Peters describes a fourth phase, bio-informational capitalism, based 'on a self-organising and self-replicating code that harnesses both the results of the information and new biology revolutions and brings them together' (2012: 105). Eugene Thacker and Alexander R. Galloway (2007: 101) wonder what will come after Deleuze's societies of control, when bioinformatics replaces computers and hypertrophy replaces political disturbances.

4. For Braidotti, the 'virus or parasite constitutes a model of a symbiotic relationship that defeats binary oppositions. It is a simulacrum that duplicates itself to infinity without any representational pretensions' (2002: 227).

5. Bardini's premise is 'Cyberpositive', which serves as an epigraph for this chapter. He credits SF author David Gerrold for first using the term 'virus' in relation to computers in his novel *When HARLIE Was One* (1972).

6. Bardini does indeed speak of 'the viral ontology of the capitalism of the fourth kind' (2011: 182).

7. Jeffrey Boase and Barry Wellman (2001: 40) compare how three types of viruses (biological, computer, marketing) are spread and controlled, and the consequences of infection. The relevant sections of their comparative table are reproduced here.

	Biological	*Computer*	*Marketing*
Spread	Disease	Destruction	Fashions
Tracing	Very difficult	Reverse messaging	Financial reward
Mutations	Natural	Deliberately created	New business model
Networking	Physical isolation	Social isolation	Network overload
Trojans	Protect against infection	Form of computer virus	Brand name

    Pathogenicity and pathogenesis remain constant despite the difference in vector. The virus adapts itself to benefit capital, which recycles and profits from its own chaos.

8. In biocomputing 'biology becomes a medium' – 'the DNA is fully biological [rather than digital] and the entire process of computation takes place in the test tube' so that the DNA has a digital output (Thacker 2003: 51).

9. In this sense it is an extrapolation of biocomputing but also of bioinformatics, which uses digitised, simulated DNA, manipulated by computers, with a biological output (Thacker 2003: 51).

10. The Deleuzian rhetoric is no coincidence – Cooper draws on *The Fold*.

11. *Antiviral*'s promotional slogan reads: 'What if you could feel like they do . . . We can help.' Consumers don't want to look like celebrities, they want to be affected by them. It is biological contagion and desire that are fetishised, even in their grotesque forms: the deformed body, the viral face.

12. Baudrillard reviewed Monod's *Chance and Necessity* in 1971 in *Utopie*, reproduced here in *Utopia Deferred*. Parts of the argument are repeated elsewhere (*SED*, *FF*) to develop a critique of Deleuze and Foucault.

13. Baudrillard's transaesthetic (*TE*: 15–21) is evident in the conjoining of beauty and deformity when Dorian explains that healthy tulips have solid-coloured petals, while the violet pattern on his yellow tulip is a result of viral infection.

14. The film thereby extrapolates the real-life story of Henrietta Lacks, to whom Arvid gestures earlier in the film. Lacks's cancer cells, cultured after her death, were extraordinary in that, unlike most cells, they did not die, but continued to grow. The cells have since been put to extensive use by medical science. See Rebecca Skloot (2010) and Baudrillard (2011b: 36).

Coda

The imminent remake of *Videodrome* promises to 'modernise the concept, infus[ing] it with the possibilities of nano-technology and blow it up into a large-scale sci-fi action thriller' (Fleming 2009: 1). Like cyberpunk itself, Cronenberg's film devours its own logic, so that, by the end, the New Flesh isn't flesh at all, but a cerebrocortical discharge into corporate messianism. So too there is something autocannibalistic about remaking a film about the subsumption of existence by imagistic technologies. *Videodrome*'s analogue technology has never circumscribed its uncontrollable flesh, yet one can only assume that nanotechnology will be complemented by digital technologies and platforms. Deleuzian schizoanalytical readings of the film are inevitable, and I trust that my own work shows the extent to which capital provides the internal animation of Cronenberg's film and, more than likely, its hideous progeny. If Baudrillard is to play the role of antagonist in a repetition of becoming-Deleuzian, then he will be a more challenging obstacle on this occasion. The question raised by the remake is what a cyberpunk film might look like in the biotech century. For biopunk to cannibalise its cyberdaddy might be the next evolutionary step, and a schizophrenic one at that. Against the interminable abstraction of value biocapitalism has planned for us, with a renewed appreciation and sympathy for the meat, a bio-punked *Videodrome* might well redistribute its psychic and corporeal coordinates away from the cul-de-sac of capitalist virtual reality. Then we might discover of what the New Flesh is truly capable.

The Shape of Punk to Come

I got a bone to pick with capitalism, and a few to break. (Refused, 1998)

Becoming-Deleuzian demands a thorough reappraisal of Baudrillard's place in SF studies and, combined with the mutations of the genre, a need to rethink cyberpunk as the literature and cinema of late capitalism. Many of cyberpunk's once-progressive impulses have proven

241

as technologically naïve as they are politically harmful. Deleuze and Baudrillard have more to offer this discourse than unlicensed desire and revelries in virtual reality. This is why the opening move of the book was to reinscribe cyberpunk into the broader critical apparatus of control. Burgess's and Kubrick's *A Clockwork Orange* are the most replete elaborations of control, as evidenced by their linguistic, auditory, perceptual and pharmaceutical schizo fluxes and accompanying reterritorialisations.

Baudrillard is far from the most congenial of theoretical interlocutors. I have argued here for a more rigorous engagement with his thought, which is usually confined in SF studies to *Simulacra and Simulation*. As the formative sites of becoming-Deleuzian, Ballard's *Crash* and Cronenberg's *Videodrome* demand a reassertion of Deleuze's schizophrenic interplay of desire and capital, extending also to Cronenberg's take on Ballard. Baudrillard here proves the more systematic thinker and critically valuable resource. He also provides the necessary distance from and antipathy towards what easily becomes the discourse of beautiful souls. As these chapters show, attempts to replace Baudrillard with Deleuze are uninformed by Baudrillard's own critiques of the latter. Placing these at the centre of becoming-Deleuzian yields a richer analysis of both thinkers and overturns long-held assumptions about both texts and critics: the basic insight of Baudrillard's controversial essay on Ballard is that, for all its eroticism, *Crash* remains profoundly devoid of passion.

Incompetent observers readily take Baudrillard for the supreme advocate of the simulacrum rather than its hostile analyst. Simulation is an all-pervading concept, but is itself more fragile than customarily acknowledged. Once its foundations in psychoanalysis and political economy are restored, the simulacrum re-emerges as contestable terrain. Returning to my own more sympathetic sense of Baudrillard's schizophrenic, and to the cracks in the simulacrum exposed in *Crash* and *Fahrenheit 451*, what becomes apparent is the near-total dependence on consensual delusion – the simulation pact. Nomadism is a poor substitute for political contestation, but it does at least indicate that simulation is a state of affairs from which we can be extricated, either by active confrontation, as in *Videodrome*, or by injections of reversibility and contingency, as in *Crash*. The Baudrillard I have thus pursued is 'less Post-Marxist than he recognises' (Murray and Schuler 1988: 327). In much the same way, the Deleuze I put to work is less the one of petty perversions than the one who reaffirms the central Marxian polemic of *Capitalism and Schizophrenia*.

In an essay first published in 1993, Jameson proposed as a 'form of philosophical hygiene that for ten years or so we simply stop using the two words, *power* and the *body*':

> Nothing is more disembodied than such references to the body, except where [...] it generates some real visceral effects [...]; materialism is scarcely achieved by the corporeal litany [...] [and] should not be confused with a historical materialism that turns on *praxis* and on the mode of production. (2008: 626)

For Jameson 'what lies around us are rather images and information stereotypes of the body, which are themselves the most powerful source of interference when it comes to a full phenomenological approach to the body itself' (ibid. 626–7). Appeals to the body as the only authentic form of materialism fall short of its simulacral reproduction and reinscribe on a corporeal level the more familiar concept of solipsism. Later, Jameson adds that the 'problem with the body as a positive slogan is that the body itself, as a unified entity, is an Imaginary concept (in Lacan's sense); it is what Deleuze calls a "body without organs", an empty totality that organises the world without participating in it' (ibid. 652). For Jameson, the body serves a series of ideological functions, formed in the very process of its mediated encounters; power he puts in Foucauldian terms, observing that 'if everything is power, then we neither require that reminder, nor can it retain any of its demystifying force [...] Wouldn't it be more useful', therefore, to 'look at the structure of the multinational corporations themselves, with a view toward determining the mode of influence and production of a properly corporate culture?' (ibid. 627).

If the lapsing of Jameson's long moratorium permits us to redress the body, we discover a highly cathected and financially lucrative object of corporate interest and investment, for which biocapital introduces itself as the mediating process and ideological overdetermination. *Antiviral* brings this to the fore, the inner and outer spaces of the body and the edifice of the simulacrum increasingly one and the same material for the extraction and valorisation of surplus. The film effects a double movement whereby biomaterial becomes a pure, abstracted simulacrum, the value and affects of which radiate and infect indiscriminately across a range of forms; but this very process introduces corporeal intimacy and abjection, making the body once more a political platform from which to speak and act.

Biocapitalism is a new name for an old problem, but one that poses new challenges for Marxism. If not grasped as a subgenre, biopunk might nonetheless be profitably understood as a syndrome of this new space, a 'meeting place or crossing point of manifestations issuing from very different origins and arising within variable contexts' (Deleuze 1989: 14). Short of providing solutions to biocapitalism, biopunk provides the raw materials from which to formulate new questions and concepts, and touches the raw nerves that stimulate the cartographic impulse of cognitive mapping.

Biopunk is a phenomenon necessarily approached politically, historically and schizophrenically, less in Jameson's sense of being enslaved to a perpetual present than in Deleuze and Guattari's that 'no one has ever been as deeply involved in history as the schizo', who 'remain[s] at that unbearable point where the mind touches matter and lives its every intensity' (AO: 21, 20). Rather than basking in an all-too-familiar schizophrenic splendour, the schizophrenic process confronts a particular historical moment. *Frankenstein* provided an important source of inspiration for the cyberpunks. With the diminishing purchase of cyberpunk on our contemporary structures of feeling, imbuing the text with a renewed subgeneric teleology rehabilitates its critical impulse. In the process, *Frankenstein* as both novel and myth acquires an alternative historical and generic leverage for analyses of the economic and libidinal exchanges between biopunk and biocapitalism. The critical value of this gesture is its capacity to identify biopunk within the foundational SF text. Underscoring the accretion of axioms across a genealogy, beginning with Shelley, and thence to *Doctor Moreau* and *Island of Lost Souls*, we arrive at its contemporary form, *Splice*, which signifies a radical break with the Frankenstein barrier, disturbing and reinforcing the extent to which the schizophrenic process and emergent forms of capital animate one another.

We need not visit any further violence on what is already an anaemic grasp of history. Yet 'the events that restore a thing to life are not the same as those that gave rise to it in the first place' (AO: 261). Recasting Čapek's *R.U.R.* as the first credible biopunk text is less an exercise in historical revisionism than a mapping of the mutating influences and inspirations. Above all, it places class consciousness at the very beginnings of biopunk, and that is itself a worthwhile project. The schizophrenic lines traced thence to *The Repossession Mambo*, *Repo Men* and *Never Let Me Go* are ones whose terminus is the 'becoming-private of the organs' (AO: 144).

Coda

Tracing these lines, even into oblivion, is the increasingly unhappy, though necessary, task of schizoanalysis, but also the more enduring labour demanded of cognitive mapping. The biopunk texts in this book, and the exchanges between them, are not the only stories to be told about biocapitalism, but they speak to the future of our fascination with schizophrenia, and to a deeper appreciation for the private neuroses and social investments that labour under a 'disorder whose cardinal feature', Woods notes, 'is its opacity' (2011: 221).

The deleterious lines traced are out of sympathy with the more joyous paths of deterritorialisation pursued by most Deleuzians, but they respond to the urgent presentiment that the supple distinctions between paranoiac breakdowns and schizophrenic breakthroughs have become increasingly hardcoded into biocapitalism itself. At *Antiviral*'s conclusion, simultaneously pathologically creative and cruel, one cannot escape the feeling of being seduced and abandoned. Does its final image denote sex, survival, communion or an ongoing engagement with the afterlife of the body?[1] The more these lines traverse one another, the more they become a mass confusion of circuitry, harder to unravel. This increasingly lends itself to uncharitable readings of schizophrenia. The introduction of suffering as a key analytic variable into the schizophrenic process underscores that 'provided the hatred is strong enough something can be salvaged, a great joy which is not the ambivalent joy of hatred, but the joy of wanting to destroy whatever mutilates life' (Deleuze 1988: 23). This renewed sense of schizophrenia, attuned to its own shameful failures, is the degree zero from which to fail again, but also to fail better, so that we might 'not feel ourselves outside of our time but continue to undergo shameful compromises with it', and this 'feeling of shame is one of philosophy's most powerful motifs' (Deleuze and Guattari 1994: 108).

This is the best way to grasp the fourth order, in which schizophrenia remains our central problem and governing passion. Here we find biocapitalism's highest assertion, but also a host of artistic originalities that allow us to think through its challenges. Baudrillard ably points to both the monstrous intensity and the banality of this new *mise en scène*, providing its theoretical rationale, but not to how it might be changed. For this very reason, I prefaced my analysis of *Antiviral* with Deleuze's faith in a new cinema that might give us reasons to believe in the world, one where the 'body is no longer the obstacle that separates thought from itself, that which it has to overcome to reach thinking [. . .] It is through the body (and no

245

longer through the intermediary of the body) that cinema forms its alliance with the spirit, with thought' (*TI*: 182). This precise sense of *through the body* is the schizophrenic intensity of biocapitalism, the seemingly boundless processes of abstraction which retain as their precondition the notion of labour power, but also reacquire the injunction that the worker is '*labour* personified' who, like a punk, confronts the machinations of alienation 'as a rebel and experiences it as a process of enslavement' (Marx 1982: 989–90).

I began this book with the observation that SF provides a 'snapshot' of capital. Captured at the interval between instinct and thought, a snapshot's affective power comes from apprehending an event as it unfolds, extracting a particle from a constellation of causal relations. Snapshots are perpetually in the middle of one thing becoming something else. They offer up a fragment of a becoming that changes our perception of its multiplicity of forces, prying it open, or careering along its surface. Snapshots are not taken contemplatively, but they can be disarming. On its own, each text is a snapshot and, in this book, I have analysed SF texts that either ignite us with their vitality or disturb us with their unspeakable misery. Indeed, the basic insight of dialectical thought is not only that these two animate one another by providing a necessary contradiction, but also that the contradiction is itself the condition of possibility. More than a matter of perspective – Baudrillardian or Deleuzian, as has been the case here – or the casual trauma of cognitive dissonance, the revelation of the dialectic is not necessarily a synthesis, but only that there can be no vitality without the danger of this misery, while the promise of vitality alone makes misery worth enduring. This neither transforms our self-disgust and hatred into nihilism or inaction nor propels us into equally unbearable ecstasy. Rather, it equips us with the patience and dedication required for the careful, ongoing analysis of capitalism's history, present, and future developments. From its origins to its contemporary form, from cyberpunk to biopunk, control to contagion, SF provides a crucial perspective from which to carry out this work.

Note

1. Claire Perkins asked me this question when she read this chapter. I don't have the answer, but that's less important than the question itself. My thanks to Claire.

References

Agamben, G. (1998) [1995], *Homo Sacer: Sovereign Power and Bare Life*, trans. D. Heller-Roazen, Stanford: Stanford University Press.

—(2005) [2003], *State of Exception*, trans. K. Attell, Chicago: University of Chicago Press.

Aldiss, B. W. (2001) [1986], *Trillion Year Spree: The History of Science Fiction*, London: House of Stratus.

Althusser, L. and É. Balibar (1997) [1968], *Reading Capital*, trans. B. Brewster, London: Verso.

Anderson, M. (dir.) (1976), *Logan's Run* [film], United States: MGM.

Angenot, M. (1979), 'The Absent Paradigm: An Introduction to the Semiotics of Science Fiction', *Science Fiction Studies*, 6(1), 9–19.

Bacigalupi, P. (2011) [2009], *The Windup Girl*, San Francisco: Night Shade Books.

Badiou, A. (2000) [1997], *Deleuze: The Clamour of Being*, trans. L. Burchill, Minneapolis: University of Minnesota Press.

Baker, B. (2005), 'Ray Bradbury: *Fahrenheit 451*', in D. Seed (ed.), *A Companion to Science Fiction*, Oxford: Blackwell Publishing, pp. 489–99.

Ballard, J. G. (1984), 'Introduction to *Crash*', *RE/Search*, 8/9, 96–8.

—(1990) [1970], *The Atrocity Exhibition*, London: Fourth Estate.

—(1995) [1973], *Crash*, London: Vintage.

Banerjee, S. B. (2008), 'Necrocapitalism', *Organization Studies*, 29(12), 1541–63.

Bardini, T. (2011), *Junkware*, Minneapolis: University of Minnesota Press.

Barker, M., J. Arthurs and R. Harindranath (2001), *The Crash Controversy: Censorship Campaigns and Film Reception*, New York: Wallflower Press.

Bashford, A. and C. Hooker (2001), 'Introduction: Contagion, Modernity and Postmodernity', in A. Bashford and C. Hooker (eds), *Contagion: Historical and Cultural Studies*, London: Routledge, pp. 1–12.

Baudrillard, J. (1975) [1973], *The Mirror of Production*, trans. M. Poster, St Louis: Telos Press.

—(1981) [1972], *For a Critique of the Political Economy of the Sign*, trans. C. Levin, St Louis: Telos Press.

—(1983a), *In the Shadow of the Silent Majorities . . . or the End of the Social, and Other Essays*, trans. P. Foss, P. Patton and J. Johnston, New York: Semiotext(e).

—(1983b), *Simulations*, trans. P. Foss, P. Patton and P. Beitchman, New York: Semiotext(e).

—(1987) [1977], *Forget Foucault*, New York: Semiotext(e).

—(1990) [1979], *Seduction*, trans. B. Singer, New York: St. Martin's Press.

—(1991), 'Two Essays', trans. A. B. Evans, *Science Fiction Studies*, 18(3), 309–20.

—(1993a) [1990], *The Transparency of Evil: Essays on Extreme Phenomena*, trans. J. Benedict, New York: Verso.

—(1993b), *Baudrillard Live: Selected Interviews*, ed. M. Gane, London: Routledge.

—(1994a) [1981], *Simulacra and Simulation*, trans. S. F. Glaser, Ann Arbor: University of Michigan Press.

—(1994b) [1992], *The Illusion of the End*, trans. C. Turner, Oxford: Polity Press.

—(1995) [1991], *The Gulf War Did Not Take Place*, trans. P. Patton, Indianapolis: Indiana University Press.

—(1997), 'Aesthetic Illusion and Virtual Reality', in N. Zurbrugg (ed.), *Jean Baudrillard, Art and Artefact*, Brisbane: Institute of Modern Art, pp. 19–27.

—(2000), *The Vital Illusion*, ed. J. Witwer, New York: Columbia University Press.

—(2002) [2000], *Screened Out*, trans. C. Turner, New York: Verso.

—(2003a) [1987], *Cool Memories*, trans. C. Turner, London: Verso.

—(2003b) [2002], *The Spirit of Terrorism and Other Essays*, trans. C. Turner, New York: Verso.

—(2004a) [2001], *Fragments: Conversations with François L'Yvonnet*, trans. C. Turner, London: Routledge.

—(2004b), 'This is the Fourth World War: The *Der Spiegel* Interview with Jean Baudrillard', trans. S. Gandesha, *International Journal of Baudrillard Studies*, 1(1); retrieved from <http://www2.ubishops.ca/baudrillardstudies/vol1_1/spiegel.htm> (last accessed 14 October 2015).

—(2005a) [1968], *The System of Objects*, trans. J. Benedict, London: Verso.

—(2005b), *The Conspiracy of Art*, trans. A. Hodges, New York: Semiotext(e).

—(2006a) [2005], *Cool Memories V (2000–2005)*, trans. C. Turner, Cambridge: Polity Press.

—(2006b), *Utopia Deferred: Writings from Utopie (1967–1968)*, trans. S. Kendall, New York: Semiotext(e).

—(2007) [2005], *The Intelligence of Evil or the Lucidity Pact*, trans. C. Turner, London: Berg.

—(2008a) [1983], *Fatal Strategies*, trans. P. Beitchman and W. G. J. Niesluchowski, Los Angeles: Semiotext(e).

—(2008b), 'The Violence of Images, Violence Against the Image', trans. P. Foss, *artUS*, 23, 38–45.

References

—(2009) [1970], *The Consumer Society: Myths and Structures*, trans. C. Turner, London: Sage.

—(2010a) [1986], *America*, trans. C. Turner, New York: Verso.

—(2010b), *The Agony of Power*, trans. A. Hodges, Los Angeles: Semiotext(e).

—(2011a) [1976], *Symbolic Exchange and Death*, trans. I. H. Grant, London: Sage.

—(2011b) [1999], *Impossible Exchange*, trans. C. Turner, New York: Verso.

—(2012) [1987], *The Ecstasy of Communication*, trans. B. Schütze and C. Schütze, Los Angeles: Semiotext(e).

Bauman, Z. (2011), *Culture in a Liquid Modern World*, trans. L. Bauman, Cambridge: Polity Press.

Baxter, J. (2009), *J. G. Ballard's Surrealist Imagination: Spectacular Authorship*, Burlington: Ashgate.

Bay, M. (dir.) (2005), *The Island* [film], United States: DreamWorks.

Bear, G. (2001) [1985], *Blood Music*, London: Gollancz.

Beaulieu, A. (2011), 'The Status of Animals in Deleuze's Thought', *Journal for Critical Animal Studies*, 9(1/2), 69–88.

Beckett, S. (1989), *Nohow On*, London: Calder.

Best, S. and D. Kellner (2001), *The Postmodern Adventure: Science, Technology, and Cultural Studies at the Third Millennium*, London: Routledge.

Biel, R. (2012), *The Entropy of Capitalism*, Boston: Brill.

Big Black (composers) (1987), *Songs About Fucking* [LP], United States: Touch and Go.

Birke, L. (1994), *Feminism, Animals and Science: The Naming of the Shrew*, Buckingham: Open University Press.

Black, S. (2009), 'Ishiguro's Inhuman Aesthetics', *Modern Fiction Studies*, 55(4), 785–807.

Boase, J. and B. Wellman (2001), 'A Plague of Viruses: Biological, Computer and Marketing', *Current Sociology*, 49(6), 39–55.

Bök, C. (2002), *'Pataphysics: The Poetics of an Imaginary Science*, Evanston: Northwestern University Press.

Boltanski, L. and È Chiapello (2007) [1999], *The New Spirit of Capitalism*, trans. G. Elliott, London: Verso.

Botting, F. and S. Wilson (1998), 'Automatic Lover', *Screen*, 39(2), 186–92.

Bould, M. (2005), 'Burning Too: Consuming *Fahrenheit 451*', *Essays and Studies*, 58, 96–122.

—(2008), 'Science Fiction Television in the United Kingdom', in J. P. Telotte (ed.), *The Essential Science Fiction Television Reader*, Kentucky: University Press of Kentucky, pp. 209–30.

—(2009), 'Introduction' and 'Appendices', in M. Bould and C. Miéville (eds), *Red Planets: Marxism and Science Fiction*, Middletown, CT: Wesleyan University Press, pp. 1–26 and 249–79.

Boyle, D. (dir.) (2002), *28 Days Later* [film], United Kingdom: DNA Films and British Film Council.

Bradbury, R. (2004) [1953], *Fahrenheit 451*, London: Voyager.

Braidotti, R. (2002) [1994], *Metamorphoses: Towards a Materialist Theory of Becoming*, Cambridge: Polity Press.

—(2007), 'Bio-Power and Necro-Politics: Reflections on an Ethics of Sustainability'; retrieved from <http://www.springerin.at/dyn/heft_text. php?textid=1928&lang=en> (last accessed 8 October 2015).

Brians, E. (2011), 'The "Virtual" Body and the Strange Persistence of the Flesh: Deleuze, Cyberspace and the Posthuman', in L. Guillaume and J. Hughes (eds), *Deleuze and the Body*, Edinburgh: Edinburgh University Press, pp. 120–43.

Brooks, M. (2006), *World War Z: An Oral History of the Zombie War*, New York: Three Rivers Press.

Browning, G. and A. Kilmister (2006), *Critical and Post-Critical Political Economy*, Basingstoke: Palgrave Macmillan.

Browning, J. (2005), 'Hello, Dolly' [review of the book *Never Let Me Go*, by Kazuo Ishiguro], *Village Voice*; retrieved from <http://www.villagevoice. com/2005-03-22/books/hello-dolly/full/> (last accessed 8 October 2015).

Buchanan, I. (2000), *Deleuzism: A Metacommentary*, Durham, NC: Duke University Press.

—(2008), *Deleuze and Guattari's Anti-Oedipus: A Reader's Guide*, London: Continuum.

Bukatman, S. (1993), *Terminal Identity: The Virtual Subject in Postmodern Science Fiction*, Durham, NC: Duke University Press.

—(2003) [1990], 'Who Programs You? The Science Fiction of the Spectacle', in A. Kuhn (ed.), *Alien Zone: Cultural Theory and Contemporary Science Fiction Cinema*, London: Verso, pp. 196–213.

Burgess, A. (1975), 'On the Hopelessness of Turning Good Books into Films', *New York Times*, 20 April, pp. 14–15.

—(2000) [1962], *A Clockwork Orange*, London: Penguin.

Burroughs, W. S. (1966a) [1961], *The Soft Machine*, New York: Grove Press.

—(1966b) [1964], *Nova Express*, London: Cape.

—(1967) [1962], *The Ticket that Exploded*, New York: Grove Press.

—(1974), 'Control', in *The Job: Interviews with William S. Burroughs*, New York: Grove Press, pp. 38–48.

—(1979), *Blade Runner (a movie)*, Berkeley: Blue Wind Press.

—(1998), 'The Limits of Control', in J. Grauerholz and I. Silverberg (eds), *Word Virus: The William S. Burroughs Reader*, New York: Grove Press, pp. 339–41.

—(2001) [1959], *Naked Lunch*, New York: Grove Press.

References

—(2002) [1953], *Junky*, New York: Penguin.
Butler, A. M. (2009), 'Jean Baudrillard (1929–2007)', in M. Bould, A. M. Butler, A. Roberts and S. Vint (eds), *Fifty Key Figures in Science Fiction*, Abingdon: Routledge, pp. 22–6.
Butler, J. (1993), *Bodies that Matter: On the Discursive Limits of 'Sex'*, New York: Routledge.
Butler, O. (1997a) [1987], *Dawn*, New York: Warner Books.
—(1997b) [1988], *Adult Rights*, New York: Warner Books.
—(1997c) [1989], *Imago*, New York: Warner Books.
Butler, R. (2010), 'Foucault + Dead Power', in R. G. Smith (ed.), *The Baudrillard Dictionary*, Edinburgh: Edinburgh University Press, pp. 78–80.
Callinicos, A. (2001), 'Toni Negri in Perspective', *International Socialism*, 2(92); retrieved from <http://www.marxists.org/history/etol/writers/cal linicos/2001/xx/toninegri.htm> (last accessed 8 October 2015).
Campbell, T. (2008), '*Bíos*, Immunity, Life: The Thought of Robert Esposito', in R. Esposito, *Bíos: Biopolitics and Philosophy*, trans. T. Campbell, Minneapolis: University of Minnesota Press, pp. vii–xlii.
Campus, M. (dir.) (1972), *Z.P.G.* [film], United Kingdom: Sagittarius Productions Inc.
Čapek, K. (1961) [1920], *R.U.R. (Rossum's Universal Robots)*, trans. P. Selver, in J. and K. Čapek, *R.U.R. and The Insect Play*, London: Oxford University Press, pp. 1–104.
—(1996) [1935], 'The Author of the Robots Defends Himself', trans. C. Simsa, *Science Fiction Studies*, 23(1), 143–4.
Carroll, R. (2010), 'Imitations of Life: Cloning, Heterosexuality and the Human in Kazuo Ishiguro's *Never Let Me Go*', *Journal of Gender Studies*, 19(1), 59–71.
Chatman, S. (1978), *Story and Discourse: Narrative Structure in Fiction and Film*, Ithaca: Cornell University Press.
—(1990), *Coming to Terms: The Rhetoric of Narrative in Fiction and Film*, Ithaca: Cornell University Press.
Clarke, J. (2009), *The Paradox of the Posthuman: Science Fiction/Techno-Horror Films and Visual Media*, Saarbrücken: VDM Verlag Dr Müller Aktiengesellschaft & Co. KG.
Clemens, J. and D. Pettman (2004), *Avoiding the Subject: Media, Culture and the Object*, Amsterdam: Amsterdam University Press.
Colman, F. J. (2005), 'Feminism', in A. Parr (ed.), *The Deleuze Dictionary*, Edinburgh: Edinburgh University Press, pp. 100–2.
Comaroff, J. and J. L. Comaroff (2001), 'Millennial Capitalism: First Thoughts on a Second Coming', in J. Comaroff and J. L. Comaroff (eds), *Millennial Capitalism and the Culture of Neoliberalism*, Durham, NC: Duke University Press, pp. 1–56.
Constable, C. (2009), *Adapting Philosophy: Jean Baudrillard and The Matrix Trilogy*, Manchester: Manchester University Press.

—(2011), 'Theory as Style: Adapting *Crash* via Baudrillard and Cronenberg', in H. Carel and G. Tuck (eds), *New Takes in Film-Philosophy*, New York: Palgrave Macmillan, pp. 135–53.

Cook, R. K. (1977), *Coma*, London: Macmillan.

Cooper, M. (2008), *Life as Surplus: Biotechnology and Capitalism in the Neoliberal Era*, Seattle: University of Washington Press.

Coppola, F. F. (dir.) (1979), *Apocalypse Now* [film], United States: Zoetrope Studios.

Creed, B. (1998), 'Anal Wounds, Metallic Kisses', *Screen*, 39(2), 175–9.

Crisp, C. G. (1972), *François Truffaut*, London: November Books.

Cronenberg, B. (dir.) (2012), *Antiviral* [film], Canada: Alliance Films.

Cronenberg, D. (dir.) (1983), *Videodrome* [film], Canada: Canadian Film Development Corporation.

—(1986), *The Fly* [film], United States: Brooksfilms and SLM Production Group.

—(1996), *Crash* [film], Canada and United Kingdom: The Movie Network and Telefilm Canada.

Csicsery-Ronay Jr, I. (1991a), 'Editorial Introduction: Postmodernism's SF/SF's Postmodernism', *Science Fiction Studies*, 18(3), 305–8.

—(1991b), 'The SF of Theory: Baudrillard and Haraway', *Science Fiction Studies*, 18(3), 387–404.

—(1994) [1991], 'Cyberpunk and Neuromanticism', in L. McCaffery (ed.), *Storming the Reality Studio: A Casebook of Cyberpunk and Postmodern Science Fiction*, Durham, NC: Duke University Press, pp. 182–93.

—(2008), *The Seven Beauties of Science Fiction*, Middletown, CT: Wesleyan University Press.

Cuarón, A. (dir.) (2006), *Children of Men* [film], United Kingdom and United States: Strike Entertainment and Hit and Run Productions.

Cubitt, S. (2001), *Simulation and Social Theory*, London: Sage.

Cusset, F. (2008), *French Theory: How Foucault, Derrida, Deleuze, & Co. Transformed the Intellectual Life of the United States*, trans. J. Fort, Minneapolis: University of Minnesota Press.

Dawkins, R. (2006) [1986], *The Blind Watchmaker*, London: Penguin.

Deleuze, G. (1988) [1986], *Foucault*, trans. S. Hand, Minneapolis: University of Minnesota Press.

—(1989) [1967], *Masochism: Coldness and Cruelty & Venus in Furs*, trans. J. McNeil, New York: Zone Books.

—(1992) [1990], 'Postscript on the Societies of Control', *October*, 59, 3–7.

—(1993) [1988], *The Fold: Leibniz and the Baroque*, trans. T. Conley, London: Athlone Press.

—(1995) [1990], *Negotiations: 1972–1990*, trans. M. Joughin, New York: Columbia University Press.

—(1998) [1993], *Essays Critical and Clinical*, trans. D. W. Smith and M. A. Greco, London: Verso.

References

—(2001), 'What is a Creative Act?', in S. Lotringer and S. Cohen (eds), *French Theory in America*, New York: Routledge, pp. 99–107.

—(2003) [1981], *Francis Bacon: The Logic of Sensation*, trans. D. W. Smith, London: Bloomsbury.

—(2004) [1969], *The Logic of Sense*, trans. M. Lester and C. Stivale, London: Continuum.

—(2006) [2004], *Two Regimes of Madness: Text and Interviews 1975–1995*, trans. A. Hodges and M. Taormina, New York: Semiotext(e).

—(2011) [1968], *Difference and Repetition*, trans. P. Patton, London: Continuum.

—(2012a) [1983], *Cinema 1: The Movement-Image*, trans. H. Tomlinson and B. Habberjam, New York: Continuum.

—(2012b) [1986], *Cinema 2: The Time-Image*, trans. H. Tomlinson and R. Galeta, New York: Continuum.

Deleuze, G. and F. Guattari (1986) [1975], *Kafka: Toward a Minor Literature*, trans. D. Polan, Minneapolis: University of Minnesota Press.

—(1994) [1991], *What is Philosophy?*, trans. H. Tomlinson and G. Burchell, New York: Columbia University Press.

—(2004) [1980], *A Thousand Plateaus: Capitalism and Schizophrenia*, trans. B. Massumi, New York: Continuum.

—(2009) [1972], *Anti-Oedipus: Capitalism and Schizophrenia*, trans. R. Hurley, M. Seem and H. R. Lane, New York: Penguin.

Deleuze, G. and C. Parnet (1987) [1977], *Dialogues*, trans. H. Tomlinson and B. Habberjam, New York: Columbia University Press.

Delville, M. (1998), *J. G. Ballard*, Plymouth: Northcote House and The British Council.

Derrida, J. (1973) [1967], *Speech and Phenomena, and Other Essays on Husserl's Theory of Signs*, trans. D. B. Allison, Evanston: Northwestern University Press.

—(1978) [1967], *Writing and Difference*, trans. A. Bass, London: Routledge.

—(1982), 'Différance', in *Margins of Philosophy*, trans. A. Bass, Chicago: University of Chicago Press, pp. 1–17.

Di Filippo, P. (1996), 'Ribofunk: The Manifesto'; retrieved from <http://www.dvara.net/hk/ribofunk.asp> (last accessed 6 November 2015).

Dick, P. K. (1996) [1968], *Do Androids Dream of Electric Sheep?*, London: Voyager.

Diocaretz, M. and S. Herbrechter (eds) (2006), *The Matrix in Theory*, New York: Rodopi.

Donaldson, R. (dir.) (1995), *Species* [film], United States: MGM.

Dosse, F. (2010) [2007], *Gilles Deleuze & Félix Guattari: Intersecting Lives*, trans. D. Glassman, New York: Columbia University Press.

Durham, S. (1998), *Phantom Communities: The Simulacrum and the Limits of Postmodernism*, Stanford: Stanford University Press.

During, E. (2001), 'Blackboxing in Theory: Deleuze versus Deleuze', in

S. Lotringer and S. Cohen (eds), *French Theory in America*, New York: Routledge, pp. 163–90.

During, S. (ed.) (2007), *The Cultural Studies Reader*, 3rd edn, London: Routledge.

Eatough, M. (2011), 'The Time that Remains: Organ Donation, Temporal Duration, and *Bildung* in Kazuo Ishiguro's *Never Let Me Go*', *Literature and Medicine*, 29(1), 132–60.

Economides, L. (2009), 'Recycled Creatures and Rogue Genomes: Biotechnology in Mary Shelley's *Frankenstein* and David Mitchell's *Cloud Atlas*', *Literature Compass*, 6(3), 615–31.

Eddleman, S. (2009), The Postmodern Turn in Cronenberg's Cinema: Possibility in Bodies', *Shift*, 2, 1–20.

Edelman, V. (1996), 'Touch Goes High-Tech', *Psychology Today*, 29(1), 59.

Egan, G. (1992), *Quarantine*, London: Gollancz.

—(1994), *Permutation City*, London: Millennium.

—(1995), *Distress*, London: Gollancz.

—(1999), *Teranesia*, London: Gollancz.

Ehrlich, P. R. (1968), *The Population Bomb*, London: Ballantine Books.

Engels, F. (1962), 'The Part Played by Labour in the Transition from Ape to Man', in K. Marx and F. Engels, *Selected Works, Volume II*, Moscow: Foreign Languages Publishing House, pp. 80–92.

Enzensberger, H. M. (1974), *The Consciousness Industry: On Literature, Politics and the Media*, New York: Seabury Press.

Eribon, D. (1991) [1989], *Michel Foucault*, trans. B. Wing, Cambridge, MA: Harvard University Press.

Esposito, R. (2008) [2004], *Bíos: Biopolitics and Philosophy*, trans. T. Campbell, Minneapolis: University of Minnesota Press.

Fekete, J. (1994), *Moral Panic: Biopolitics Rising*, Montreal: R. Davies Publishing.

Ferreira, A. (2008), 'Primate Tales: Interspecies Pregnancy and Chimerical Beings', *Science Fiction Studies*, 35(2), 223–37.

Fincher, D. (dir.) (1999), *Fight Club* [film], United States and Germany: Regency Enterprise and Linson Films.

Fisher, M. (2009), *Capitalist Realism: Is There No Alternative?*, Washington: Zero Books.

—(2012), 'Precarious Dystopias: *The Hunger Games*, *In Time*, and *Never Let Me Go*', *Film Quarterly*, 65(4), 27–33.

Fiveson, R. S. (dir.) (1979), *Parts: The Clonus Horror* [film], United States: Group 1 International Distribution Organization Ltd.

Fleischer, R. (dir.) (1973), *Soylent Green* [film], United States: MGM.

Fleming, M. (2009), 'U Cues up Redo of "Videodrome"', *Daily Variety*, 27 April, pp. 1 and 9.

Flieger, J. A. (2000), 'Becoming-Woman: Deleuze and the Molecular

References

Unconscious', in I. Buchanan and C. Colebrook (eds), *Deleuze and Feminist Theory*, Edinburgh: Edinburgh University Press, pp. 38–63.
—(2005), *Is Oedipus Online? Siting Freud after Freud*, Cambridge, MA: The MIT Press.
Fluet, L. (2007), 'Immaterial Labors: Ishiguro, Class, and Affect', *NOVEL: A Forum on Fiction*, 40(3), 265–88.
Fordham, J. (2010), '1 + 1 = 3', *CineFex*, 122, 11–32.
Forry, S. (1990), *Hideous Progenies: Dramatizations of Frankenstein from Mary Shelley to the Present*, Philadelphia: University of Pennsylvania Press.
Forster, M. (dir.) (2013), *World War Z* [film], United States and United Kingdom: Skydance Productions, Hemisphere Media Capital, GK Films and Plan B Entertainment.
Fotopoulos, T. and A. Gezerlis (2002), 'Hardt and Negri's *Empire*: A New Communist Manifesto or a Reformist Welcome to Neoliberal Globalisation?', *Democracy & Nature*, 8(2), 319–30.
Foucault, M. (1977), *Language, Counter-Memory, Practice: Selected Essays and Interviews*, ed. D. F. Bouchard, trans. D. F. Bouchard and S. Simon, Ithaca: Cornell University Press.
—(1978) [1976], *The History of Sexuality, Vol. 1: An Introduction*, trans. R. Hurley, New York: Pantheon Books.
—(1980), *Power/Knowledge: Selected Interviews and Other Writings, 1972–1977*, ed. C. Gordon, New York: Pantheon Books.
—(1995) [1975], *Discipline and Punish: The Birth of the Prison*, trans. A. Sheridan, New York: Vintage Books.
—(2003) [1997], *Society Must Be Defended: Lectures at the Collège de France, 1975–1976*, trans. D. Macey, New York: Picador.
—(2008) [2004], *The Birth of Biopolitics: Lectures at the Collège de France, 1978–1979*, ed. M. Senellart, trans. G. Burchell, New York: Picador.
Frankenheimer, J. (dir.) (1996), *The Island of Dr. Moreau* [film], United States: New Line Cinema.
Franklin, S. (2006), 'The Cyborg Embryo: Our Path to Transbiology', *Theory Culture Society*, 23(7/8), 167–87.
Freedman, C. (2000), *Critical Theory and Science Fiction*, Middletown, CT: Wesleyan University Press.
Freud, S. (1922), 'A Child is Being Beaten', *The Journal of Nervous and Mental Disease*, 56(4), 405–6.
—(1995), *The Freud Reader*, ed. P. Gay, London: Vintage.
—(2002) [1930], *Civilisation and Its Discontents*, trans. D. McLintock, London: Penguin Books.
Freud, S. and J. Breuer (2004), *Studies in Hysteria*, trans. N. Luckhurst, London: Penguin Books.
Fudge, E. (1999), 'Calling Creatures by their True Names: Bacon, the New Science and the Beast in Man', in S. Wiseman, R. Gilbert and E. Fudge

(eds), *At the Borders of Human: Beasts and Natural Philosophy in the Early Modern Period*, London: Macmillan, pp. 91–109.

Gane, M. (2000), *Jean Baudrillard: In Radical Uncertainty*, London: Pluto Press.

Garcia, E. (2009), *The Repossession Mambo*, New York: Harper Collins.

Gasiorek, A. (2005), *J. G. Ballard*, Manchester: Manchester University Press.

Genosko, G. (1999), *McLuhan and Baudrillard: The Masters of Implosion*, London: Routledge.

Gerrold, D. (1972), *When HARLIE Was One*, New York: Ballantine Books.

Gibson, W. (1984), *Neuromancer*, New York: Ace Books.

Gilbert, S. and S. Gubar (1984), *The Madwoman in the Attic: The Woman Writer and the Nineteenth-Century Literary Imagination*, New Haven: Yale University Press.

Gingeras, A. M. (2001), 'Disappearing Acts: The French Theory Effect in the Art World', in S. Lotringer and S. Cohen (eds), *French Theory in America*, New York: Routledge, pp. 259–70.

Gleaves, D. H. and E. Hernandez (1999), 'Recent Reformulations of Freud's Development and Abandonment of his Seduction Theory: Historical/ Scientific Clarification or a Continued Assault on Truth?', *History of Psychology*, 2(4), 324–54.

Godard, J.-L. (dir.) (1967), *Weekend* [film], France: Athos Films.

Goh, R. B. H. (2000), '"Clockwork" Language Reconsidered: Iconicity and Narrative in Anthony Burgess's "A Clockwork Orange"', *Journal of Narrative Theory*, 30(2), 263–80.

Gomel, E. (2000), 'From Dr. Moreau to Dr. Mengele: The Biological Sublime', *Poetics Today*, 21(2), 393–421.

Gonzalez, P. B. (2010), '*Fahrenheit 451*: A Brave New World for the New Man', *Senses of Cinema*, 55; retrieved from <http://sensesofcinema. com/2010/feature-articles/fahrenheit-451-a-brave-new-world-for-the-new-man-2/> (last accessed 9 October 2015).

Gordon, S. (dir.) (1985), *Re-Animator* [film], United States: Empire Pictures.

Grace, V. (2000), *Baudrillard's Challenge: A Feminist Reading*, New York: Routledge.

Grebowicz, M. (2010), 'When Species Meat: Confronting Bestiality Pornography', *Humanimalia*, 1(2), 1–17.

Griffith, G. (2009), 'Science and the Cultural Imaginary: The Case of Kazuo Ishiguro's *Never Let Me Go*', *Textual Practice*, 23(4), 645–63.

Grosz, E. (1994), *Volatile Bodies: Toward a Corporal Feminism*, Sydney: Allen & Unwin.

Grünberg, S. (2006), *David Cronenberg: Interviews with Serge Grünberg*, London: Plexus.

References

Guattari, F. (2006), *The Anti-Oedipus Papers*, ed. S. Nadaud, trans. K. Gotman, Los Angeles: Semiotext(e).

—(2009), *Chaosophy: Texts and Interviews 1972–1977*, ed. S. Lotringer, trans. D. L. Sweet, J. Becker and T. Adkins, Los Angeles: Semiotext(e).

Haddow, G., A. Bruce, J. Calvert, S. H. E. Harmon and W. Marsden (2010), 'Not "Human" Enough to be Human but not "Animal" Enough to be Animal: The Case of the HFEA, Cybrids and Xenotransplantation in the UK', *New Genetics and Society*, 29(1), 3–17.

Hageman, A. (2012), 'The Challenge of Imagining Ecological Future: Paolo Bacigalupi's *The Windup Girl*', *Science Fiction Studies*, 39(2), 283–303.

Hallward, P. (2006), *Out of this World: Deleuze and Philosophy of Creation*, London: Verso.

Ham, M. (2004), 'Excess and Resistance in Feminised Bodies: David Cronenberg's *Videodrome* and Jean Baudrillard's *Seduction*', *Senses of Cinema*, 30; retrieved from <http://sensesofcinema.com/2004/30/videodrome_seduction/> (last accessed 9 October 2015).

Hamilton, S. N. (2003), 'Traces of the Future: Biotechnology, Science Fiction and the Media', *Science Fiction Studies*, 20(2), 267–82.

Hansen, M. (2001), 'Internal Resonance, or Three Steps Towards a Non-Viral Becoming', *Culture Machine*, 3; retrieved from <http://www.culturemachine.net/index.php/cm/article/viewArticle/429/446> (last accessed 9 October 2015).

Haraway, D. J. (1991), *Simians, Cyborgs, and Women: The Reinvention of Nature*, New York: Routledge.

—(2007), *When Species Meet*, Minneapolis: University of Minnesota Press.

Hardt, M. (2010), 'The Common in Communism', in C. Douzinas and S. Žižek (eds), *The Idea of Communism*, London: Verso, pp. 131–44.

Hardt, M. and A. Negri (2001) [2000], *Empire*, Cambridge, MA: Harvard University Press.

Harrison, H. (2007) [1966], *Make Room! Make Room!*, New York: Orb.

Harrison, N. (2001), 'Readers as *Résistants*: *Fahrenheit 451*, Censorship, and Identification', *Studies in French Cinema*, 1(1), 54–61.

Harvey, D. (1989), *The Condition of Postmodernity: An Enquiry into the Origins of Cultural Change*, Oxford: Basil Blackwell.

—(2006) [1982], *The Limits to Capital*, London: Verso.

—(2010), *The Enigma of Capital and the Crises of Capitalism*, London: Profile Books.

Hayles, N. K. (1991), 'The Borders of Madness', *Science Fiction Studies*, 18(3), 321–3.

—(1999), *How We Became Posthuman: Virtual Bodies in Cybernetics, Literature, and Informatics*, Chicago: University of Chicago Press.

Heller, C. (2005), 'McDonalds, MTV, and Monsanto: Resisting Biotechnology in the Age of Informational Capital'; retrieved from <http://www.social-ecology.org/2005/01/mcdonalds-mtv-and-mon

santo-resisting-biotechnology-in-the-age-of-informational-capital/> (last accessed 9 October 2015).

Helmreich, S. (2000), 'Flexible Infections: Computer Viruses, Human Bodies, Nation-States, Evolutionary Capitalism', *Science, Technology, & Human Values*, 25(4), 472–91.

—(2008), 'Species of Biocapital', *Science as Culture*, 17(4), 463–78.

Henenlotter, F. (dir.) (1990), *Frankenhooker* [film], United States: Levins-Henenlotter.

—(2008), *Bad Biology* [film], United States: Media Blasters and Fever Dreams.

Hitchcock, A. (dir.) (1958), *Vertigo* [film], United States: Paramount Pictures.

Hollinger, V. (1994) [1991], 'Cybernetic Deconstructions: Cyberpunk and Postmodernism', in L. McCaffery (ed.), *Storming the Reality Studio: A Casebook of Cyberpunk and Postmodern Science Fiction*, Durham, NC: Duke University Press, pp. 203–18.

—(2010), 'Retrofitting *Frankenstein*', in G. J. Murphy and S. Vint (eds), *Beyond Cyberpunk: New Critical Perspectives*, New York: Routledge, pp. 191–210.

Holmberg, T. (2011), 'Unfamiliar Biological Futurities: Animals in Techno-Science', *Humanimalia*, 2(2), 60–6.

Holmqvist, N. (2008) [2006], *The Unit*, trans. M. Delargy, New York: Other Press.

Holtmeier, M. (2009), 'Scars, Cars, and Bodies without Organs: Techno-colonialism in J. G. Ballard's *Crash*', *Leonardo Electronic Almanac*, 16(4/5), 1–9.

Horkheimer, M. and T. W. Adorno (2002) [1944], *Dialectic of Enlightenment*, ed. G. S. Noerr, trans. E. Jephcott, Stanford: Stanford University Press.

Houellebecq, M. (2000) [1998], *Atomised*, trans. F. Wynne, London: Vintage.

Hughes, E. (1993), 'A Cypherpunk's Manifesto'; retrieved from <http://www.activism.net/cypherpunk/manifesto.html> (last accessed 9 October 2015).

Huxley, A. (1983) [1932], *Brave New World*, London: Granada.

Hyman, S. E. (1963), 'Glossary of Nadsat Language', in A. Burgess, *A Clockwork Orange*, New York: Ballantine, pp. 185–91.

Irigaray, L. (1980), 'Book review of *Seduction*', *Histoires d'Elles*, 21 (March); quoted in V. Grace (2000), *Baudrillard's Challenge: A Feminist Reading*, New York: Routledge.

Isaacs, N. D. (1973), 'Unstuck in Time: *Clockwork Orange* and *Slaughterhouse Five*', *Literature/Film Quarterly*, 1, 122–31.

Ishiguro, K. (2005), *Never Let Me Go*, New York: Alred A. Knopf.

Jain, D. (ed.) (2009), *Deleuze and Marx: Deleuze Studies Volume 3:*

References

2009 (Supplement), Edinburgh: Edinburgh University Press, pp. 1–7.

James, P. D. (1992), *The Children of Men*, London: Faber and Faber.

Jameson, F. (1992), *The Geopolitical Aesthetic: Cinema and Space in the World System*, Bloomington: Indiana University Press.

—(1996) [1991], *Postmodernism, or, The Cultural Logic of Late Capitalism*, London: Verso.

—(1997), 'Culture and Finance Capital', *Critical Inquiry*, 24(1), 246–65.

—(2007) [2005], *Archaeologies of the Future: The Desire Called Utopia and Other Science Fictions*, London: Verso.

—(2008), *The Ideologies of Theory*, London: Verso.

—(2009), *Valences of the Dialectic*, London: Verso.

Jeunet, J.-P. (dir.) (1997), *Alien: Resurrection* [film], United States: Brandywine Productions.

Joseph, M. K. (1998), 'Introduction', in M. Shelley, *Frankenstein; or, The Modern Prometheus*, Oxford: Oxford University Press, pp. v–viii.

Kafka, F. (2007), *Metamorphosis and Other Stories*, trans. M. Hofman, London: Penguin Books.

Kellner, D. (1989a), *Jean Baudrillard: From Marxism to Postmodernism and Beyond*, Southampton: Polity Press.

—(1989b), 'David Cronenberg: Panic Horror and the Postmodern Body', *Canadian Journal of Political and Social Theory*, 13(3), 89–101.

—(1994), 'Introduction: Jean Baudrillard in the Fin-De-Millennium', in D. Kellner (ed.), *Baudrillard: A Critical Reader*, London: Blackwell, pp. 1–24.

—(2000), *Media Culture: Cultural Studies, Identity and Politics between the Modern and the Postmodern*, New York: Routledge.

Kenton, E. C. (dir.) (1932), *Island of Lost Souls* [film], United States: Paramount Pictures.

Kirby, D. (2000), 'The New Eugenics in Cinema: Genetic Determinism and Gene Therapy in *GATTACA*', *Science Fiction Studies*, 27(2), 193–215.

—(2002), 'Are We Not Men? The Horror of Eugenics in *The Island of Dr. Moreau*', *Paradoxa*, 17, 93–107.

Kirtchev, C. A. (1997), 'A Cyberpunk Manifesto'; retrieved from <http://project.cyberpunk.ru/idb/cyberpunk_manifesto.html> (last accessed 9 October 2015).

Kittler, F. A. (1999) [1986], *Gramophone, Film, Typewriter*, trans. G. Winthrop-Young and M. Wutz, Stanford: Stanford University Press.

—(2012) [2002], *Optical Media: Berlin Lectures 1999*, trans. A. Enns, Cambridge: Polity Press.

Kroker, A. and D. Cook (1986), *The Postmodern Scene: Excremental Culture and Hyper-Aesthetics*, New York: St. Martin's Press.

Kubrick, S. (dir.) (1971), *A Clockwork Orange* [film], United Kingdom: Hawk Films.

Lacan, J. (1977), *Écrits*, trans. A. Sheridan, London: Tavistock.

—(1992) [1986], *The Seminar of Jacques Lacan, Book VII: The Ethics of Psychoanalysis 1959–1960*, ed. J. Miller, trans. D. Porter, London: W.W. Norton & Company.

—(1998) [1973], *The Seminar of Jacques Lacan, Book XI: The Four Fundamental Concepts of Psychoanalysis*, ed. J. Miller, trans. A. Sheridan, London: W.W. Norton & Company.

Land, N. (1998), 'Cybergothic', in J. B. Dixon and E. J. Cassidy (eds), *Virtual Futures: Cyberotics, Technology, and Post-Human Pragmatism*, London: Routledge, pp. 103–15.

Landon, B. (2004), 'Less is More: Much Less is Much More: The Insistent Allure of Nanotechnology Narratives in Science Fiction', in N. K. Hayles (ed.), *Nanotechnology: Implications of the New Technoscience*, Bristol: Intellect Books, pp. 131–46.

Lang, F. (dir.) (1927), *Metropolis* [film], Germany: UFA and Universal Pictures.

Lansbury, C. (1985), *The Old Brown Dog: Women, Workers, and Vivisection in Edwardian England*, Madison: University of Wisconsin Press.

Laplanche, J. (1989) [1987], *New Foundations for Psychoanalysis*, trans. D. Macey, New York: Basil Blackwell.

—(1999), *Essays on Otherness*, trans. J. Fletcher, New York: Routledge.

—(2001), 'An Interview with Jean Laplanche [Interview with C. Caruth]', *Postmodern Culture*, 11(2); retrieved from <http://pmc.iath.virginia.edu/text-only/issue.101/11.2caruth.txt> (last accessed 9 October 2015).

Latham, R. (2002), *Consuming Youth: Vampires, Cyborgs, and the Culture of Consumption*, Chicago: University of Chicago Press.

Latour, B. (1993) [1991], *We Have Never Been Modern*, trans. C. Porter, Cambridge, MA: Harvard University Press.

Lederer, S. E. and R. M. Ratzan (2005), 'Mary Shelley: *Frankenstein: Or, the Modern Prometheus*', in D. Seed (ed.), *A Companion to Science Fiction*, Oxford: Blackwell Publishing, pp. 455–65.

Leeson, L. H. (dir.) (2002), *Teknolust* [film], United States: Velocity Entertainment.

Levin, C. (1996), *Jean Baudrillard: A Study in Cultural Metaphysics*, New York: Prentice Hall.

Lotringer, S. (2001), 'Doing Theory', in S. Lotringer and S. Cohen (eds), *French Theory in America*, New York: Routledge, pp. 125–62.

—(2003), 'Better Than Life: My '80s', *Artforum International*, 41(8), 194–7 and 252–3.

—(2008), 'Remember Foucault', *October*, 126, 3–22.

Lovecraft, H. P. (2002), *The Call of Cthulhu and Other Weird Stories*, London: Penguin Books.

Luckhurst, R. (1997), *The Angle Between Two Walls: The Fiction of J. G. Ballard*, New York: St. Martin's Press.

References

—(2005), 'J. G. Ballard: *Crash*', in D. Seed (ed.), *A Companion to Science Fiction*, Oxford: Blackwell Publishing, pp. 512–21.

Lykke, N. (1996), 'Between Monsters, Goddesses and Cyborgs: Feminist Confrontations with Science', in N. Lykke and R. Braidotti (eds), *Between Monsters, Goddesses and Cyborgs: Feminist Confrontations with Science, Medicine and Cyberspace*, London: Zed Books, pp. 13–29.

Lyotard, J.-F. (1993) [1974], *Libidinal Economy*, trans. I. H. Grant, Indianapolis: Indiana University Press.

MacCormack, P. (2009), 'Cinemasochism: Submissive Spectatorship as Unthought', in D. N. Rodowick (ed.), *Afterimages of Gilles Deleuze's Film Philosophy*, Minneapolis: University of Minnesota Press, pp. 157–76.

McGuigan, J. (2009), *Cool Capitalism*, London: Pluto Press.

McHale, B. (1992), *Constructing Postmodernism*, New York: Routledge.

McMurtry, J. (2013), *The Cancer Stage of Capitalism: From Crisis to Cure*, 2nd edn, London: Pluto Press.

McNally, D. (2011), *Monsters of the Market: Zombies, Vampires and Global Capitalism*, Boston: Brill.

Mann, D. (dir.) (1971), *Willard* [film], United States: Cinerama Releasing Corporation.

Marcuse, H. (1969) [1965], 'Repressive Tolerance', in R. P. Wolff, B. Moore Jr and H. Marcuse, *A Critique of Pure Tolerance*, London: Jonathan Cape, pp. 93–138.

—(2007) [1964], *One-Dimensional Man: Studies in the Ideology of Advanced Industrial Societies*, New York: Routledge.

Marks, J. (2006), 'Information and Resistance: Deleuze, the Virtual and Cybernetics', in I. Buchanan and A. Parr (eds), *Deleuze and the Contemporary World*, Edinburgh: Edinburgh University Press, pp. 194–213.

Marshall, P. A., D. C. Thomasma and A. S. Darr (1996), 'Marketing Human Organs: The Autonomy Paradox', *Theoretical Medicine*, 17, 1–18.

Marx, K. (1950), 'Wage Labour and Capital', in K. Marx and F. Engels, *Selected Works, Volume 1*, Moscow: Foreign Languages Publishing House, pp. 66–97.

—(1971) [1939], *Grundrisse: Outlines of the Critique of Political Economy*, trans. D. McLellan, London: Macmillan.

—(1975a), '"Critical Criticism" as the Tranquillity of Knowledge, or "Critical Criticism" as Herr Edgar', in K. Marx and F. Engels, *Collected Works, Volume 4*, trans. J. Cohen et al., New York: International Publishers, pp. 19–54.

—(1975b), *Early Writings*, trans. R. Livingstone and G. Benton, New York: Vintage Books.

—(1976), 'The Poverty of Philosophy: Answer to the *Philosophy of Poverty* by M. Proudhon', in K. Marx and F. Engels, *Collected Works, Volume 6*, trans. J. Cohen et al., New York: International Publishers, pp. 105–212.

—(1982) [1867], *Capital: A Critique of Political Economy, Volume 1*, trans. B. Fowkes, New York: Penguin.

—(1991) [1894], *Capital: A Critique of Political Economy, Volume 3*, trans. D. Fernbach, New York: Penguin.

Marx, K. and F. Engels (1950), 'Manifesto of the Communist Party', in K. Marx and F. Engels, *Selected Works, Volume 1*, Moscow: Foreign Languages Publishing House, pp. 32–61.

Massumi, B. (1987), 'Realer than Real: The Simulacrum According to Deleuze and Guattari', *Copyright*, 1; retrieved from <http://www.brian-massumi.com/english/essays.html> (last accessed 9 October 2015).

Matheson, R. (2002) [1956], *The Shrinking Man*, London: Gollancz.

Mbembé, J.-A. and L. Meintjes (2003), 'Necropolitics', *Public Culture*, 15(1), 11–40.

Melehy, H. (1995), 'Images Without: Deleuzian Becoming, Science Fiction Cinema in the Eighties', *Postmodern Culture*, 5(2); retrieved from <http://pmc.iath.virginia.edu/text-only/issue.195/melehy.195> (last accessed 9 October 2015).

Melville, H. (2007) [1851], *Moby-Dick; or, The Whale*, London: Vintage Books.

Merrin, W. (2005), *Baudrillard and the Media: A Critical Introduction*, Cambridge: Polity Press.

Meyer, A. (2009), 'Eric Garcia's *The Repossession Mambo* [review]', *Crikey*; retrieved from <http://blogs.crikey.com.au/literaryminded/2009/08/11/eric-garcias-the-repossession-mambo/> (last accessed 9 October 2015).

Meyers, W. E. (1980), *Aliens and Linguists: Language Study and Science Fiction*, Athens, GA: University of Georgia Press.

Milburn, C. (2005), 'Nano/Splatter: Disintegrating the Postbiological Body', *New Literary History*, 36(2), 283–311.

Milner, A. (1999), *Class*, London: Sage.

—(2005), *Literature, Culture and Society*, 2nd edn, London: Routledge.

—(2012), *Locating Science Fiction*, Liverpool: Liverpool University Press.

Monod, J. (1972) [1970], *Chance and Necessity: An Essay on the Natural Philosophy of Modern Biology*, trans. A. Wainhouse, London: Collins.

More, T. (1995) [1516], *Utopia: Latin Text and an English Translation*, ed. G. M. Logan, R. M. Adams and C. H. Miller, Cambridge: Cambridge University Press.

Morris, M. (1984), 'Room 101 or a Few Worst Things in the World', in A. Frankovits (ed.), *Seduced and Abandoned: The Baudrillard Scene*, Sydney: Stonemoss Services, pp. 91–117.

Mulvey, L. (1989), *Visual and Other Pleasures*, Bloomington: Indiana University Press.

Murphy, G. J. and S. Vint (2010), 'Introduction: The Sea Change(s) of Cyberpunk', in G. J. Murphy and S. Vint (eds), *Beyond Cyberpunk: New Critical Perspectives*, New York: Routledge, pp. xi–xviii.

Murray, P. and J. A. Schuler (1988), 'Post-Marxism in a French Context', *History of European Ideas*, 9(3), 321–34.

Natali, V. (dir.) (2009), *Splice* [film], Canada and France: Dark Castle Entertainment and Gaumont.

Newitz, A. (2001), 'Biopunk'; retrieved from <http://web.archive.org/web/20021220190353/http://www.sfbg.com/SFLife/tech/71.html> (last accessed 9 October 2015).

Niccol, A. (dir.) (1997), *Gattaca* [film], United States: Jersey Films.

Nolan, W. F. (1999) [1967], *Logan's Run*, New York: Buccaneer Books.

Norris, C. (1990), *What's Wrong With Postmodernism? Critical Theory and the Ends of Philosophy*, London: Harvester Wheatsheaf.

Noys, B. (2008), 'Crimes of the Near Future: Baudrillard/Ballard', *International Journal of Baudrillard Studies*, 5(1); retrieved from <http://www2.ubishops.ca/baudrillardstudies/vol5_1/v5-1-article8-Noys.html> (last accessed 14 October 2015).

—(2010), *The Persistence of the Negative*, Edinburgh: Edinburgh University Press.

—(2014), *Malign Velocities: Accelerationism and Capitalism*, Croydon: Zero Books.

O'Flinn, P. (2005), 'Production and Reproduction: The Case of *Frankenstein*', in F. Botting (ed.), *Frankenstein: Contemporary Critical Essays*, London: Macmillan, pp. 21–44.

Orwell, G. (1993) [1949], *Nineteen Eighty-Four*, Maryborough: Penguin Books.

—(2000), *The Collected Essays, Journalism and Letters of George Orwell, Vol. 4: In Front of Your Nose, 1945–1950*, ed. S. Orwell and I. Angus, Boston: D. R. Godine.

Overell, R. (2014), *Affective Intensities in Extreme Music Scenes: Cases from Australia and Japan*, New York: Palgrave Macmillan.

Owens, C. (1998), 'The Discourse of Others: Feminists and Postmodernism', in H. Foster (ed.), *The Anti-Aesthetic: Essays on Postmodern Culture*, New York: The New Press, pp. 65–92.

Parrinder, P. (1995), *Shadows of the Future: H. G. Wells, Science Fiction and Prophecy*, Liverpool: Liverpool University Press.

Pasquinelli, M. (2008), *Animal Spirits: A Bestiary of the Commons*, Rotterdam: NAi Publishers.

Patterson, M. L. (2010), 'A Biopunk Manifesto'; retrieved from <http://maradydd.livejournal.com/496085.html> (last accessed 9 October 2015).

Pawlett, W. (2007), *Jean Baudrillard: Against Banality*, London: Routledge.

Perelberg, R. J. (2005), 'Introduction', in R. J. Perelberg (ed.), *Freud: A Modern Reader*, London: Whurr Publishers, pp. 1–28.

Peters, M. A. (2012), 'Bio-informational Capitalism', *Thesis Eleven*, 110(1), 98–111.

Peters, M. A. and P. Venkatesan (2010), 'Biocapitalism and the Politics of Life', *Geopolitics, History and International Relations*, 2(2), 100–22.
Picart, C. J. S. (2003), *Remaking the Frankenstein Myth: Between Laughter and Horror*, Albany: State University of New York Press.
Pisters, P. (2012), *The Neuro-Image: A Deleuzian Film-Philosophy of Digital Screen Culture*, Stanford: Stanford University Press.
Plant, S. and N. Land (1994), 'Cyberpositive'; retrieved from <http://www.sterneck.net/cyber/plant-land-cyber/> (last accessed 9 October 2015).
Poiana, P. (2008), 'Seduction and the Scandal: Two Kinds of Relation with the Thing', *Angelaki: Journal of the Theoretical Humanities*, 13(3), 53–65.
Polanksi, R. (dir.) (1974), *Chinatown* [film], United States: Paramount Pictures.
Powell, A. (2005), *Deleuze and Horror Film*, Edinburgh: Edinburgh University Press.
—(2008), 'Off Your Face: Schizoanalysis, Faciality and Film', in I. Buchanan and P. MacCormack (eds), *Deleuze and the Schizoanalysis of Cinema*, New York: Continuum, pp. 116–29.
Puchner, M. (2008), 'When We Were Clones', *Raritan: A Quarterly Review*, 27(4), 34–49.
Rabinow, P. and N. Rose (2006), 'Biopower Today', *BioSocieties*, 1, 195–217.
Radford, M. (dir.) (1984), *Nineteen Eighty-Four* [film], United Kingdom: Virgin Films.
Refused (composers) (1998), *The Shape of Punk to Come* [CD], Sweden: Burning Heart.
Reichardt, J. (1994), 'Artificial Life and the Myth of Frankenstein', in S. Bann (ed.), *Frankenstein, Creation and Monstrosity*, London: Reaktion Books, pp. 136–57.
Rifkin, J. (1998), *The Biotech Century: Harnessing the Gene and Remaking the World*, New York: Jeremy P. Tarcher and Putnam.
Rikowski, G. (2003), 'Alien Life: Marx and the Future of the Human', *Historical Materialism*, 11(2), 121–64.
Rodley, C. (ed.) (1997) [1992], *Cronenberg on Cronenberg*, Boston: Faber and Faber.
Rodowick, D. N. (1997), *Gilles Deleuze's Time Machine*, Durham, NC: Duke University Press.
Rojek, C. and B. S. Turner (1993), 'Introduction: Regret Baudrillard?', in C. Rojek and B. S. Turner (eds), *Forget Baudrillard?*, London: Routledge, pp. ix–xviii.
Rollin, B. E. (1995), *The Frankenstein Syndrome: Ethical and Social Issues in the Genetic Engineering of Animals*, Cambridge: Cambridge University Press.

References

Romanek, M. (dir.) (2010), *Never Let Me Go* [film], United Kingdom and United States: DNA Films and Film4.

Rose, N. (2007), *The Politics of Life Itself: Biomedicine, Power, and Subjectivity in the Twenty-First Century*, Princeton: Princeton University Press.

Ross, A. (2012), 'Agamben's Political Paradigm of the Camp: Its Features and Reasons', *Constellations*, 19(3), 421–34.

Ruddick, N. (1992), 'Ballard/*Crash*/Baudrillard', *Science Fiction Studies*, 19(3), 354–60.

Sample, I. (2007), 'Frankenstein's Mycoplasma', *The Guardian*, 8 June; quoted in S. Žižek (2010), *Living in the End Times*, New York: Verso.

Sapochnik, M. (dir.) (2010), *Repo Men* [film], United States and Canada: Relativity Media and Stuber Pictures.

Saussure, F. de (1960) [1916], *Course in General Linguistics*, ed. C. Bally and A. Sechehaye, trans. W. Baskin, London: Peter Owen.

Savat, D. and M. Poster (eds) (2009), *Deleuze and New Technology*, Edinburgh: Edinburgh University Press.

Scheper-Hughes, N. (2004), 'Bodies for Sale – Whole or in Parts', in N. Scheper-Hughes and L. Wacquant (eds), *Commodifying Bodies*, London: Sage, pp. 1–8.

Scott, R. (dir.) (1982), *Blade Runner* [film], United States: The Ladd Company.

Sellars, S. and D. F. J. O'Hara (2012), *Extreme Metaphors: Interviews with J. G. Ballard, 1967–2008*, London: Fourth Estate.

Seyfer, T. (2004), 'What Are Chimeras and Hybrids?', *Ethics and Medics*, 29(7); in A. Ferreira (2008), 'Primate Tales: Interspecies Pregnancy and Chimerical Beings', *Science Fiction Studies*, 35(2), 223–37.

Sharon, T. (2011), 'A Schizoanalysis of Emerging Biotechnologies: Renaturalized Nature, the Disclosed Secret of Life, and Technologically Authentic Selfhood', *Configurations*, 19, 431–60.

Sharp, L. (2000), 'The Commodification of the Body and its Parts', *Annual Review of Anthropology*, 29, 287–328.

—(2006), *Strange Harvest: Organ Transplants, Denatured Bodies, and the Transformed Self*, Berkeley: University of California Press.

Shaviro, S. (1993), *The Cinematic Body*, Minneapolis: University of Minnesota Press.

Shelley, M. (1998) [1818], *Frankenstein; or, The Modern Prometheus*, Oxford: Oxford University Press.

Short, S. (2005), *Cyborg Cinema and Contemporary Subjectivity*, New York: Palgrave Macmillan.

Shukin, N. (2009), *Animal Capital: Rendering Life in Biopolitical Times*, Minneapolis: University of Minnesota Press.

Silverman, K. and H. Farocki (1998), *Speaking about Godard*, New York: New York University Press.

Skloot, R. (2010), *The Immortal Life of Henrietta Lacks*, Sydney: Picador.

Slusser, G. (1992), 'The Frankenstein Barrier', in G. Slusser and T. Shippey (eds), *Fiction 2000: Cyberpunk and the Future of Narrative*, London: University of Georgia Press, pp. 46–71.

—(1994) [1991], 'Literary MTV', in L. McCaffery (ed.), *Storming the Reality Studio: A Casebook of Cyberpunk and Postmodern Science Fiction*, Durham, NC: Duke University Press, pp. 334–42.

Smith, D. W. (2004), 'The Inverse Side of the Structure: Žižek on Deleuze and Lacan', *Criticism*, 46(4), 635–50.

Sobchack, V. (1991), 'Baudrillard's Obscenity', *Science Fiction Studies*, 18(3), 327–9.

—(1998), 'Beating the Meat/Surviving the Text, or How to Get Out of this Century Alive', in P. Treichler, L. Cartwright and C. Penley (eds), *The Visible Woman: Imaging Technologies, Gender and Science*, New York: New York University Press, pp. 310–20.

—(2004) [1987], *Screening Space: The American Science Fiction Film*, 2nd edn, London: Rutgers University Press.

Soderbergh, S. (dir.) (2011), *Contagion* [film], United States and United Arab Emirates: Participant Media, Imagenation Abu Dhabi and Double Feature Films.

Spierig, M. and P. Spierig (dirs) (2009), *Daybreakers* [film], Australia and United States: Lionsgate, Screen Australia, Pictures in Paradise, Film Finance Corporation Australia, Pacific Film and Television Commission, Furst Films.

Spiller, N. (ed.) (2002), *Cyber Reader: Critical Writings for the Digital Era*, London: Phaidon.

Squier, S. (1998), 'Interspecies Reproduction: Xenogenic Desire and the Feminist Implications of Hybrids', *Cultural Studies*, 12(1), 360–81.

Stacey, J. (2010), *The Cinematic Life of the Gene*, Durham, NC: Duke University Press.

Staiger, J. (2003), 'Hybrid or Inbred: The Purity Hypothesis and Hollywood Genre History', in B. K. Grant (ed.), *Film Genre Reader III*, Austin: University of Texas Press, pp. 185–99.

Stam, R., R. Burgoyne and S. Flitterman-Lewis (1992), *New Vocabularies in Film Semiotics: Structuralism, Post-structuralism and Beyond*, London: Routledge.

Sterling, B. (1996) [1985], *Schismatrix*, New York: Ace Books.

Stiegler, B. (2013) [2006], *Uncontrollable Societies of Disaffected Individuals: Disbelief and Discredit, Volume 2*, trans. D. Ross, Cambridge: Polity Press.

Stockwell, P. (2000), *The Poetics of Science Fiction*, Harlow: Longman.

Studlar, G. (1984), 'Masochism and the Perverse Pleasures of Cinema', *Quarterly Review of Film Studies*, 9(4), 267–82.

References

Styhre, A. and M. Sundgren (2011), *Venturing into the Bioeconomy: Professions, Innovation, Identity*, Basingstoke: Palgrave Macmillan.

Sunder Rajan, K. (2007) [2006], *Biocapital: The Construction of Postgenomic Life*, Durham, NC: Duke University Press.

Suvin, D. (1979), *Metamorphoses of Science Fiction: On the Poetics and History of a Literary Genre*, New Haven: Yale University Press.

—(1994) [1991], 'On Gibson and Cyberpunk SF', in L. McCaffery (ed.), *Storming the Reality Studio: A Casebook of Cyberpunk and Postmodern Science Fiction*, Durham, NC: Duke University Press, pp. 349–65.

Taylor, D. (dir.) (1977), *The Island of Doctor Moreau* [film], United States: American International Pictures.

Thacker, E. (2003), 'What is Biomedia?', *Configurations*, 11(1), 47–79.

—(2005), *The Global Genome: Biotechnology, Politics and Culture*, Cambridge, MA: The MIT Press.

Thacker, E. and A. R. Galloway (2007), *The Exploit: A Theory of Networks*, Minneapolis: University of Minnesota Press.

Theall, D. F. (2001), 'Marshall McLuhan, Canadian Schizo-Jansenist and Pseudo-Joycean Precursor of and Preparer for the Dissemination of French Theory in North America', in S. Lotringer and S. Cohen (eds), *French Theory in America*, New York: Routledge, pp. 111–24.

Thoburn, N. (2003), *Deleuze, Marx and Politics*, New York: Routledge.

Thomas, C. (1992), 'Baudrillard's Seduction of Foucault', in W. Stearns and W. Chaloupka (eds), *Jean Baudrillard: The Disappearance of Art and Politics*, New York: St. Martin's Press, pp. 131–45.

Thoret, J. (2011), 'The Seventies Reloaded: (What does the cinema think about when it dreams of Baudrillard?)', *Senses of Cinema*, 59; retrieved from <http://sensesofcinema.com/2011/feature-articles/the-seventies-reloaded-what-does-the-cinema-think-about-when-it-dreams-of-baudrillard/> (last accessed 9 October 2015).

Trifonova, T. (2003), 'Is There a Subject in Hyperreality?', *Postmodern Culture*, 13(3); retrieved from <http://pmc.iath.virginia.edu/issue.503/13.3trifonova.html> (last accessed 9 October 2015).

Truffaut, F. (dir.) (1966), *Fahrenheit 451* [film], United States: Anglo Enterprises and Vineyard Film Ltd.

Turney, J. (1998), *Frankenstein's Footsteps: Science, Genetics, and Popular Culture*, New Haven: Yale University Press.

Vandenberghe, F. (2008), 'Deleuzian Capitalism', *Philosophy & Social Criticism*, 34(8), 877–903.

Varga, D. (2003), 'The Deleuzean Experience of Cronenberg's *Crash* and Wenders' *The End of Violence*', in M. Shiel and T. Fitzmaurice (eds), *Screening the City*, London: Verso, pp. 262–83.

Vaughan, M. H. (2010), 'The Paradox of Film: An Industry of Sex, a Form of Seduction (Notes on Jean Baudrillard's *Seduction* and the Cinema)', *Film-Philosophy*, 14(2), 41–61.

Vint, S. (2010a), *Animal Alterity: Science Fiction and the Question of the Animal*, Liverpool: Liverpool University Press.

—(2010b), '"The Mainstream Finds its Own Uses for Things": Cyberpunk and Commodification' and 'Afterword: The World Gibson Made', in G. J. Murphy and S. Vint (eds), *Beyond Cyberpunk: New Critical Perspectives*, New York: Routledge, pp. 95–115 and 228–33.

—(2011a), *Repo Men* [review], *Science Fiction Film and Television*, 4(2), 306–9.

—(2011b), 'Science Fiction and Biopolitics', *Science Fiction Film and Television*, 4(2), 161–72.

Voela, A. (2013), 'Antigone and her Double, Lacan and Baudrillard', *Journal for Cultural Research*, 17(3), 219–33.

Wachowski, L. and A. Wachowski (dirs) (1999), *The Matrix* [film], United States and Australia: Village Roadshow Pictures and Silver Pictures.

Wardle, P. (1997), 'Cronenberg's *Crash*', *Cinefantastique*, 28(10), 26–31.

Weatherill, R. (2000), 'The Seduction of Therapy', *British Journal of Psychotherapy*, 16(3), 263–73.

Weinstone, A. (2004), *Avatar Bodies: A Tantra for Posthumanism*, Minneapolis: University of Minnesota Press.

Wells, H. G. (1978), *The Complete Science Fiction Treasury of H. G. Wells*, New York: Avenel Books.

—(2004) [1896], *The Island of Doctor Moreau*, London: Phoenix.

Whale, J. (dir.) (1931), *Frankenstein* [film], United States: Universal Pictures.

—(1933), *The Invisible Man* [film], United States: Universal Pictures.

—(1935), *Bride of Frankenstein* [film], United States: Universal Pictures.

Whalen, T. (2007), 'The Consequences of Passivity: Re-evaluating Truffaut's *Fahrenheit 451*', *Literature/Film Quarterly*, 35(3), 181–90.

Wilde, O. (1974) [1890], *The Picture of Dorian Gray*, London: Oxford University Press.

Williams, R. (2003) [1974], *Television: Technology and Cultural Form*, New York: Routledge.

—(2010), *Tenses of Imagination: Raymond Williams on Science Fiction, Utopia and Dystopia*, ed. A. Milner, Berlin: Peter Lang.

Winterbottom, M. (dir.) (2003), *Code 46* [film], United Kingdom: BBC Films and Revolution Films.

Wohlsen, M. (2011), *Biopunk: DIY Scientists Hack the Software of Life*, New York: Current.

Wolfe, C. (2010), *What is Posthumanism?*, Minneapolis: University of Minnesota Press.

Wolfe, G. K. (1979), *The Known and the Unknown: The Iconography of Science Fiction*, Kent, OH: Kent State University Press.

Woods, A. (2011), *The Sublime Object of Psychiatry: Schizophrenia in Clinical and Cultural Theory*, Oxford: Oxford University Press.

References

Yuzna, B. (dir.) (1990), *Bride of Re-Animator* [film], United States: Wild Street Pictures.

—(2003), *Beyond Re-Animator* [film], Spain: Castelao Producciones and Fantastic Factory.

Žižek, S. (2000) [1999], *The Ticklish Subject: The Absent Centre of Political Ontology*, New York: Verso.

—(2002), *Welcome to the Desert of the Real: Five Essays on September 11 and Related Dates*, New York: Verso.

—(2004), 'From Politics to Biopolitics ... and Back', *South Atlantic Quarterly*, 103(2/3), 501–21.

—(2008), 'The Prospects of Radical Politics Today', *International Journal of Baudrillard Studies*, 5(1); retrieved from <http://www2.ubishops. ca/baudrillardstudies/vol5_1/v5-1-article3-zizek.html> (last accessed 14 October 2015).

—(2009), *First as Tragedy, Then as Farce*, New York: Verso.

—(2010), *Living in the End Times*, New York: Verso.

—(2012a) [2004], *Organs without Bodies: On Deleuze and Consequences*, New York: Routledge.

—(2012b), *The Year of Dreaming Dangerously*, New York: Verso.

—(2013) [2012], *Less than Nothing: Hegel and the Shadow of Dialectical Materialism*, New York: Verso.

Index

Index

Index

Wolfe, C., 134, 136–7, 155
Wolfe, G. K., 155
Woods, A., 16, 19

xenotransplantation, 143

Žižek, S., 2, 27n, 34, 51, 59, 100n, 113, 158–9, 164, 171n, 180, 186, 201, 203, 208
on Deleuze, 24–5n, 158
zōe, 210